Without Hope

I would like to dedicate this book to the Galway Rape Crisis Centre and to all victims of child sexual abuse. I hope that this book will make it easier for other victims to come forward and tell their stories.

Without Hope

A Childhood Ruined by the Man
she should Trust the Most

BARBARA NAUGHTON

EBURY
PRESS

3 5 7 9 10 8 6 4 2

Published in 2010 by Ebury Press, an imprint of Ebury Publishing
A Random House Group company
First published in Ireland by Merlin Publishing in 2008

The Random House Group Limited Reg. No. 954009

Addresses for companies within the Random House Group can
be found at www.randomhouse.co.uk

A CIP catalogue record for this book is available from
the British Library

The Random House Group Limited supports The Forest
Stewardship Council (FSC), the leading international forest
certification organisation. All our titles that are printed on
Greenpeace approved FSC certified paper carry the FSC logo.
Our paper procurement policy can be found at
www.rbooks.co.uk/environment

Mixed Sources
Product group from well-managed
forests and other controlled sources
www.fsc.org   Cert no. TT-COC-2139
© 1996 Forest Stewardship Council
FSC

Printed in the UK by CPI Cox & Wyman, Reading, RG1 8EX

ISBN 9780091932534

To buy books by your favourite authors and register for offers visit
www.rbooks.co.uk

Contents

Prologue

Connemara, Galway, 1985

One night I woke up because I heard someone crying. It was really dark. I heard a bang on the floor and then an eerie silence. It left me with an uncomfortable feeling in my chest. I hugged my favourite teddy bear Vefin and wished I was still asleep.

I was troubled, looking around my bedroom in the dark. Despite my fear and my desire to stay in bed, all my instincts urged me to go and investigate. I was afraid something bad had happened to my mam.

I slowly opened my bedroom door and began edging towards the kitchen. It was still very quiet and it was so dark I could barely see ahead of me.

Suddenly I heard my father's voice.

'Barbara?' he seemed to whisper from right beside me.

I was frightened. I jumped and looked around me to find the voice but I couldn't see him. I made my way down the hall, towards the sitting room. I could just see my father's shadow lying on the couch. I didn't want to go near him but I was worried about Mam.

I edged into the room, moving towards the kitchen. I thought I could see something on the floor.

As I passed by my father, he spoke again.

'Don't go into the kitchen,' he ordered. He reached out his hand and pulled me towards him on the sofa. He touched me on the side of my stomach. I felt uncomfortable as he then moved his hands around my chest area. I looked at my father's face in surprise and I moved away from him.

'Come closer, come here.' He reached out and pulled me to him again.

I could smell alcohol from his breath and his face was red. I knew he'd been drinking again. Mam had always told us to stay quiet and do what he said when he'd taken drink.

He took my hand and held it.

'What are you doing out of bed?' he asked.

I was too scared to reply. I looked towards the right side of the sitting room, the entry to the kitchen. My instinct guided me there and I pulled away from my father.

He tried to block me from entering the small scullery but I got past him.

I switched on the light and screamed when I saw my mother lying face down on the floor. She wasn't moving and looked really cold.

I cried and fell on my knees beside her. I held her hand and began saying 'Mam, Mam' but she didn't wake up.

I kept calling her name and squeezing her hand until she finally stirred. She opened her eyes and saw me staring at her. She began to look around but seemed a bit dizzy. She was green-looking and I thought she was going to get sick. One of her eyes was all red and puffy-looking.

My father shouted at me from the sitting room: 'Barbara, get back to bed.'

He sounded very angry.

I was frightened but I kept staring at my mother. I wanted to make sure she was awake. I pulled at her and tried to help her up off the floor but she grabbed her side and couldn't seem to move.

'Just leave her alone and go on back to bed,' my father yelled again from the couch.

Mam smiled up at me and whispered: 'Go back to bed, love.'

I moved past my father on the sofa. He tried to grab my hand again as I walked by but I ran around him. As soon as I was back in bed I closed my eyes and pretended to be asleep. My heart was racing. I was scared and very worried about my mother who was still lying on the scullery floor.

The following morning when I got out of bed, I walked into the sitting room. Mam was sitting on the edge of the couch, gazing out the window. Her eye was black and swollen. She was still holding her side.

My brothers were sitting quietly beside her.

'Did you hear any noises last night?' I asked them.

'No,' Paul replied.

'We were fast asleep,' Patrick agreed.

I looked at them in surprise. We all slept in bunk beds in the same room. I was sure the loud noise would have woken them up as well.

My mother looked at me directly and said: 'Barbara saved my life last night. She was the only one that got out of bed to help me.'

I sighed with relief when I heard my mother saying that but I still felt helpless.

There was silence in the house between my parents for days afterwards.

We all knew it would happen again.

ONE

A Bag of Ice

I was born in Kinnvarra, Camus, a small rural village in the west of Galway on August 25, 1978. My father came from a large family in Kinnvarra and had 11 siblings. My mother also came from a big family. The village was situated in the Gaeltacht, an Irish-speaking region, and I was brought up speaking Irish as my first language. Our house was in quite a remote area. We lived at the top of a hill, with a lake just down from the house on the other side. The local shop was at the bottom of the hill, with the church and the pub about three miles away. My father's Uncle Colin was married to Delia who lived at the bottom of the hill in a small house.

It was a beautiful area but we didn't notice that growing up. We always thought it was a bit quiet. When I look back I don't remember anything very exciting happening when I was very young. One of my few earliest memories is the day I started school.

When the morning arrived I remember I got dressed in a hurry and joined my parents and two brothers for breakfast. My younger sister Alison, the baby, was having a nap. She was five years younger than me. Patrick was a year older than me, so he was already going to school but I don't remember him telling me anything about it. Paul was a year younger than me so he had to wait another year.

After breakfast, I went into the sitting room where my father was cleaning out the ashes from the grate, as he always did. I stood for a while watching him and then asked: 'Did you like going to school?'

'No, I didn't. I hated my teachers,' he replied. 'They used to beat me for nothing.'

I remember I got a fright when he said that. This wasn't what everyone else had told me about school.

'You'll be in school until three o'clock, but don't worry the teachers will probably be soft on you because it's your first day.'

I was scared at the idea that the teachers would beat me but I didn't say anything. I found my mother who was preparing my lunch and my little school satchel and asked: 'Why did the teachers in my father's school beat him?'

'Don't listen to your father. Get your coat now because we're about to leave.'

As my mother and I walked towards the hall door, my father appeared from the sitting room and asked: 'Don't you think that she's a little young to be starting school?'

My mother replied: 'Well, five years old is the age I see all the children from the neighbourhood starting school.'

I was getting more afraid by the minute but my mother guided me out the door, ignoring him.

After what I felt was a long walk down the hill, we finally arrived outside the gates of the National School. I was nervous and when my mother told me to run into the school and join the other children, I looked up at her, crying, and said: 'Please, don't leave me.'

She looked down at me, with sympathy in her eyes.

'You'll make lots of new friends and I'll be back to collect you in a couple of hours.'

I was not convinced and pleaded with her to take me home. Suddenly, a tall woman approached, holding a young girl's hand and told me that she would bring me into the school. The young girl smiled at me, grabbed my hand and led me inside. At the door, I turned and saw my mother walking away, with her brown bucket in her hand. She was going to the well to get water before she went home. There was a post box beside it so there was always the idea of killing two birds with one stone: drop by the well while you're going to the post box. We didn't drink water from the tap because my father said it was poisoned.

When I entered the school I was amazed at the size of it. There were loads of children running around everywhere as well.

The tall woman led me into a room and told me that this was my classroom. I looked around, trying to take it all in. There were 20 other children seated in the room. I recognised a couple of them from the area, as Kinnvarra is quite small.

Seconds later, another tall woman arrived. She introduced herself as Miss Carter and told us that she was our teacher. She appeared very friendly and I immediately felt better.

From then on, my first day in National School was a delight. Miss Carter allowed all of us to draw pictures and play with our teddies until our parents collected us later that day. As we were walking home, I told my mother all about my first day and all the children I had met.

When we got back to the house, we found my father lying on the couch. Looking back, it's a wonder how my father filled his days, as he never worked much in his life. The only things I remember him doing are tinkering about with cars or applying his handyman skills to 'upgrading' our home. He didn't ask me about school and I walked past him and went to my room.

It was around this time that my mother started working in a fish factory. She worked there seasonally, usually from October to February. She had to wear big Wellingtons. I remember them because I tried them on one day and fell over as they were too big. The fish factory was about three miles away from the house. Even with two cars sitting outside the house, my father would never collect her from work. Her cousin would sometimes drop her home. She would come home shivering with the cold and her hands were freezing ice blocks. I remember how cold they felt. As soon as she was in the door, she would change out of her 'fish clothes' and sit beside the fire to warm up.

When Christmas arrived, Paul and I decided to stay up to see if we could catch Santa delivering our presents. We got bored waiting and decided to investigate. We had been told Santa could be very quiet. We went towards the sitting room to see if anything had been left under the tree. We bumped into each other in the hall and laughed. I overheard Mam say: 'Oh no, I thought they would be asleep.'

For once we didn't care who knew we were out of bed. We were both scrambling about in our bedrooms when we heard Patrick shouting at us from the sitting room: 'You're wasting your time in the bedrooms. Come here, you lunatics!'

We raced into the sitting room and sure enough the presents had been right in front of our eyes all the time. The first thing I spotted was a doll in a push walker with a little bottle on the stand. I lifted her out of the walker and rushed around the sitting room kissing her. I was so happy with my present and Paul had got the bike he had been longing for.

We were the two happiest children in Connemara.

When we had finished admiring our presents, we decided to tuck into the box of chocolates that had been left in the room. We stayed up until it got bright playing with our new toys. Mam finally came to get us for breakfast.

I suddenly thought about my little sister Alison and asked Mam: 'What did Santa leave for her?'

Mam showed me a box of jelly sweets: 'Santa knows that she loves them.'

On St Stephen's Day, my father came into my bedroom and spotted me playing with two dolls I had gotten for Christmas. Without warning, my father grabbed them and said: 'They look like they're shivering from the cold. We'd better put them into the oven and heat them up.'

I screamed at him: 'Stop, Daddy, please.'

He ignored my screams and left my bedroom.

I followed behind him as he went into the kitchen. He put my two new dolls onto the roasting tray my mother had used for our Christmas turkey and shoved it into the oven. I kept screaming at him to stop, but he only laughed.

A few minutes later, he opened the oven and retrieved the melting dolls. They had been badly burnt. I tried to pull the tray away from him and rescue them but he laughed again and went off to show the burned dolls to my brother.

At this stage, I was bawling crying. He put the tray on the kitchen table and I reached for the dolls.

My father started to laugh and said: 'You can't touch them now, you fool.'

Later that evening when my mother returned home, I told her what had happened. She told me that the dolls were destroyed and not to be whining.

As spring arrived, we were all looking forward to the good weather as it rained all the time in Galway during the winter months. There seemed to be a great atmosphere in Kinnvarra. People in my village visited each other on a daily basis and there was always something exciting happening. Our neighbours would always throw a nice party whenever a child had a birthday. The locals also loved to know what was going on with everyone. If someone was sick, while there would be a flood of compassion, they would love this bit of hot gossip.

My father wouldn't talk to the locals because he said: 'All they talk about is cows.' Our relatives visited regularly, including my great-granny who lived across the road from our home. When our parents went to Spiddal or Galway City, my father's family generally did the babysitting because they lived beside us. His parents had 12 children altogether and all five of his brothers still lived there except for Joe who lived in England. We never saw him.

I was very close to my Aunt Sally, my father's youngest sister. Although she was two years older than me, we got on really well. I used to love spending time with her. I really admired her and thought she was really intelligent. I always used to have a great time with her playing in her garden, doing drama scenes and singing. She told me wonderful stories and she'd act them out as well which always made them more interesting to listen to.

During that spring, I remember my granny calling my brothers and me into her house.

'Oh no, what did we do wrong?' we muttered to each other. However, when we arrived, our granny gave us all a bag of Tayto crisps. I used to love looking at the image of the Tayto man on the bags. Patrick went to open his bag and I shouted: 'Careful, Patrick, don't hurt the Tayto man!'

Granny just laughed. She was looking after us

because Mam was in hospital having Suzanne, my youngest sister. As the youngest of five children, Suzanne had to make a lot of effort to get herself heard but this seemed no problem to her. When my mother returned from hospital with the new baby, I barely recognised her as she had lost so much weight. I remember sitting beside Mam on the couch and peering into the bundle in her arms.

'Where did the new baby come from, Mam?' I asked.

My granny intervened: 'Your mammy bought the baby from the shop at the bottom of the hill.'

But I was not convinced. I had never seen a baby on any of the shelves in the shop.

Mam just laughed at my confusion but nobody explained where the baby had really come from. My mother then handed me my little sister to hold. I tried to be really careful.

Moments later, Paul rushed into the house and asked: 'Is the new baby a boy or a girl?'

'A little girl, you have another little sister,' my mother replied.

A look of disappointment crossed Paul's face.

'Ha, ha, there are three girls in the house now. We're stronger than you,' I said.

'You should have another boy,' Paul said to Mam. 'Send the girl away. All girls are troublemakers.'

I smiled when I heard this and it annoyed him.

As he left the room, he said: 'Mam, can't you see the troublemaker smiling?'

I just kept on smiling. He got angrier and stormed out of the room.

Some of the times I liked my little brother and other times he annoyed me. The times Paul and I got on, my father used to tell him to hit me. From time to time, my father did his best to keep us fighting.

I don't remember many days from my early childhood.
Looking back a lot of it is a blur but I do remember some
days very clearly for one reason or another. How I felt
when I saw other girls dressed up in white dresses is very
vivid in my mind. Looking back, I must have been at
Patrick's First Communion. When I saw the girls in their
pretty white dresses, I asked Mam what was going on. I
wanted to find out how you got to wear a dress like that.

'They're making their First Communion, Barbara.
That'll be you next year,' she told me.

As I sat looking at the girls in the neighbourhood
dressed up and looking so happy, I remember thinking:
'But will Daddy let me?'

I put that thought out of my mind and was just as
excited as the rest of the class when we started
preparing for our First Communion the following year.
Miss Carter arranged music classes for us so we could
sing at the service. I was a regular member of the class
choir at this stage, as we could join at a very young age.
I loved singing and we performed in the local church in
Kinnvarra, Camus. I wanted to become a famous
Country and Western singer, like the American Country
and Western ones I sometimes watched on our
television. I would watch the Country Music Awards at
eight o'clock every Sunday night with my mother.
Sometimes I would try to sing along or sing a song
myself but my father would shout over: 'Shut up' or
'You can't sing anyway.' I used to run out to the fields
to sing where he couldn't hear me.

A few weeks before my First Communion, I came
home from school with my brothers after finishing
singing lessons to find that my parents had gone out. I
remembered that they had told us they were going
shopping and might not be home when we got back
from school. Unusually, we couldn't find the front door

key to get in. It was normally under the mat on the front doorstep. We checked under the geranium pot for the key, but found nothing.

'Let's stay at Granny's until they get back,' Patrick said.

We jumped over the low wall that separated our two houses and ran towards Granny's house. I loved going to see Granny. I'd make up any excuse to go and see her. She was always nice to me. Granddad was a different matter and I hoped he wasn't at home. He was mean and always told us to be quiet.

We found her sitting beside the kitchen window, knitting.

'Ah there yis are,' she said as she looked up from her knitting. 'Come on in and sit down. Do you want some orange? Get yourselves a glass there.'

I got a glass of orange and sat down beside her. The boys had run off outside.

'What are you knitting?' I asked.

'A pair of gloves for your Uncle Tommy,' she replied. 'He has to go to Galway City for a job interview next week.'

Tommy was my father's brother. I liked him because he always played games with us.

'I'm learning how to knit in school but I only work with two needles,' I said. 'I might get to use three needles next year when I'm eight.'

'I learned how to use three needles in school when I was about your age,' she replied. 'It's sometimes easier to use three, like when you're knitting a jumper. I'll teach you how to use three if you like.'

'I'm knitting a scarf because our teacher said it was the easiest thing for us to start on.'

'Are you looking forward to your Holy Communion?' she asked.

'I'm looking forward to wearing the beautiful white dress and white gloves that Mam said she'd get for me,' I said happily.

I was all set to tell her about my dream dress but our parents came home shortly afterwards. I always felt safe at Granny's and I didn't want to leave. Reluctantly, I picked up my school bag and went home.

Patrick, Paul and I helped carry in the weekly shopping, as we always did, while Mam looked after Alison. My brothers and I checked every bag for sweets, but sadly found nothing.

I was marking the calendar every day, counting down for the big day to come. It was the beginning of May and there was a great stretch in the evening. There were only two more weeks to go when I woke up one night. I could hear shouting and crying. I slept in the room next door to my parents' bedroom and I listened to my father shouting. By the sound of his voice, I knew he had been drinking.

Suddenly, there was the sound of a thud and then everything went quiet.

I was frightened and couldn't sleep afterwards. My brothers slept in the bunk beds across from me and I looked over to see if they were awake. They didn't move. Perhaps they were awake and wanted to pretend they hadn't heard all that shouting. I glanced at them again, wondering if they were really awake but I didn't say anything.

The next morning, I heard my father rushing around the house whistling. Even then, I had learnt that if my father whistled he was either up to something or had already done something wrong. As I lay in bed, listening to his energetic whistling, an uncomfortable feeling gripped my chest. I jumped out of bed and dressed quickly.

I went into the kitchen. My father went by carrying a bag of ice towards my parents' bedroom, with a look of concern on his face. I was really worried when I saw it. He closed the door behind him. I followed and knocked on the bedroom door, asking if I could come in.

Patrick passed in the hallway and said: 'Ssssh! Leave it. Don't go in.'

I didn't listen to him and opened the bedroom door. I spotted my mother on the bed, holding an ice pack to her arm.

'What happened, Mam?' I asked. As soon as the words were out of my mouth, I saw the bedside clock lying on the floor.

'It's all right Barbara. I fell and hurt my arm,' she replied.

I knew she was lying and that my father had thrown the clock at her.

I hated him hurting her. I remember thinking, if only I was older, I could have attacked him. I looked at my mother's arm again and felt full of rage.

My father told me to get out.

Later that afternoon, my father went off somewhere. There was always a better atmosphere in the house when he was gone. Even Mam was happier – we could turn the radio up and all relax a bit. When he was there, we were afraid of him and tip-toed around the house. There was no energy when he was there.

'What happened last night, Mam?' I asked.

'I fell off the chair, Barbara. I was reaching for something on top of the cupboard.'

I knew my mother was lying, but at that stage of my life had no understanding of adult relationships. I didn't press her on the issue.

For days afterwards, the atmosphere in the house was horrible. My parents would pass each other without speaking. My father moped around the place. He was cursing all the time and giving out about silly little things, like ranting about a piece of paper on the floor. If the car didn't start, he would rave to whichever one of us was in the car at the time. I couldn't understand why my father behaved like this. His moods changed in a matter of seconds.

I tried to stay out of his way because I was afraid he'd say I couldn't make my First Communion. I began to wish that we could just move away with Mam.

Eventually, a few days later, they started talking again. We could stop walking on eggshells. I was glad when things got a little better. There were only a few days to go on my Communion Calendar and I'd been worried that they wouldn't come.

On the day before my Holy Communion, I sat on my bed and looked at the cards that I had received. There were cards from all my relatives, but the most beautiful one of all was from Mam and Dad. I opened it and read the verse written inside:

'May the Lord Jesus bless and protect you today and all the days of your life.'

I've never forgotten those words.

Underneath Mam had written, 'To Barbara, with lots of love, from Mam and Dad'. I counted the kisses and there were seven altogether, one for every year of my life.

I remember feeling surprised when I saw the kisses because my mam didn't give us many hugs. When I finished reading all the cards, I picked up a heart-shaped rosary box that my granny had given me for my Holy Communion. There were a set of rosary beads inside. I opened up the box and lifted the crystal beads up by their silver cross. They glittered like the colours of the rainbow in the sun. I twirled the cross and the colours changed and danced about the ceiling and walls. I put out my hand and slowly lowered the beads onto my palm. They were like jewels winking in the sun.

Mam said that I could only use the beads for feast days as they were too delicate for everyday praying. I carefully placed them back into their box and tucked them into the corner of a shoebox. My new rosary beads were my most precious possession. I knew my granny really cared for me. She would 'make a fuss of you' and was very laidback and easygoing. I would use any excuse to go over the wall next door. She had some funny habits that used to make me laugh. One of them was an odd thing she did at every meal – she'd always look underneath her plate when there was food on it. To this day I've no idea why she did it. Granddad was very different. He was rude and would row with people. I remember one time a man in the village said to me: 'Your grandfather's an awful man.'

I went to sleep that night dreaming of my special day to come. The following morning, when I woke up, I got dressed in my Communion clothes.

'Where did you buy the dress, Mam?' I asked her, as I stepped into it.

'A family member gave it to me,' she replied.

I knew the other girls in my class would have new dresses but I was used to getting other people's clothes. People from the village often came to the house with clothes for us. I was just happy to have a pretty white dress.

After breakfast, I was in the kitchen when my father asked me to follow him outside.

As we walked towards the front door, my father held my hand.

'Close your eyes,' he instructed.

I wondered what he had done.

He told me to open them and I saw our dark blue car, looking as good as new. Even the centres of the wheels were shining. I wondered why my father had gone to this effort. I was soon to find out.

As we came back into the kitchen, my father turned to me and said: 'I won't be standing at the altar with you today, Barbara.'

I immediately looked at my mother in confusion. All the mams and dads stand beside their child while they get their First Communion. That was the way we had practised in school.

'What does he mean, Mam?' I asked. She was sitting at the kitchen table with Alison in her lap.

'Your father doesn't like the Church, Barbara,' she replied. 'But he should come with us.'

She looked directly at him.

'I've no intention of stepping foot in that church. I never stood at the altar for your brother Patrick either,' he replied.

'But Mam,' I pleaded. 'Miss Carter says both parents have to stand with their children. Please, Mam.'

'I'll be waiting in the car,' he said.

With that, my father left the house.

This was the first time in my life that I remember feeling that my father had little affection for me or my siblings. This was the most important day of my life and he wouldn't come into the church with me like all the other fathers. He didn't care about me; all he cared about was himself. I felt sad and embarrassed.

Later that morning my Aunt Baba, my mother's sister, called around to go to the church with us. Dad drove us all down. When we arrived outside the church, he parked the car and said: 'I'll wait in the car till the ceremony is over.'

I got out of the car without a word.

As soon as my mother, aunt and I entered the church, we noticed how all the other children and parents were dressed so nicely. Many of the mothers were wearing nice hats but mine wasn't. We continued up the aisle and took our seats directly in front of the altar.

The Mass began and it soon became the turn of my school gang to stand in front of the altar. As we received our First Communion, all the other children's parents were there, unless one of them was dead. The only one missing was my father. I felt so disappointed that he hadn't come to the church.

When the Mass finished, I got several cards from my friends and relatives. As I stood on the altar with my classmates, my Aunt Baba took several photographs but it just didn't feel the same without my father there as well. I looked around and saw all my classmates getting their photos taken with their parents. I felt so let down.

Outside the church, many more photographs were taken. My father joined us and, after some persuading from my mother, he agreed to be in some of them. I then ran over to a group of my classmates who were gathered together outside the church. When I had finished talking to them, my mother and I walked towards the car, where my father was talking to some of his friends.

'Come on over to our house this evening for drinks,' I heard him say to one of them. My father's friend also had two daughters making their Communion that day.

When we arrived back at the house, Mam started tidying it for the visitors. I wasn't allowed to help her as I was wearing my white dress, but I also wasn't allowed out in the garden to play so it was a bit boring.

When they arrived that evening, they took more

photos of me with their daughters. After having something to eat, we all went to the local pub. I had a great time in the pub with the girls as our parents sat in a corner, drinking and chatting. We played some of the machines and we tried to learn how to play pool against my brothers. I remember announcing proudly to the girls: 'From this day on we'll be able to receive Communion every week.'

I remember one day towards the end of that year, Mam and I were sitting beside the fire. She was rubbing her hands together and putting them in front of the fire. I asked her to tell me how she had met my father.

'Well it was in the Poitín Still, which was a dance hall near Spiddal…' My father interrupted at this point. We hadn't noticed him coming into the room.

'I never wanted to go out with you,' he told my mother. 'You stuck money in my back pocket to pay us in so we could go places but I told you I didn't want you.'

Mam looked embarrassed and said: 'Shh, Patsie, not in front of the child.'

The conversation died there and I knew better than to bring it up again.

Over the following week, as I lay in bed at night, I began to hear strange noises. I told my parents about them at breakfast the next morning.

'You must be imagining them,' they told me.

For the following couple of nights, I decided to remain awake to investigate what was causing these noises. On the first night, I heard the squeaks of a little animal at my bedroom door and footsteps on the linoleum. It took a good while for the noise to stop. The following night, as I lay in bed, the little critter returned. Again, I could hear his little feet scratching on the linoleum. This time, I decided to see if I could catch the little devil.

I got out of bed and crept towards my bedroom door. I could still hear the little creature's claws. I opened the door as quickly as I could and spotted a mouse. We stared at each other for a split second and then he suddenly scampered off. I tried to follow him but he disappeared from view.

The following morning, I told my mother and father: 'I spotted the mouse last night. I knew I wasn't imagining the sounds.'

'I did find some mouse droppings on the linoleum this morning,' Mam said. She turned to my father: 'You'd better put down a couple of traps to catch him.'

I hadn't realised that this would be the end of my furry little friend visiting me during the night.

I was really sad when my father caught him.

It was only a few weeks after this that my mother was obliged to stay in Galway Hospital again. She was there for several nights. I found out later that this was as a result of my father's violence.

While she was away, my father seemed to be spending more and more time in the pub. One night, after he came home, he tried to climb onto one of the bunk beds in our room. As he was staggering up, he slipped and fell. He lay on the ground and didn't move.

I approached him and started to shake him until he started groaning. He cuddled me and then headed towards his own bedroom.

As a child of eight, I lay on my bed, feeling sorry for my father. I innocently believed he missed my mother.

Sadly, I was shortly to realise that this was not the case.

TWO

Learning the Facts of Life

One Sunday morning in May 1987, Mam told me I had to stay back from Mass.

'Your room is an absolute disgrace. Your clothes are thrown all over the room. You're going to stay at home and clean it up while the rest of us go off to Mass.'

It was a few months before my ninth birthday. I'd been given my own small bedroom because my father said I was getting too big to share with my brothers. My two little sisters shared the fourth bedroom.

'Fine,' I replied. At that stage, I didn't mind whether or not I could go.

I grabbed my skipping rope and skipped down to my room. I rushed around stuffing my clothes anywhere they could fit, even under my bed and in my big teddy bear's pocket. I tidied my toys away too so the room would look clean when Mam returned. In a matter of minutes my room was as tidy as a doll's house. The only thing left to do was hide Vefin, my favourite teddy bear. Mam always went on about 'that scruffy old teddy' and threatened to throw him out every time she spring-cleaned the room. So I wrapped him in his blanket and tucked him into the corner of my wardrobe to hide him. I knew he was safe in there, hidden from her.

But I was not safe.

I had my back to the bedroom door as I stretched on my tippy-toes to push Vefin as far back into the wardrobe as possible. I didn't realise my father was in the room until he put his hand on my shoulder. I jumped.

I don't remember everything that happened next. I've a memory of the fear I felt when he told me to follow him into the sitting room. I thought I must be in trouble as he looked so serious when he pushed me onto the couch.

I didn't know what was happening when he put his knee on the couch. I thought, 'He's going to squash me.' He was a big, heavy-set man and when he lay on top of me there was so much weight. I was trapped. I couldn't breathe properly.

I was sinking down into the couch.

I couldn't move. I didn't understand why he was pushing my skirt up. 'This is not right,' I kept thinking to myself.

I didn't want to look at him.

I tried to switch off from what was going on when he pulled down my knickers. It was such a horrible feeling.

I knew my father shouldn't be doing this.

I felt broken. It was as if my heart was being ripped out of me.

Then there was terrible pain. I felt as if something was overwhelming me. It was so sore.

I started screaming and crying out loud. I begged him to leave me alone.

'Daddy, please don't. Stop. Please Daddy.'

I tried to push him away but I wasn't strong enough.

He wouldn't listen. My father showed no pity as I kept crying. He didn't care and just told me to keep quiet.

Afterwards, I felt numb. From far away I heard him telling me to fix my skirt. I was dizzy.

The frozen feeling inside wouldn't allow me to speak but part of me wanted to run out of the house and scream. My head felt strange.

My father's voice was like an echo talking to me from the other side of the house. He was promising that he wouldn't hurt me again.

'What just happened here is perfectly normal. Sure, people put up with all sorts in their own homes. There's no need to tell anyone about this, is there?' he asked.

I couldn't say anything.

He got angry when I didn't answer. 'Don't say anything to your mam,' he growled.

I was too scared to speak. I nodded.

He went on and on for ages. I really wanted everyone to come home from Mass.

'Children all over Ireland have to deal with a lot worse,' he told me. 'Sure some children are beaten black and blue every day.'

After a while, I think he must have thought he'd gotten through to me because he got up and left me huddled on the couch.

I sat there like that until Mam and the rest of the family came home.

My father was sitting across from me, giving me the evil eye. He was trying to make sure that I put a bright face on for my mother. He wanted me to look happy.

For the rest of the day my father kept warning me to keep up this act. I was in such pain and he kept calling me aside and saying: 'You look miserable, put a "happy face" on for your mam.'

I couldn't look him in the face.

I felt sick.

I hated him.

I nodded along to his orders so I could get away from him as fast as possible.

I went to bed early that night and as I was lying there in the dark I thought back to my father's words.

'I'd prefer to be beaten black and blue all day, every day, than have him hurt me like that again,' I thought.

In the days that followed I felt confused. A huge sadness built up inside me. I tried to convince myself it wouldn't happen again but I felt so uneasy. I tried not to be left in the house alone with my father.

Two weeks later it happened again, in my bedroom this time. The rest of the family were out of the house. Mam was visiting relations with Alison and Suzanne. My two brothers were outside in the garden playing soccer with my Aunt Sally. I longed to go out and play soccer with them in the garden. Sadly, my father said I wasn't allowed.

I had a feeling inside that something bad was about to happen. I tried to sneak out, but my father told me again to stay in the house.

I was scared and went into my bedroom. I lay on my bed with my arms wrapped around Vefin. I was facing the wall but I heard the door open. I squeezed my eyes shut and prayed it was one of my brothers.

'Barbara?'

My heart sank as my father came over to the bed.

'Come on, get up,' he said.

He pulled me off the bed and undressed me. I could hear my brothers outside as he forced himself on me again. I was upset because I couldn't do anything. I wanted to scream and cry but I felt so powerless. It was very painful and I felt sore again. I remember wishing so much that I'd disobeyed him and gone outside where it was safe.

When he was finished he helped me put my clothes back on because I couldn't stop crying.

I felt the same numbness as before.

'Jesus Christ Almighty, you'd think you were going

to have a heart attack or something, you look awful pale,' he said.

It was a lovely sunny day but I felt like everything was dark.

'Dry up your eyes and go out and play with your brothers,' he told me. 'But don't tell them anything.'

He got up off the bed and left the room. I could hear him whistling as he went down the hall.

I began to tune into the noises outside and heard my brothers laughing. I didn't want to play soccer anymore. I didn't even want to go outside. The pain was terrible.

I slowly walked into the sitting room and fell on to the chair. I was taking deep breaths, when Patrick came in and asked was I coming out.

'No thanks,' I said.

I couldn't tell him why I didn't want to join them because I knew we weren't really alone. My father was holding up the wall with his ear to the door. This was what he did any time I tried to talk to anyone else in my family. I had heard him pushing in the door slowly. It was his way of letting me know he was around.

From that day on, my father made every effort to restrict my freedom. He also always made sure he knew all my comings and goings. The following morning stands out in my memory because it was from this time on that I began to feel uncomfortable with everything. I felt dirty and disgusting. I didn't want to be me. I hated myself. I thought it was my fault that he was doing these things.

I sat at our kitchen table trying to eat breakfast but I couldn't; I had no interest in food. As I was getting ready for school, my mind was whirling with all the things my father had told me about how it was all normal. I didn't know what to believe. I remember thinking, 'Do other children really have to do things like that with their fathers?'

I was only eight years of age and my head was full of these thoughts.

Later that afternoon, as I sat on the steps outside the school, I just didn't feel like doing anything. I didn't want to play football, chasing or things like that. I couldn't stop wondering why my father was hurting me. I wasn't even excited that we almost had our summer holidays.

As the abuse kept happening, I began to feel like I was being punished for doing something wrong. My mother was away a lot at the time. She seemed to keep disappearing and we'd be told she'd gone shopping or to visit relatives. I found out later that she was in hospital because of his beatings.

One of the nights she was gone, my father wouldn't let me go to bed. My sisters were already asleep but he kept me in the sitting room and told the boys to get out.

They were jealous that I was getting to stay up late. I tried to go with them but that just annoyed him.

'Sit down and do what you're told,' he shouted.

He started to describe things that women had to put up with and how they suffered.

'Men tear the clothes off a woman with a knife if she refuses to have sex with him. There are no sane men out there. Sure, men only abuse women and use them like rubber dolls,' he told me.

I didn't know what he meant by rubber dolls. I was just worried that he was going to do something to my dolls or teddies next if I didn't do what he wanted.

My father made me feel sick.

He talked about a few of our neighbours and told me they were cheating on their wives.

I knew that was something bad.

He moved from his chair and sat down beside me on the couch. I can still remember the smell of the glass of homemade *poitín* in his hand.

I tried to edge away, nodding to show I was listening to his stories. I was praying he wouldn't notice but he grabbed my knee.

I went still and tried to make myself as small as a mouse.

The more he drank, the worse it got.

He brought out a pornographic video and insisted on showing it to me. I didn't want to look at it and tried to turn my face away. He told me that I had to watch it as I needed to learn the facts of life.

He kept re-playing the film, even though he knew I didn't want to watch it and that it was making me cry.

I turned my head away from the video. I hoped he wouldn't realise I wasn't watching because I knew it would make him angry.

He finally turned the video off and reached for me. I knew he was going to try and hurt me again.

I panicked.

I jumped up and ran to my bedroom.

'Daddy, leave me alone, you're hurting me and I don't like it,' I screamed.

He dragged me into my brothers' bedroom, where both Patrick and Paul were asleep. He woke them up and started showing them pictures of naked women having sex. They rubbed the sleep out of their eyes and looked confused. When they saw the pictures, they didn't know what to say.

It was horrible.

I ran out of the room and got into my bed. I could still hear my father laughing, while he stood there, with drink on him, in their bedroom. I heard him tell them that he wanted me to see the pictures as well.

I prayed that he would fall over or pass out but he came back into my bedroom. He held up the scary pictures. He kept talking and wouldn't let me go to sleep.

He was standing right in front of me and I was shaking.

'Women have had to suffer putting up with men for centuries, not to mention childbearing. When they get married, they have to endure constant pain and misery,' he told me.

I kept the covers pulled right up to my chin and hugged Vefin.

I couldn't stop thinking that he was going to grab me but Patrick and Paul were still awake. Eventually, he grew tired. He was swaying on his feet as he stumbled out the door.

As months passed, I felt my life was falling apart. I don't even remember my ninth birthday but I do remember the first time I realised how bad I felt inside.

I was kept after school one day for being bold. The teacher's daughter, I don't remember her name, tried to cheer me up.

'How old are you?' she asked.

I looked away.

'Stand up, let me see how tall you are,' she tried again.

But I felt too sad to even talk to her.

That evening, when I arrived home from school, Sean Delapp, was sitting in our house chatting to my mother. He was an old fellow from the neighbourhood, who used to visit us occasionally. As soon as I entered the house, I knew if he was in the sitting room as I could smell his pipe smoke. I liked the smell of the pipe. He was such a lovely person and wonderful company. He was also one of the few people that my father didn't give out about.

I was always happy to see him. I said hello, threw my bag on the couch and ran out into the garden. While I was playing in the garden, I bumped my head off a big rock. When I put my hand to my forehead, I noticed there was blood on it.

I screamed with fright and ran in to my mother, who was in the sitting room. She looked at me and immediately stood up and brought me into the kitchen where she dabbed my forehead with a damp sponge. She then dried it with a towel.

Sean came into the kitchen, a look of concern on his face. He said: 'Don't be afraid, you'll be fine.'

It felt comforting when he said that.

A few days later I was playing with my brothers in the garden when Sean walked up towards our gate. We used to run up to him excitedly. As we chatted to him, a silver van pulled up outside our gate. A man rolled the window down and enquired about a certain house in the neighbourhood. After we pointed out the house, he said to me: 'Would you mind coming with me and showing me?'

I didn't know what to do. Thank God Sean was standing there and heard everything. He intervened, saying: 'I don't think that's necessary at all. In fact, I'll break this stick over your back if you don't leave at once.'

When the van had gone, Sean went in to my mother and told her about the incident.

She said: 'I heard on the radio that kids were missing from the Clifden area.'

I was shaken by the incident and so thankful he'd said something. He was a very kind person as was his entire family. I never saw them fighting or arguing. I remember Patrick tried a few puffs of his pipe and got sick afterwards.

Sean only started laughing.

'That's the best thing that could've happened to you. It'll put you off cigarettes for life,' he told him and he was right.

He enjoyed telling us interesting stories. I learned a lot from him. He came out with wonderful sayings like 'It's always a new broom that sweeps clean first' or 'A fly would never enter a sealed mouth'.

We never tired of his company.

One day followed another and I tried to do normal things. Going to school every day got me away from my father but it was hard concentrating. At least I was safe when I was there. Some days, I walked home with my brothers. Other times, I walked with one of my friends, Gemma, who was heading in the same direction. Gemma was a year ahead of me in school and she had a bubbly personality. Although I never discussed my father's behaviour with her, I found it helped me to talk to her about all the gossip and all the small school things that were happening in my life. The journey was a little longer when I walked home with Gemma but it was definitely worth it. We generally parted at a fork in the road – laughing about Gemma taking the high road and me taking the low road. I hated having to turn in the opposite direction to go home.

As soon as I saw the house, I would feel dread build up inside me. I'd start to walk slower. No matter what time I walked into the house, it always felt cold. My father would step out, smiling and chatting away, while making tea and slicing bread. He would then ask if my brothers were far behind me. I came to realise that he was trying to find out how much time he would have with me on his own. I always replied that they were right behind me. If my father thought that I was lying, he would generally touch me. After he was done, my father's tirades would follow. He would rant at me, giving out about men's behaviour and talking about how horrible they were. He would usually complain about his own marriage and Mam, claiming it was all a horrible accident.

'My marriage is a curse, it should never have happened,' he would tell me.

I never said anything and tried to only half-listen.

Every time it happened, I thought to myself that the only accident was him coming into this world.

I started to faint at Mass around that time. One Sunday morning, as I stood on the altar, I felt light-headed. Suddenly my vision blurred and my legs went from under me. I awoke in a stranger's arms, outside the church. My mother was standing in front of me with her hands on her face, wondering what had happened.

Since my father didn't go to Mass, he wasn't there. He used to stay home and peel the potatoes to go into a big pot of stew. He'd begin to peel them before we'd leave the house but when we returned from Mass, he would generally still be standing there, with potato peel all over the kitchen.

'How come it takes you so long to peel a few potatoes? Sure you were doing them when we left,' my mother would ask him.

He always told her that he had been doing other housework: 'Do you not understand how tough this work is for a man being kept on his feet all the time?'

Later that week, my parents drove me to the local surgery. My doctor asked how I felt before I fainted and where I was getting pains.

'I see flashing white lights for minutes and then I get the warning signs and I know I'm going to faint,' I replied. 'If I try to ask for help, I can't seem to speak and before I know it I'm waking up in someone's arms, outside the church.'

He told me that he would have to send me to hospital to investigate my fainting problems.

I remember neighbours dropping in for a cuppa and asking my parents if there had been any follow-up done about my fainting episodes. My parents would tell them that the doctor had referred me to the local outpatient's clinic for further examinations. I think they only took me there once.

Weeks later, I fainted again at Mass. I remember waking up in the arms of the same man from Camus who had helped me the first time. I had been queuing up at the altar to get Communion with my brothers when it happened. I remember pinching Paul and giving him a sign that I'd felt a tightness in my chest but he just looked away. My mother had been late arriving so she wasn't nearby. I'd felt myself falling forward and the young fair-haired man caught me.

Mass was nearly over at this stage so he carried me outside. When it had finished, my mother came out and ran over to where I was lying on the ground. I couldn't understand why she hadn't come out earlier. I was worried when I woke up in the arms of the young man from Camus. He was looking around him, nervously asking where my parents were, when suddenly my mother came out of nowhere with my brothers.

'Is there something wrong with this child? This isn't the first time she's fainted like this.' He was looking up at my mother.

'Her condition is being looked after by a doctor,' she reassured him.

I knew this wasn't true but I didn't dare say anything. Since my last visit to the doctor, nothing else had happened. I later learnt that the hospital had sent letters trying to arrange an appointment for me and my father had burnt them.

When we arrived home that afternoon, she told my father what had happened.

'She shouldn't be going to Mass in that condition. She should stay at home in future, until she gets better,' he said.

Mam agreed so that was the end of me going to Mass for the next few weeks.

I was scared and wished I could stop myself fainting because I knew what would happen if I was in the house alone with my father. Sure enough, after the rest of the family went off to Mass that first Sunday morning, my father came into my bedroom.

He started off by telling me about what had happened in the pub the previous night.

I was dreading him touching me.

I pretended to listen and even asked questions to keep him talking. I tried to keep myself covered with a blanket, so he couldn't come near me.

It was no good – when he had got a conversation going he gradually eased his way onto the bed. Suddenly he told me to push up in the bed. I had no choice as he lay in beside me and forced himself on me.

As he turned me over, I tried telling him to stop but my voice was muffled. He was on top of me and my face was pressed into the bed. I couldn't breathe and tried to turn my face to the wall to catch a breath.

He wasn't interested in how I felt or how painful it was.

It was agony.

I felt myself going dizzy again and I must have fainted because the next thing I remember was him shaking me. I told him I was going to be sick and he went off to the kitchen to get me a basin.

I was shaking and felt filthy. He had used my body even though I kept telling him to stop. I didn't understand why my father was treating me like this.

After I got sick, he sat down beside me and started telling me the same old stories but this time he apologised and asked me: 'What effect is this having on you?'

I mumbled: 'It's hurting me. It's bothering me.'

He blamed the drink, even though he wasn't drunk at all. There was no alcohol in his system that morning.

'It has nothing to do with drink, you do this to me when you're sober,' I said, crying.

'I'm sorry, I'm going to stop. I will, I'll stop.'

He then said, 'I know this is why you get sick. It has a major effect on you. Would you be happy if I left you alone?'

I thought he really meant it. 'Yes, I would be happy if you left me alone,' I replied.

He rambled on like this tirelessly, like a broken record, the same thing all the time.

I was trembling at this stage, I felt like I was going to vomit again. I was crying my eyes out.

He tried to take my mind off what he had done to me by starting to bad-mouth my mother's family.

I could barely hear what he was saying because I was in such a state. He stopped after a while and I could see that his face was going red. I knew he was getting angry because I was still bawling crying and couldn't stop.

We both knew the rest of the family would be back any minute.

My father must have started worrying that I was in such a state that I would tell someone about what he was doing to me. He shouted: 'One word about this to anybody and I'll drown you in the lake right out there.' He jabbed his finger out the window, towards the lake beside our house.

I believed him completely.

'And don't think of running over to tell anyone next door because my family reports everything back to me. Sure they wouldn't even believe you anyway.'

I'd stopped crying at this stage I was so scared.

Suddenly, we heard the sound of our car driving up the lane. Mam and my brothers and sisters were returning from Mass.

My father quickly ran out of my room, saying as he went: 'You know what I mean. Keep your mouth shut and get that horrible sad face off and put on a bright face quickly for them. I'm warning you; don't give them anything to be suspicious of.'

As soon as the rest of the family entered the house, my father's demeanour changed completely. Gone was the raging, threatening monster and out came the pleasant, good-humoured husband and father.

He was very conversational and asked Mam who she had spotted at Mass. I saw my mother's face brighten, as it always did whenever my father behaved kindly towards her, when I walked into the kitchen.

Mam then looked at my face and told my father that I looked quite pale.

'Ah she's fine,' my father replied.

'But do you not think she's a bit quiet?' Mam asked. 'Are you OK, Barbara?'

I didn't say anything because I was afraid of my father, who was glaring at me behind my mother's back.

My father's humour changed and he shouted: 'Jesus

Christ Almighty. What the fuck are you thinking? I didn't say a word to her.'

My mother immediately went quiet and said nothing more.

Later that evening over dinner, my father watched me picking at my food. I don't know how I managed to eat with him staring at me all the time. I felt sick to the stomach and uncomfortable. I was still in a lot of pain. I knew everyone in the family had to behave in a certain way to keep my father happy and I could feel all of that as we sat at the table. Nobody said a word because of the atmosphere.

Whenever I looked in his direction, I noticed a dirty look on his face. I began to daydream. I did this a lot and it seemed to help. Sometimes my mind would wander into space, thinking about nothing, and other times I would think about running away from my father. After a while I realised that the rest of my family were looking at me, wondering what I was doing, which brought me back down to earth. I stopped thinking about being somewhere far away and tried to concentrate on eating my dinner.

My mother gave me an impatient look but she didn't say anything.

The following day, I went in the car with my mother to visit her mother. My granny, who was in her mid-70s, was a hard-working lady. She'd spend hours cutting seaweed and turf and had a fondness for brewing *poitin*. She lived nine miles from our house and I seldom had a dull moment with her. She told great stories and I really enjoyed listening to her.

Sadly, I didn't get the opportunity to visit her as much as I would have liked. My father always ensured that I was kept at home as much as possible. He always seemed to find some household job I had to do immediately if there was any chance of going to my granny's.

I felt very sad about it because we weren't able to see my other granny either.

My father's family were always rowing with one another. Usually the rows were just over small things and quite childish but they could still last for months. Weeks would go by with members of my father's family not speaking to one another. When my father was rowing with a family member, it affected my relationship with my relatives. Due to the current row, because of a fight my father had had with his brother over a car, I wasn't allowed to talk to my Aunt Sally. Sadly, Sally was not allowed to speak to us once a row broke out between our parents. I used to feel really bad when she'd pass me on the road and turn her head in the opposite direction. She would also pass me in school and not say a word. I hated it and I knew our entire family was suffering because of my father's childish behaviour.

To try to cheer us up, Patrick used to draw white hopscotch boxes on the ground outside our house. He put the numbers one to nine in different boxes and told us to jump in the boxes that he chalked. I worked hard at it, trying to keep my balance as I jumped from box to box. We knew how to do it because we used to watch the older kids playing it. Whenever we were bored or feeling bad at home, we played hopscotch. Paul and I also developed another new pastime. We would roll a barrel to the top of a hill and one of us would jump into it. The other would roll the barrel to the bottom of the hill. We had great fun and it always made me feel better. It kept my mind off other matters.

One day, after playing hopscotch, Paul and I went into the house to see if we could find anything nice to eat. We climbed onto the sink to look in the cupboard. We spotted a sweet cake so we asked my mother if we could have a piece. I told her that the cake was in little crusts and that I'd love to eat it.

'Go ahead the two of you. You can finish it outside. It's a gorgeous day,' she said.

We were so happy to have the cake. We were only allowed to eat sweet things at the weekend. The birds kept flying around us for food.

I remember such a feeling of ease while we sat in the field enjoying the sweet cake. My father wasn't around to shout at us.

With all the trouble at home, I began to lose interest in school. I'd stopped fainting so I was able to go back to Mass but that didn't help me in the classroom. I was in third class and my mind wasn't allowing me to concentrate properly. Some mornings I could no longer hear the teacher talking. As the end of the school year approached, even though Gemma tried to help me, I was struggling to keep up. Much as I tried to keep joking away in my usual manner, it became extremely difficult. I don't remember any of the teachers asking me what was wrong or going to see my parents. I don't think it would have made any difference if they had.

I didn't think things could get any worse but one day Gemma called to my front door. When she came in, my family, for no apparent reason, were awkward with her. My brothers and sisters kept glancing in my direction, as if to say: 'Why have you invited this person into our house?' They said very little and didn't once try to talk to her.

It was awful and she left quite quickly. I was really embarrassed and thought that now I wouldn't even have a friend at school.

She wasn't long gone when my father called me into the kitchen. I knew it wasn't going to be for anything good.

He said to Mam: 'Where did Barbara get the idea that she could bring her friends to the house?'

My mother, easily intimidated by my father, looked at him blankly. She didn't say anything so he turned to me and said: 'You're not allowed to invite anyone to this house without my permission.'

I knew immediately that he would never give his permission.

He continued: 'Your friends from school might come in and start stealing things.' At that stage, I understood why my father didn't want any of my friends around our house. He tried to cover it up and shouted, in his usual manner: 'If I didn't have any friends growing up as a child, why should you?'

I looked at Mam. It was unfair and I hoped she'd say something.

'You must obey your father's rules,' she said.

I couldn't answer back because I was afraid my father might hit me.

That was the last time one of my friends came to the house.

THREE

The Lake

Christmas was one of the few times of the year I could relax. My father usually didn't come near me because there was too much going on in the house. We were always busy getting everything ready and relations dropped in and out at all hours. At night I'd often have cousins or my sisters sharing my room so he couldn't get me alone. Most of my good childhood memories are wrapped around Christmas time.

We had some strange happenings in our house on my tenth Christmas. We got up at around eight that morning and started looking for our presents.

My father shouted at us from my parents' bedroom: 'Stop running around! And stop turning everything upside down, making it look like we've been burgled.'

We went into their bedroom and looked around to see if we could find our presents but there was nothing there.

Mam was laughing as she watched us. Our father's head emerged from under the blankets. He looked at Paul and said to him: 'I know what Santa left for you. It's a bag of turf. I saw him early this morning.'

He took any opportunity to annoy Paul. My father was laughing at him; he was delighted when Paul got annoyed. I could hear my father telling him that he was wasting his time and that he'd tried to explain to him all year that he wasn't going to get anything from Santa.

'If Santa did that, I'll attack him when he puts his big fat legs down the chimney next year,' Paul said.

Mam joked: 'Well, I guess you all should go back to

bed and not waste time looking for something that isn't
there.'

My brothers were lifting the blankets, checking
under every single bed in the house.

Paul shouted: 'Wouldn't you think he would have
put them in our bedrooms instead of messing about?
There was this sort of messing last year too. It sickens
me.'

Patrick said: 'Paul, did you hear the footsteps last
night?'

'I thought I heard something,' Paul replied.

'I don't know, but I noticed one thing; the bloody
bottle of Coke that Mam left out of the fridge last night
for him is empty on the table,' Patrick agreed.

'No wonder he's so fat! He left damn all for us. All
he does is eat and drink,' Paul replied. 'Did you write a
letter to him last night because I can't see that on the
windowsill?'

I told him if the letters were gone, that meant Santa
had read them and we'd gotten something.

We went into the boys' bedroom and Patrick was
raging that he couldn't find any presents. He yanked
the curtain open and suddenly a big white bag fell out.
He jumped with joy until he realised that it was Paul's
name on the bag.

He was raging: 'I mustn't have gotten anything
because this was the last place I had to look. I've
searched everywhere else in this house! Frig that tinker,
Santa!'

Paul wasn't listening to him because he was too busy
opening his presents.

Patrick jumped back up onto his bunk bed, giving
out about not getting any presents. In his frustration, he
found himself kicking a plastic bag at his feet, under the
blanket. He was so caught up in looking around the

house for his presents that he'd never even thought of looking at the end of his bed. He began shouting at Paul.

'I bet this is your bag of socks, get rid of them off my bed.'

Patrick pulled the blanket and realised that it wasn't a bag of socks at all, but his presents. He shouted with joy.

I found my own toys under a little mat outside my bedroom. They were well wrapped and as I pulled them apart, I spotted a green-haired golliwog smiling at me. I was delighted with my doll and told my mother: 'It's the same golliwog that the teacher has in a box at school and she lets me play with it whenever I want to.'

After I pulled the doll out of the bag, I spotted a colouring book and markers and a little blue dolphin that I could wind up. I was delighted with all my presents.

We had a lovely dinner on Christmas Day because Mam was such a good cook. My granny came around to us that evening. She'd made us some homemade butter which was delicious.

I hated taking down the decorations after Christmas. I could feel the Christmas warmth disappear, as the lights that used to shine from the Christmas tree vanished. I wished we could leave them up all year round.

I placed the little angel back in the bag and wished it was next Christmas already.

We were back in school when, a few nights later, I thought I saw a shadow pass outside my door. My father was out at the pub so I knew he wasn't prowling around.

With my fists clenched around my blue plastic rosary beads, I started praying that it would go away. It disappeared but I'd got such a fright I couldn't sleep. It was about an hour later when I heard my father coming home. I called on every saint not to let him near my room but the saints must have been somewhere else. At first he tried tip-toeing on the lino but I could still hear him walking into my bedroom.

I pretended to be asleep but he started shaking me.

'Wake up, wake up,' he whispered.

I could smell the alcohol off his breath.

He said: 'Get up, Barbara.'

I was frightened and didn't move.

He realised that I was pretending to be asleep. My father pulled me out of the bed by the legs and shook me to make sure that I was fully awake. He pulled up my nightclothes, pushed me back on the bed and raped me.

I made a noise and he told me to keep my mouth shut so that my mother couldn't hear anything that went on.

I felt so helpless. He was hurting me and I didn't know how I could endure the pain anymore. I had tears flowing from my eyes but he didn't stop. I tried to tell myself that it wasn't happening and that I was only imagining it. I tried to escape in my mind but the pain was too bad.

It kept bringing me back.

I was only ten years of age, thinking an animal wouldn't do this to its young. I begged him to stop.

It was the most horrible night of pain for me. When he was finished, he stood up, put his trousers on and left. He was probably afraid that my brothers, who were sleeping in the room next to me, might have overheard him. The walls in our house were quite thin.

I heard him go into the kitchen and start to cook something for himself.

Later that night, after I thought he'd gone to bed, I went into the bathroom. I locked the door behind me and tried to wash myself. As I looked at myself in the mirror I suddenly got sick. I felt so weak that I fainted. I hadn't done that in months.

I woke up just as my father burst the bathroom door in. He lifted me off the ground as my mother walked in behind him.

I asked her what happened and she told me that I fainted.

'Your father had to break the door down when he heard the bang of you falling on the floor,' she said.

He asked me: 'Are you all right, Barbara?' He was pretending that nothing had happened earlier in the night.

I still felt dirty, even after having a cold shower. I was also shaking from the cold.

I didn't answer him.

'I'm going to bed,' I said to my mother and rushed down the hall to my bedroom.

The following day in school was very difficult. I couldn't stop thinking about what had happened. There was a feeling of emptiness inside me. I couldn't have fun with the rest of my classmates. I was also very tired because I'd been awake all night. I was glad that none of my friends seemed to notice because I didn't want to talk about it.

That evening, I told Mam: 'I really don't want to sleep in that room on my own anymore.'

I'd tried telling her this before but she kept saying how lucky I was to have my own room. This time I told her about the shadow I'd seen the night before.

'I'm too scared to sleep,' I said.

She replied: 'Barbara, I've told you there's nothing to be scared of.'

I kept talking about how frightened I was until my mother finally relented and allowed me to sleep beside her. I felt comfortable there and was finally able to relax.

A couple of hours later, however, a car coming up the driveway woke me up. I knew it was my father. I stared at the curtain and could see the reflection of the car lights on the wall. But this time, because Mam was there, I wasn't frightened.

When my father came into the bedroom, he asked: 'Why isn't she in her own bed?'

Mam explained to him: 'She was upset because she was seeing a shadow outside her room. She wouldn't sleep a wink if we left her in there.'

He gave me a strange look but he got into bed, the other side of my mother.

I felt safe with Mam in between us and drifted back to sleep.

The next morning, my father brought up the shadow when the rest of my family were out of the house: 'So what's this about a shadow outside your bedroom?' He appeared anxious. 'You shouldn't be making up stories and telling them to your mother.'

I told him all about the shadow and what I had actually seen: 'And I noticed that it didn't come past the arch in the door.'

He replied: 'It must've been your imagination.'

Later that evening, as we were all watching television, my father called me into his bedroom. As he pretended to sort the clothes in his wardrobe, he started giving out to me.

'What have I done wrong?' I asked him.

'Take that miserable-looking face off while you're watching TV with the rest of them,' he replied. 'Don't forget I'll be watching you all the time.'

My father didn't have to tell me this; I already knew. I felt suffocated by my father constantly watching me.

Another way my father liked to keep me under his eye was to cut my hair. My father liked keeping my and my sisters' haircut very short, like a boy's, which I hated. I think he did it because he wanted us to look horrible.

I remember going into school one Monday morning after having a particularly severe haircut over the weekend. The other children in the class laughed at me. One girl from the neighbourhood stood up and said: 'Don't mind the stupid things the others are saying, they're only jealous.'

I think she realised how I was badly affected by these remarks.

Some people would ask me who had cut my hair and they were surprised when I'd tell them that my father did it. I remember one particular time, when a boy, who was standing outside the school at lunchtime, laughed at my hair. I ran into the toilet crying and didn't come out for 20 minutes. That week, the other two classes came into our classroom for a Mass the priest was reading. I will never forget the words he said: 'If a person's hair is short it doesn't mean that they're different from anybody else and it doesn't mean that a person is ugly.'

He must have noticed that I was very shy and uncomfortable about my hair.

I remember one of the teachers tried to make me feel better as well. One afternoon, she came over to me and asked: 'Are you not going to join the other girls in the yard?'

She was trying to cheer me up because she probably noticed that I had been sitting, staring into space, on my own.

'Some of the boys were laughing at my hair. They said it's ugly and I look like a boy,' I said.

'Don't mind them,' she told me.

I was really grateful she'd tried to help me. It made me feel better so I joined my friends and tried to put it behind me.

When I returned home that afternoon, I complained to Mam about my hair: 'It's too short, Mam. Everyone in school is laughing at me.'

My mother offered little support. Instead she complained to my father about having to listen to me moaning. She said that she was getting the blame about my hair and that she shouldn't have to put up with me saying that I looked like a boy.

My father then turned to me and said: 'Stop giving out about your hair to your mother – your constant whinging is driving her mad.'

Sometimes I thought Mam was as bad as my father. She would report back to my father every time I complained to her about his behaviour. At times I would barely have the story finished and she'd be approaching him reciting back what I had said.

When my hair began to grow a little soon afterwards, my father got a chair one Saturday and told me to sit on it. His hairdressing salon was outside the shed in our back garden. He began to cut my hair very short, ignoring my protests: 'Stop giving out, sure it has to be cut.'

Patrick came around to the back garden and pleaded with my father to leave my hair alone.

'Her hair looks nice as it is; it doesn't need a cut,' he said.

My father ignored Patrick's comments and continued with the scissors. My lovely curls dropped to the ground.

Patrick still pleaded, but it didn't matter to my father how it looked. He didn't care how much I hated it short. There was nobody that was going to change his mind. As soon as my hair passed my shoulders, out came the scissors. He did the same to my sisters' hair and I could see they hated it too. But what could we do?

That summer, my entire family worked on the bog near our house, turning turf. After turning it, my father told us to bring all the bags of turf down the hill to the main road. He said it would save him from having to waste petrol driving the tractor up the hill to get them. I remember my mother walking in front of us, carrying a heavy bag on her back. Thankfully she had to stop from time to time to rest and we'd all get to sit down.

I hated working on the bog. It was strenuous and dirty work and our hands used to be filthy. The weight I had to carry on my back was so heavy that I would be breathless by the time I reached the main road. We were too young to be carrying such heavy bags. After a day's work I would have a backache.

On one occasion, I remember my father telling my mother that we needed to collect as many bags of turf as possible as the weather was going to deteriorate. I remember him saying: 'Let me know if they don't do much work. Don't give them a chance to sit around yapping. That's all they ever do.'

When we came home that night, my mother told my father: 'Barbara did most of the work today, she worked very hard.'

I suppose I was working very quickly with anger. I hated being there and just wanted to get the job done as fast as possible. I didn't want to have to face the place again.

My father commented: 'I noticed that Barbara certainly works as hard as her granny.' It was rare praise from him.

The summer was speeding by and it was almost the end of July before we knew it. I used to have a lovely time going for walks with our dog Blackie. We'd never had any pets before we got him earlier that year. He was a gorgeous black and white dog. My father hated Blackie. He never had any interest in animals and the only way my mother convinced him to have a dog was to say that it would keep the cows out of our garden. She said a dog would be ideal to keep them away. We all loved him.

Mam made a little kennel for Blackie beside our house. I used to go out every day after dinner and give him the potato skins. He would wag his tail whenever I fed him. As far as I can remember, my father never even bought dog food for him.

My parents also got some hens from friends and Paul and I enjoyed feeding them crushed bread.

One day, as I walked around the house to feed the hens, I spotted my father in the garden with one of his brothers. As I got closer, I realised that he was cutting the heads off the poor hens with a knife. My father was holding one of the hens and cutting his little head off with a pocket knife.

I ran into the house crying: 'Mam, go out and stop him, he's hurting the hens.'

She told me: 'That's what people do all the time for food.'

'But I love the hens; I don't want them to be hurt,' I pleaded with her.

My mother walked out and stood at the side of the house.

'Barbara's upset over you hurting the hens,' she called up to him.

A wicked smile crossed my father's face as he continued to chop their heads off.

The same afternoon he mentioned that he wanted to get rid of Blackie. I was afraid that he would do something awful to him too.

My father claimed that poor Blackie was useless around the house. My Uncle Tommy tried to tell him that my sisters and I would miss him but I knew he wasn't listening. My father then walked towards the wall to look at Granny's house. Her dog, a terrier, was sitting outside her door and my father was staring at him.

'I'd like to drown that terrier with Blackie,' he said to Uncle Tommy.

'She needs that dog around the house,' my uncle replied.

He left the terrier alone but my father's mind was made up about Blackie.

Later that day, he got a rope and tied it around the dog's neck. Then he tied the rope to the back of the car and drove off.

Poor Blackie tried to free himself, but he couldn't do it. I was standing at the side of our house when I saw him being dragged along. The poor thing was struggling to stay on his feet. I started screaming hysterically and Alison came outside. She was only four years old at the time and she began bawling crying when she saw that Blackie was hurt.

I was shaking with shock and I couldn't believe what I was seeing. My mother ran out and looked sad when she saw how my sister and I were reacting.

'Your father has to do it, girls, because he feels that Blackie will bring dust in the house and that it might bring back your asthma attacks, Alison.'

'That's not right,' I cried. 'Alison hasn't had one in ages. Besides, Blackie has his own little home outside the house, not bothering anyone.'

I wanted to believe that my father wouldn't actually kill him. When he suddenly stopped the car in the middle of the road I thought he might have changed his mind after hearing my sister and me crying.

I should have known better.

He pulled out fast again and I could see him watching Blackie struggling, trying to free himself from the heavy rope. I was stunned when I heard my father laughing loudly.

Blackie stopped moving soon after that.

I started walking towards the car. I wanted to take care of Blackie. I was hoping he wasn't really dead and that I could nurse him back to life. Before I reached him, my father got out, threw his body into the back and drove off.

He returned home shortly afterwards and wouldn't say where he'd left Blackie. My mother told him how badly I reacted and pointed at Alison, sitting, quietly crying. He repeated what Mam had said: 'That dog wasn't good for your asthma condition.'

Mam then told him that I'd said it wasn't a good excuse and he gave me a dirty look.

He moved over to Alison and started trying to console her. I was devastated after watching Blackie die and seeing his attempt to manipulate my sister disgusted me.

I hated him.

The same evening, he did it again – this time to Granny's terrier from next door. I think he did it because he knew that I liked playing with Granny's dog and I used to pet him a lot. I ran to the back of the house when I heard the noise. My father had tied the same rope around the terrier's neck and was laughing again. No doubt, my father was finding the whole experience very amusing. When he'd made enough fun of the poor animal he threw him into the back of the car and drove off again.

I knew that he was probably going to drown him. I thought that's what had happened to Blackie.

When he came back, my mother told him I'd been watching.

'The girl couldn't believe you were doing that,' she said.

All he said was: 'That's Blackie gone now and your granny's dog for you. He's dead now. He didn't float on top of the water for long; he went down quickly.'

Alison was still crying about Blackie so my father must have felt a little guilty. He promised to buy her sweets and went off to get them. When he came back, he tried to tell her again that Blackie had to go as his hair was aggravating her asthma. She seemed to accept it and had a few sweets. What could she do – Blackie was gone.

It took a long time for me to forget him after that. I used to look at the spot where Blackie had been tied up and feel miserable. I missed sneaking out of the house and feeding him. I'd still look for him every time I came home.

None of us asked for a new dog.

Later that week, my father called over to his mother's house and met up with three men already there from the neighbourhood. They all went over to a shed across from Granny's house. I was standing outside our house so I could see what was going on.

I heard him tell the others: 'I'm going to set a trap for the bird, look at this.' They were confused and didn't understand what he was going to do.

I watched as he placed a piece of cheese in the trap and left it on top of the shed. As the men stood there, they gradually became bored waiting for the birds to come down and grab the cheese so my father decided to replace the cheese with some bread. This time a bird approached the snare. As it tried to pull the piece of bread out of the trap, his legs got caught. My father started roaring laughing as he pulled the trap down. He continued laughing as the poor creature struggled to fly away.

I felt so sorry for the poor bird.

My father stood laughing over the little bird. When he finally released it from the trap, it ran around trying to lift its wings and fly. It had damaged its wing. The more the poor bird struggled, the more laughter I heard from my father.

He seemed to want to attack every creature in sight for some reason. A few days later, my father asked his friends to give him some medication so that he could give it to his father's donkey. Initially I thought it was a joke but he gave the poor donkey half a bottle of anti-depressant tablets. After a few minutes, it fell to the ground.

The following morning, when my grandfather came out, he discovered the donkey lying on the ground, motionless. He stood there, surprised, wondering what had happened.

I spotted my father standing behind the wall, laughing at my grandfather.

Grandfather asked him: 'Jesus, do you know what happened to the donkey? That's very strange; I wonder how it happened.'

He kicked the donkey and tried to wake him up but the poor animal was long past caring.

I don't know whether my granddad ever found out

what my father had done. He might have suspected because in many ways my grandfather was just like my father. Most of our neighbours used to fetch water from the well that belonged to my great-grandmother, my father's grandmother. They all had water in their houses but they liked the water from the well and they'd also heard that tap water was poisonous. However, my grandfather stopped them from doing it. He was trying to keep the well to himself.

He was a rather taciturn character at the best of times. Whenever a neighbour visited his house, he would either ignore them completely, begin reading a newspaper or higher the volume on the television. By this stage, he had managed to alienate himself from every one of his neighbours in the locality. I remember, soon after his donkey died, a deaf and dumb lady came to try and fetch water from the well. My grandfather shouted sarcastic remarks at her and called her names until she ran off.

The following week, my brothers and I were watching him baling hay in a field across from his house. When my Aunt Sally spotted us sitting on the wall, she walked over and began chatting. As we were talking, our grandfather finished up and returned to their house.

When we saw him going in, we decided to play a game in the field. We began rolling around in the hay and were having a great time until our grandfather spotted us. He came out of the house and began roaring at us. We all scattered in different directions. He chased after us and caught my aunt. He grabbed hold of her and slapped her hard across the face. Her glasses fell to the ground.

My brothers and I felt sorry for Sally as she wiped the tears from her eyes. He then yelled at her: 'Now go back to the house.'

We quickly jumped over the wall and returned home.

I hoped I didn't turn out like him.

One Sunday afternoon, a few weeks later, Mam decided to go and visit her family. She told me to get my two sisters ready. I don't remember where my brothers were that day but they weren't in the house. I didn't want to be alone with my father.

I tried to leave with them. I told my mother that I had all the housework done and that I needed to go with her.

Then I overheard him saying to my mother: 'No, no. She was bold during the week, leave her behind. That should teach her a lesson. She was cheeky.'

My mother agreed and that was that.

I stood at the window, crying, until the car disappeared from view. Once it was gone, I couldn't stay still. I ran around the house.

My father began to curse at me.

I tried to calm down and started ironing the pile of clothes my mother had left for me. I moved everything into my bedroom hoping my father would forget I was there. I had my back to the door when he came in.

I jumped, as he growled in my ear: 'If I ever hear you telling anyone about what I've done to you, I'll put a rope around your neck and throw you out into the lake over there – do you hear me?'

Even though I'd been listening to these silly threats for years, they still frightened the living daylights out of me. I nodded. Even though in the back of my mind, I knew that my father was just trying to frighten me, I couldn't help shaking whenever he started talking to me like that. He was like a broken record and I hated the kind of language he used.

After I nodded that I got the message, he pushed me onto my bed and raped me. It was in my bedroom again. I wished I'd just kept ironing in the kitchen.

I felt so sick, looking at the clock ticking and trying to pretend I was somewhere else.

When he had finished, he spoke to me about his marriage with Mam again.

'My marriage never worked. The reason I want to be with you is because you're such a pretty child,' he said.

I turned around and asked: 'Does that give you a reason to do this thing to me?'

I thought he would flare up on me but he didn't.

He said: 'Your mother doesn't do anything for me anymore. I can't even make love to her. She puts me off.'

I asked him: 'Why do I have to put up with it?'

He replied: 'Listen, I'm never going to do this to you again, and if you fucking tell anybody, I will throw you out in the lake that's out by the house there. Your body will never be found because I'll put a block on your stomach and I'll put a rope around your neck to make sure you go down quicker.'

I was obviously in a bad state because my father was a bundle of nerves, first screaming at me and telling me to smile, then trying to console me saying it would never happen again.

He said I looked like a girl who hated the world.

When he'd left, I stood near the windowsill watching the sun go down, waiting for my mother to return. I felt trapped in the house and locked inside myself.

At the end of August, just before we had to go back to school, my father told me that he was going fishing on the lake. It was a few days after my eleventh birthday. What a place to go fishing, I thought.

He'd made so many threats about the lake that I felt uncomfortable and unhappy when he said it. I wondered what he was up to.

'I'd like to know how deep the water is. They say when you see flowers or leaves on top of the water it means that it's very deep,' he said.

In the end, he told my two brothers and me that we had to accompany him. I was really nervous about going.

When we reached the lake, we all got into the boat and headed off. Paul, Patrick and I sat beside our father as he started fishing. He had a rope in his hand when suddenly he put it around my waist.

'Now jump into the water there,' my father said.

I was terrified as I couldn't swim but I knew I'd no choice. As my head went under, the cold water entered my mouth and I began to cough. I could feel the rope tightening around my waist, pulling my body towards the water's surface. It felt very uncomfortable.

When my head finally emerged, I could see my father laughing. He looked like the devil. It was a terrifying sight.

He then pushed me down into the water for a second time.

Again, the cold water rushed into my mouth. This time, I swallowed it and began to cough. I was very frightened as I didn't trust my father. I had no idea what he was trying to do. I thought he was trying to drown me.

When I returned to the surface, I was coughing water. I could barely breathe. My eyes were sore and I was freezing. I looked pleadingly at my father, who laughed.

He pushed me under the water for a third time.

This time I began to cry. When he finally lifted me

back into the boat, tears were streaming down my cheeks. My father made some sarcastic remark to my brothers as I stood there shaking.

When I returned home later that evening, I told my mother everything that had happened.

Mam was shocked and, for once, gave out to him. My father nodded and said that he shouldn't have put me in the water.

I had nightmares about drowning for years after that.

It made all my father's threats seem real.

FOUR

The Liar

I was glad to get back to school that year as it got me away from my father. Ever since the day at the lake I'd been really afraid he'd take me there again. I knew he'd enjoyed watching me get so scared. I was still having trouble sleeping.

There were changes that year in school because a new teacher arrived. I was going into fifth class and she took over third, fourth, and fifth classes. We were all moved to the middle room that we had previously used for lunch.

Our new teacher was very kind and generous. She was really interesting and organised drama classes for us twice a week. At the time, I didn't join in. There was too much sadness in me and I felt that I couldn't do anything entertaining with my class. The new teacher tried to get me to join in a few times but I just couldn't do it.

Patrick took part in the drama group along with a few of my classmates. I really enjoyed watching the plays. They helped me to forget about what was happening for a brief time and took me away from all the bad things that were strangling my life.

In one play, Patrick played the role of a priest and another boy played the 'baddie'. While I can't remember the name of the play, one scene in particular stands out in my mind. The 'baddie' went to the priest to confess murdering his granny. He went on to tell the priest about all the evil sins that he had committed in his life. I suddenly sat up and listened when I heard him saying the line: 'Father, I have something serious to tell you. You won't like me for this; you won't believe me.'

I began to concentrate on the play. I felt the character on stage was showing me how to tell somebody about what was happening to me.

I kept thinking about it for days afterwards. I was trying to get up the courage to tell the local priest, Father Keane. I double-checked that if I told him in Confession he couldn't tell anybody else and it would be our secret. I was really tempted to do it but I was too frightened. I kept thinking about what had happened at the lake. I knew that my father would kill me if he found out I'd told somebody. In the end I decided not to do it. I didn't think the priest would believe me anyway.

I was really pleased for Patrick that the play was a success. It went from our classroom to the theatre in Galway City where they won first prize for acting in the National School's category.

The one thing I did do was dancing. I went to Irish set dancing classes at school every Sunday with Paul. I loved dancing. Most of the time we used to have two ladies teaching us and they made it great fun. They had us dancing in big groups as well as individually. For some of the time, Paul was the only boy and the other girls sometimes made fun of him, but he didn't mind, he just kept on learning. It took a while for me to get the hang of it and on our lunch breaks my friends gave me dancing lessons. Paul and I constantly practised. In the ensuing years, I won several trophies and medals, as did many girls in my class. At home, however, it was a constant struggle to try and attend dance classes on a Sunday. Fortunately, my Aunt Sally was also going. This made it easier for us because she'd call around and collect us. I remember many occasions when I was in tears, begging my mother to allow me to go to the dance classes. My father would complain about the cost of petrol or something to try to keep us at home.

He always seemed to be ranting about something. At the time, he was not working and spent much of the day in bed, sleeping. My mother tried to motivate him but gradually began to accept the inevitable, that she had married a man who was not fond of the word 'work'. During the day, while he slept, he warned all of us to be as silent as we could be and not to disturb him from his sleep.

At breakfast time, we were not allowed to eat until our father had arrived at the table. Sometimes Alison and Suzanne sneaked into the kitchen and stole some biscuits before my father arrived. My mother knew what my two sisters were doing but decided to ignore their behaviour for the sake of some peace and quiet.

I remember one afternoon we came back from school and we were all watching TV, as my father slept on the settee. Suddenly he woke up and started screaming at us: 'Are yis deaf or something? Lower the volume on the TV.'

'You,' he gestured to Paul, 'go off and get me a pen.'

Paul scrambled quickly out of the room. As we waited in the sitting room for him to come back, our father grew more impatient. After several minutes, Paul finally returned with a tiny pencil.

My father went mad. 'Jesus, Mary and Saint Joseph, look at the size of the bloody pencil he gets me. What do you have in your satchels? Apples instead of school books and pens?' My father grabbed the pencil out of Paul's hand, walked over to the TV and drew a little line beside the volume button. He turned to us and said: 'While ye are all sitting there, I might as well give you a warning in case there is any misunderstanding. If the volume goes above the mark I've just drawn on the

TV, I'll blow the television up in the field with the rest of the trash. We never had televisions when I was young. We had to do without, so why do you lot need it?'

After that it became impossible to enjoy the TV, as the volume was so low we could barely hear the person speaking. It was the same with the radio. Whenever I got the chance to be alone in the house, I had the radio blaring. I'd sing along to the pop music and it felt great.

While the weather was nice that autumn, we also had a lovely time picking blackberries. As young children, my brothers and I had watched our granny and our mother making jam. When we got back to the house, we'd copy what they used to do but we always added more sugar than we should have. Our mother generally said nothing as she knew we all had a sweet tooth.

One sunny day, when I returned home from blackberry picking, I joined Alison in the back garden. I usually played with her in the sand box and would help her put water in her doll's mouth.

I was really enjoying sitting out in the sun and playing with my little sister. We spotted an aeroplane and it seemed to be coming in our direction. We both waved our arms wildly in the air. Mam opened the window and told us: 'The plane will come closer if you keep jumping up and down. They'll think you need to be rescued.'

I felt a wonderful burst of hope but the aeroplane flew right past us.

Alison went into the house to get more water for the doll. While she was gone, I found some pieces of glass in the sand. I don't know how they got there but instead of throwing them away, I scattered them all over the sand. It was such a stupid thing to do. I don't know what I was thinking. Alison came back and walked right over the sand in her bare feet. Immediately she began to cry and I spotted blood on her feet.

I felt terrible.

I was sick with sympathy for her and tried to comfort her. My granny was walking by and heard the crying. She lifted Alison up in her arms and carried her into her house. She gave her an orange as she put a bandage on her foot. Alison stopped crying almost immediately. Granny was very good when it came to things like that. She genuinely cared for us.

I never admitted what I'd done. I just felt like such a bad person.

A few weeks later, one of my father's old schoolfriends returned home from England to live in our neighbourhood with his wife and four children. He had two teenage daughters and two sons that were our age. His children began to walk to school with us. They were really good company but sadly, at the time, I wasn't in the mood to play with any of them. They must have thought I was very stand-offish.

One morning, before school started, I sat on the school wall with my brothers and Jack, the English boy.

Patrick asked us: 'How about we all play a game? You can watch, Barbara, you're not too well at the moment.'

Jack turned to me. 'Oh, what's wrong with you?'

With that, I began to cry. Jack had hit a raw nerve. During a special school Mass a few weeks before, I'd started to vomit. The head teacher had stood up and rushed down to the back of the classroom to see what was wrong with me. I'd started crying with embarrassment. All I could think of were the other schoolchildren and their parents watching me getting sick. My Uncle Peter, Granny's youngest son, who was standing beside me at the time, had told me not to worry and to stop crying.

'Sure you didn't know you were going to be sick, it came on all of a sudden,' he said.

I hadn't attended school for a few days after that. Some medicine from the doctor's surgery stopped me vomiting but my tummy was still sore. I was mortified about the whole thing.

Jack looked very upset when he saw me crying. I realised he was only trying to be friendly and so I asked him to explain that game anyway. It was something to do with tricks with the palms of the hand but I felt so low in myself that I couldn't take it in properly. I kept crying and Patrick finally told Jack that I had problems with my health. No further questions were asked but I felt embarrassed around him after that. It was so difficult just trying to act normally at school.

My health improved over the next few weeks. I think it was because it was our turn to have the Stations of the Cross at home that year and we were so busy getting ready for it, my father left me alone. Every year, one family in our community had the Stations of the Cross in their home. The Mass would be read in the house with the family and neighbours gathered around. Mam wanted my father at the Mass but he replied: 'Sure I have better things to be doing than standing around empowering a priest.'

At the end of the service, he miraculously appeared to help himself to the food and alcohol.

I had a great time with my neighbours that night. I was going around serving tea, sandwiches and biscuits. I remember the priest, Father Keane, was a nice person. I really enjoyed the Mass. The first person I gave the sweetcake to was my teacher. Uncle Peter said that I was favouring the teacher, hoping I would not get homework, but I genuinely liked her as she was always kind. She used to visit us every now and again whenever she had the chance. She also brought a lot of magazines and other stuff with her and told Mam that it would be very helpful for me to read them.

My mother used to send me to her house on errands sometimes and would tell me to spend a while there. I couldn't enjoy these visits, however, as I had to keep an eye on my watch. I knew that my father would give out to me if I spent more than 30 minutes away from home. I always found it difficult visiting somebody's house when I was being timed. I had to constantly rush out the door to make it home in time.

A week after the Stations of the Cross Mass, I saw a white shadow appearing. It was a very bright white and looked like the shadow of a person. It seemed that there was something on its head that I couldn't see properly. I rubbed my eyes, thinking there was something wrong with my eyesight or that I was imagining things. Then I heard some noises outside my bedroom door. Patrick was in his bedroom and also heard the noises which made me feel better. I wasn't the only one.

We got out of our beds and went into the kitchen. We stared down at the kitchen floor because we could hear footsteps. We thought we might see something but there was nothing there.

When we told our family, my father turned around to Mam and said: 'Imagine that, only a week after Mass has been read here. That shows you that Mass is no good.'

Mam told him: 'Priests don't speak to get rid of ghosts.'

My father insisted: 'But the priest blessed the house

and that should've been enough to cast out anything that was unholy. I saw a ghost appear on the wall where the picture of Jesus used to be kept. The picture moves sometimes too.'

I felt my father wasn't trying to scare me for once. I think he realised that my brother and I were telling the truth. A look of concern crossed his face when I told him that I couldn't be crazy because Patrick had seen the same thing.

My brother told our parents exactly where he had heard the footsteps. Coincidentally they started near an extension my father had built a few years earlier.

My father replied: 'The old ladies used to say that nobody should build an extension from a house over a *boithrin*. The shadows could've appeared because I blocked the *boithrin*.'

My father spent days going on about it, wondering was it a result of the extension, but we all forgot about it when we heard about the burglary. Money had been stolen from our elderly neighbours while they were at Mass. The thieves had gone through the whole house and finally unearthed some money the old folks had hidden up in the attic.

I will never forget the evening, a few days later, when Patrick and I spotted our father opening the accordion with a screwdriver. Patrick was learning how to play it at school. My father could play but he told Patrick: 'I can't read notes; I prefer to play by ear.' He had a habit of sitting on the toilet seat or on his bed and playing it for a couple of hours in the afternoon. There is no doubt my father had talent on the accordion, but he seldom used it. His mind was too focused on badness.

That night, we were standing at the door of my parents' bedroom watching him. When he opened the accordion up, bundles of notes fell to the ground. He lifted them off the floor and began counting them. He looked at ease counting the notes. We approached him and Patrick asked: 'Where did all that money come from?'

'I stole it from our neighbours,' he replied. There was not a bit of shame or embarrassment as he was telling us this.

I was totally disgusted with him. My father never thought about how he would feel if it was done to him. He was a pure headcase, with no thought for the people he hurt.

'Old people have no faith in banks and have a habit of stashing money somewhere in their houses,' he told us, as he continued counting out the money.

Patrick and I were shocked.

'Aren't you afraid of getting caught?' Patrick asked.

'Ah sure the police aren't clever enough to open the accordion, they'd never figure out where the money's stashed,' he told us, delighted with himself. 'Someone from my family helped me,' he continued. 'When we first went into the house, it wasn't long before we lost hope that we'd find any cash as we hadn't come across any. Then I decided to search the attic. Up there I found a biscuit box and bingo! There was all the money! We were supposed to share whatever we found between us, but I just pocketed most of the money myself – sure wasn't it my idea to go up to the attic? I pretended I only found a couple of notes.'

Two weeks later, my father confided in me again: 'I've robbed another one of our neighbours.'

When he told me what he had done, I felt disgusted at him. I didn't know why he was telling me. I was ashamed to be related to such a man.

I remember another occasion when my mother's

sister, Peggy, dropped over to visit us. She lived in the
Lettermore area and I got on very well with her. I was
always excited when I saw her coming around. My
father never stopped picking on her when she'd come
to babysit us but she was well able to tell him where to
go.

My mother was trying on clothes for a wedding that
she had been invited to the following day and Peggy
was helping her. As they discussed the dresses, I
decided to make myself a cup of tea. I walked towards
the kitchen, but then I noticed that our bathroom door
was open. An uncomfortable thought entered my mind,
just as I heard my father's voice. He was talking to
himself.

I returned to the sitting room and told my mother
that he'd returned home.

My mother told me: 'Grand so, tell him that the
wedding tomorrow starts at 12 o'clock.' I returned to
the bathroom and watched as my father placed a plastic
bag on the windowsill. He then pulled a bundle of
paper money from the bag and began counting it. When
he spotted me, I must have given him a fright because
he yelled: 'What the hell are you doing standing there
sneaky looking?'

I didn't know what to say. 'Mam sent me in to tell
you the wedding tomorrow starts at 12,' I mumbled.

I knew without being told that he had robbed the
money. I thought it was probably from someone else
locally. Everyone had been talking about the spate of
burglaries in the area. A few of the children at school
had said something to us about our father being the
thief. Patrick had told him and he'd been furious. I was
thinking he must have moved the money out of the
accordion because he was nervous.

'Keep your mouth shut about this money or you'll

really suffer. You're the only person that knows about it so I'll know if you tell anyone,' he said.

I was in a daze as I went back to the sitting room. I sat silently looking at Aunt Peggy and Mam, wondering to myself: 'Why can't he be like a normal father and work for a living?'

With some of the money he'd stolen, he bought a cow with an unusual cocoa colour. We called her Shirley. He would always send Paul down the fields to feed her potato skins. He seldom went down himself.

One day, as my brothers and I walked home from school, a lady from the local shop approached us.

'Are you lot the owners of that cow over there?' she asked. We looked to where she was pointing and there was Shirley in the middle of the road, ambling along.

Paul, who absolutely adored the cow, dropped his school bag on the ground and ran towards Shirley. When he reached her, he patted her on the shoulder. He then led her up the road towards our house. When he had managed to lead her into our garden he relaxed and started to play with her.

It was a huge relief to Paul that nothing had happened to Shirley, as my father would have killed him.

The following weekend, on Sunday afternoon, my mother and siblings were preparing for a day out. As I was the eldest girl, my mother asked me to remain at home. She told me to clean the house and keep an eye on the dinner that was cooking on the stove.

'I'm heading out for a few hours, I'll be back later this afternoon,' Mam said.

I began to panic. Remembering what had happened last time, I had no desire to be left on my own in the house with my father. So I began to sweep immediately. I had the place spotless in less than 20 minutes. Mam next asked me to dress Alison and Suzanne, so I hurriedly put their clothes on.

Then, she turned to me and said: 'Barbara, will you mop the kitchen floor there, I don't want someone slipping on that potato skin.'

I mopped furiously until everything was in order.

'Mam, can I go with you now? I have everything cleaned,' I pleaded, just as she was preparing to leave.

'No, you have to stay at home and keep an eye on the dinner. And don't forget to take the clothes out of the washing machine and hang them on the line outside as soon as they're ready.'

I started to cry but she ignored me. She probably thought I was looking for attention.

My father gave me a peculiar look. He'd started glaring when I asked Mam if I could go with them. He began blinking his eyes and started to give out to me.

My father then announced: 'Well, I'm going to go down the mountain for a walk and check on the cow.'

I knew he never went near the cow but he left the house with the rest of the family.

I stood at the window, watching them go, crying my eyes out.

My father was waiting in the driveway, watching them going out the gate in the car. As soon as they were out of sight, he came back inside.

'Jesus, Mary and Joseph, you're crying there at the window, giving every signal that you don't want to be near me at home.'

I was too upset to speak.

His voice got louder and I felt frightened by his big, bully voice.

I knew what was to come.

Again, he started telling me horrendous stories about what women had to put up with from men.

Except this time, he was more detailed. He told me about the violent and disgusting things that happened in marriages: 'Men force themselves on women all the time, it's an everyday occurrence. It's the way it's always been.'

My father seemed to enjoy telling me all about it.

I was sickened and answered in an angry tone: 'Why should women have to accept this type of behaviour from men when they're married?'

He became angry when I answered him back; he wasn't used to that. His voice got louder by the minute, telling me that I was stupid and that I didn't understand. He shouted: 'I suppose you think men and women get married for nothing? What do you think men do to women, put them up on windowsills and look at them? Not at all, you fucking lunatic.' He worked himself into a rage.

I had become accustomed to this type of talk by now but it made me feel ill. I wasn't able to deal with it.

He called me into the bathroom. He was standing beside the bath.

I will never forget this horrible experience.

He told me to kneel on the edge of the bath and put my hands on the wall.

I refused and ran down towards the sitting room, crying.

He yelled at the top of his voice and ordered me to come back.

I was very frightened. I stayed in the sitting room. I didn't want him to come near me. Again, he shouted at me to come into the bathroom. 'You'll suffer if you don't do what I say,' he roared.

I knew he meant it so I dragged myself down to the bathroom. I was shaking and felt like fainting.

He took the bathroom mats off the floor and placed

them on the edge of the bath. He told me to kneel on them and lean against the wall. He said that it wouldn't hurt my knees if I leaned on the mats.

He was wrong but I was too afraid to move.

My father forced himself on me as I stared at the tiles on the wall.

This was a horrible experience. I can't seem to get this haunting image out of my mind.

When he was finished, he tried to talk to me.

My knees were hurting after I got off the bath. I was crying, complaining with pain. He wanted to have a normal conversation. He was annoyed when I didn't laugh at his jokes.

I was crying and he told me not to be like a child.

I felt ugly in myself.

He went to his bedroom and called me in after him. My father was sitting on the bed and put his green dressing gown on to take a bath. He used to get ready early to go out on Sunday evening.

He was trying to console me, saying that he would never do it again.

I couldn't listen to him. I'd heard the same thing, over and over from him, after he'd abused me so many times before.

I felt physically sick after what he had done to me. My face was red from crying.

He started whistling as he was walking around the bedroom. He stopped and looked at me, clearly getting annoyed.

'I'm tired of telling you to clear the miserable look off your face before your mother returns,' he growled.

We both knew that she was due back soon. As usual, he began to give out about my mother's family. I got the impression that he was trying to excuse his behaviour towards me by blaming Mam and her family. He was going on about how her family had destroyed his life: 'They've kept me down ever since I married your mother. I used to go out in a suit and tie every day until they told me I shouldn't wear good clothes. They ruined my life.'

He rambled on tirelessly: 'And I receive no support from my own family. My blood pressure is sky high and it's all because of my marriage to your mother and all the rows with my own family. The doctor told me to try and avoid all this stress and worry.'

The next minute, he started raging about my mother's grandmother, who I loved. He ranted: 'I would like to dig up her bones in the graveyard and smash her coffin. She was cruel to me, always telling me what to do.'

My memories of this woman were totally at odds with my father's hateful comments. My great-granny was a kind, giving and considerate human being. Whenever I had the opportunity to visit her, God rest her soul, she was always kind. I have a clear memory of one lovely day with her. I can still remember her waving in the doorway as I was leaving.

My father used horrible curses about her. Not only that, he was looking towards the sky as he cursed. It was as if he believed somebody was going to answer him back. He looked at the photograph of Jesus in the hallway and cursed his relations: 'Lord Jesus, please let the sky burst and hurt all those people that I hate.'

If there was money to be made in bad-mouthing and back-stabbing, my father would have been a rich man.

I sighed deeply and stumbled out of the room but he called me back.

'Don't even think of telling your mother what I've been saying to you. That's between you and me.'

My family returned soon afterwards. My father was

in the bathroom getting ready to go to the pub at 7pm. He generally went to the pub between 5.30 and 7pm, depending on which pub he was going to.

When my mother first saw me, she noticed something. She asked was I sick and called to my father: 'Is Barbara alright? Why has she got a terrible sad face on her?'

My father rushed from the bathroom quickly and said: 'What do you mean? Sad face? Sure she always looks like that.'

My mother replied: 'No, she's not usually like that.'

My father looked like he was getting angry so she dropped the issue.

When Mam left the sitting room to make tea, he said: 'Get that ugly, sad face off you and smile in front of your mother.'

I managed a half-smile and thankfully he left after his tea.

The following morning, I had to face school again. It was very difficult. I couldn't understand anything anymore. I felt my life was falling apart. I was scared and nervous. I felt that my mind was removed from places like school. I just didn't seem to belong there anymore. I knew I should try harder to concentrate and enjoy time with my friends but I couldn't do it. I didn't feel normal. I felt ugly and disgusting.

My father suddenly arrived at the school when I was playing with my friends at lunchtime. I felt embarrassed seeing him sitting outside the school gates in the car. He was staring at me. I didn't feel afraid, as I was comforted by the fact there was a lot of other children around me. But when I approached his car I felt a bit nervous. I didn't know why he was there.

He said immediately: 'I've written a letter and put

some money in it for Saint Martin. I want to ask Saint Martin for help, I want to stop doing this thing to you. Here's the evidence. I wanted to show you before I posted it so you can see the proof.'

I didn't believe him.

I knew he was trying to make me feel better again. He had told me too many times that he would stop doing this to me but somehow it always happened again. At the same time, a huge part of me desperately wanted to believe him. When he showed me proof of postage I convinced myself that this was the end of it.

Some of my friends were waiting for me at the gate. I thought I'd be able to be a normal girl now, just like them. I sighed with relief, thinking this was the end of all the horrible things in my life. I smiled at my friends as I walked towards them.

The following day, Patrick, Suzanne and I were in one of the bedrooms, sitting on the bed, when all of a sudden, we heard a stream of bad language coming from the next room. My father was sewing his trousers and he started cursing about a needle sticking in his hand. We heard him saying: 'Fuck the lot of you up there in Heaven. I know you're doing this to a man deliberately. I'd love to put a bomb up there and kill all the fakers in Heaven. There is nobody up there.'

Suzanne burst out laughing from nerves. She was only young but Patrick glared at her: 'Be quiet, I want to listen to him.' As we sat in the bedroom, my father's tirade continued. He shouted: 'One of these days I will send that holy picture flying off the wall; it's constantly staring at me. It seems to be causing too many problems. It's cursed.' He continued: 'I hope that an awful thunder storm will come and make pieces of the planet.'

He started throwing things around the bedroom.

I got an awful shock listening to him praying for badness. I hoped that the saints would burn him in hell. What shocked me the most was that he was showing such hypocrisy by speaking ill of the saints after ordering the brochures from the Saint Martin De Porres' office.

Several days later, I saw the postman coming into our garden. My mother, who was in the kitchen, also spotted him and walked out to greet him. I followed behind.

The postman handed her several letters and, after some small talk, he went off about his business.

When she opened one of the letters, I noticed some religious brochures. He had also received scapula and medals and a gold medal to put around a chain on his neck.

I asked her: 'Are they for you?'

She replied: 'No, they're for your father. He ordered them from Dublin. Remember when he had a big operation on his scalp to try and make his hair grow back? Well, he was hoping that if he said a few Novenas to St Martin that his hair would grow back.'

I realised immediately that my father had been lying. I felt betrayed and stupid for ever believing his lies.

Mam asked me: 'What did you think it was for?'

'Nothing,' I said.

'He's a LIAR,' I thought to myself.

That's all I could ever expect to hear out of his mouth – lies.

FIVE

Escaping the Monster

During the winter when the weather was bad, our parents kept us home from school. My father used to say: 'I don't want to waste bloody petrol bringing them down the road to school. It's not on.' We ended up watching cartoons like *Tom & Jerry* all day. Our only break was when anybody came in to visit us. There was one old man who used to call to our house a good bit in the bad weather. He was a homeless man and not known to anyone living in the area. He'd started calling about a year before. At first I used to get really frightened when I saw him approaching our gate. He was unshaven and his hair was all over the place. I thought he was scary-looking.

I always remember his first visit to our house. As soon as the old man approached, my mother told me to open the door. At the time, there was coloured glass in our front door and when I opened the door, I stood right behind it so he wouldn't see me. He saw my shadow behind the door, however, and stood there wondering if he should come in. My mother had then called from the kitchen: 'Barbara, have you opened the door?'

I was afraid to speak in case the old man heard me and so I said nothing.

'Hello?' the homeless man called so my mother had to rush out from the kitchen to greet him. She told me not to be so silly.

It took me a while to get used to him visiting. The first few times, when I spotted him approaching our front door, I usually ran out into the garden. I stayed there until I heard him leaving and could return to the house. My Aunt Sally was as frightened as I was. Whenever she saw him approaching their gateway, she screamed and hid behind the wall.

After he'd been visiting us for a while, however, I got used to him and enjoyed his company.

It wasn't long before our headmaster realised why we weren't turning up. On one of the rare days we went to school, he turned around and said to the class: 'I notice the Naughtons only attend school when the weather is fine.'

We were all mortified.

The headmaster contacted our parents and insisted that we attend school. He said that we should be driven to school whatever the weather conditions or he'd report us.

My father had to give in but he ranted to us about it all the time.

We were back at school a week when I arrived home one day and found the old man sitting on the couch with Paul and Patrick. He was reciting poetry. Everybody felt relaxed so I sat down and listened to a poem he recited about a dog. It made me think of Blackie.

We noticed that the homeless man hadn't turned up for a few weeks after that and we all wondered what had happened to him. Then Mam told us that she heard on the radio that a car had hit him. It was sad news just before Christmas.

We were due to break up for the holidays and the weather was quite cold. There was frost on the ground but no snow, which we were all disappointed about. One of my friends slipped while we were playing in the school playground and cut her hand. We all ran over and lifted her to her feet. After school was finished, the girl made up a story and told her mum that I had pushed her. I've no idea why she did this.

When I reached home, my parents told me that the girl had complained about me pushing her. I couldn't understand why this girl was making up lies. I started crying and told Mam exactly what had happened. I said that there were three other girls who saw it.

My father asked Mam: 'How did you deal with the girl's mother?'

'I told her that she was going to be a busy woman if she has to go from door to door complaining about everything that happens to that girl.'

Nothing more was said about it at home.

The following day, I asked the girl why she was making up this story about me pushing her. She blushed and walked away from me, which made me feel really bad. I'd only tried to be nice to her.

I took a shortcut home from school that afternoon with Gemma and I told her all about it. She just laughed and said it was all nothing, which made me feel better.

I was still finding school difficult and I was looking forward to the Christmas break. I was happy when we got our Christmas holidays a few days later. I went home and helped Mam get the decorations down from the attic. It was lovely seeing the tree going up.

We'd a great time over Christmas and the New Year. All our neighbours dropped in and there was loads of gorgeous food. It all went by too quickly.

January 6th or Little Christmas as we called it arrived in no time and we had to take everything down. It was a shock to be back in school after the long break.

My father was still going out and enjoying himself every night, even after we'd gone back to school. He came home one night and entered my bedroom. I had been almost asleep but I woke up completely when I heard the door opening. He was staggering a bit and I knew that he had been drinking.

I pretended to be sound asleep.

He stood at my window looking out.

I was starting to shake, wondering what he was planning to do. Through my half-shut eyes I could see him turning around and looking back at the bed where I was 'sleeping'.

He came over, sat on the edge and started to speak. His words were a little slurred. I didn't move and kept pretending to be asleep.

He started to nudge me.

I tried to turn over in the bed but then he started shaking me.

I opened my eyes immediately, afraid that he would start hitting me if I didn't.

He began to pull back the blankets on my bed. I was shivering as he rubbed my nightclothes and placed his hand on my stomach.

I was afraid to say anything because he was being so strange. I felt extremely uncomfortable. He started to run his hand all over my body and began to lift up my nightdress.

Suddenly, footsteps could be heard outside my bedroom door. He immediately stood up, throwing the blankets over me in the process. As he walked towards the window again, my mother came into the room.

She looked at me and then looked at my father. She immediately asked him: 'What are you doing in Barbara's bedroom at this time of night?'

'I thought I heard noises outside, I was worried that someone might be looking through the window at Barbara,' he replied.

My mam must have sensed that something was

wrong. She approached my bed, pulled up the blankets and looked at my blue nightdress.

I was looking down, pulling at my nightdress, which was caught halfway up.

I really wanted to tell her at this point but my father's violent eyes were staring at me. He was glancing like a lunatic between me and my mother.

Mam looked at the nightdress and a look of uncertainty crossed her eyes. She gave my father a strange look.

He became embarrassed and was trembling.

'You're keeping her awake, go back to bed,' she told him.

After a couple of minutes, I heard my parents arguing in their bedroom. I heard my father slapping Mam and yelling at her: 'What did you think was going on?'

My mother never talked to me about what had happened.

The following morning, I was too tired to get up for school as I had been up most of the night. It was around 4.30am before I got to sleep.

My mother let me sleep for the day. When I finally woke up, I just sat on my bed, looking out my window, until it got dark. I was tearful and found it difficult to concentrate on anything.

The atmosphere in the house hadn't changed and the next day my mother called me for school as normal. I thought she would have realised from that moment what my father was doing but she didn't ask me anything.

That weekend, my father called me outside to help him tidy the shed. I didn't want to go but I was too afraid to disobey him.

While the rest of the family were in the house, he raped me.

It was freezing.

When he was finished, he told me: 'I won't be able to have you to myself as much now as your mother's become a little suspicious. She'll be keeping a close eye on me.'

I was glad that at least she could do that much.

As I was dressing, my father spotted my mother approaching the shed.

'Hurry up, your mother's coming,' he hissed at me.

My mother opened the shed door and asked my father: 'What are you doing?'

'I've just been fixing some tools. Barbara's helping me tidy the shed,' he replied.

She looked suspiciously at my father. She'd seen the look of devilment on his face and knew he was up to something. I think she noticed that I was a little frightened and withdrawn.

She gave my father a dirty look and turned to leave, calling: 'Come on inside and help me in the house, Barbara.'

I followed her into the house with a heavy heart.

The following morning, one of my mother's first jobs was to deal with the floor. When I entered the sitting room, I found my father lying on the sofa, watching my mother working.

This was a skill he had developed over the years.

When my mother had finished, she looked at my father and said: 'Jesus, you'll sleep your life away. Come on, I'm bored, take me for a drive.'

I was amazed that she could speak so normally to him after what had happened two nights before.

He immediately lost the head. 'What do you mean you're "bored"? You sound like one of the kids, would you get lost, I just want some peace and quiet,' he ranted.

My mother disappeared into one of the bedrooms. Moments later, the front door opened and Paul came in. He dragged his mucky boots across the clean floor and I knew there was going to be trouble.

A few minutes later, Mam returned. 'Who's dirtied the floor I've just mopped?' she asked.

'Paul came in from the garden and walked across the floor,' I told her.

She called Paul from his bedroom. When he entered the sitting room, my mother asked him: 'How did you manage to muddy my clean floor?'

'I was told to bring in a bag of turf from the back garden,' he replied.

My father loved causing trouble like this.

My mother began to re-mop the sitting-room floor. As she mopped, my father called all of us into the sitting room. 'Look at that holy picture of Jesus on the wall there,' he said.

We all looked at the holy picture as he continued.

'The eyes of Jesus move when the sun shines on them. The picture must be haunted.' He turned to my mother and said: 'All the holy pictures in the house should be taken down and thrown out. They bring nothing but bad luck.'

My mother looked at him in shock. 'Don't be saying such things in front of the children. Don't turn them against the church. It's little wonder that Patrick never listens to the priest at Mass when he hears that kind of talk.'

My father smiled when he heard this.

'I'm glad he doesn't listen to the priest. Patrick has a mind of his own, he'll decide if anything is "above" him. Surely if a child can work out it's all bullshit, the rest of the people out there should know it's all fake. Priests, they're all fakers. I told you before, it's all bullshit. You go there every Sunday, for what? And why do the priests encourage women to have more children when they already have too many?'

My mother glared at my father and left the room.

I stood there looking at his face going red with anger when he realised my mother wouldn't engage with him and tried not to laugh about it.

'Your mother finds it difficult to deal with the truth,' he laughed, trying to get us to join in.

My desire to laugh was gone in a second. He'd reminded me of what happened in the shed the day before.

When my mother returned to the sitting room, she asked my father: 'Will you drive Suzanne and Alison to the crossroads for the minibus to collect them?' The minibus brought them to Oughterard for swimming lessons.

I asked my mother could I go. She nodded and I was delighted to be out of the house.

Back at school on Monday I tried to put the weekend behind me. It was a bit easier because we were told some exciting news. A social night had been arranged to celebrate the opening of the new local hall. We were happy to hear it as we'd all been really glad that a new hall was opening in Camus. We'd be able to do lots of activities, including indoor soccer and basketball, there. They were also going to hold discos and start a youth club. In the weeks leading up to it, we practised reciting poetry and telling stories in class. The school had arranged for a band to play when all the readings were finished. I was reciting a poem with Paul and singing a song.

The night finally arrived and we were all really excited. My parents had been in Rosmuc for the day but

Mam arrived home alone that evening sporting a black eye.

We all knew that our father had punched her.

'What happened, Mam?' I asked, as I made her a cup of tea.

'I only asked him a simple question and he punched me. I said I needed to know when we were going home as I had to feed the children. I was tired waiting all day for him in the pub,' she replied.

Nobody said anything. We were all getting worried because we needed the car to get down to the hall. We rehearsed the pieces we had learned for the show while we waited.

As the clock approached 8pm, when the show was to start, my father still hadn't arrived. My mother looked concerned but there was nothing she could do.

Eventually, we heard the car approaching. When my father came in, my mother said: 'Can I have the car keys?'

She put her hand out for them.

It was a tense moment. None of us dared say a word. I was really afraid that we weren't going to get to go at all but thankfully my father handed over the keys.

My mother told us to collect everything we needed and jump in the car. We all dived for the car before my father changed his mind. I was really glad he wasn't coming with us but I felt sorry for Mam.

When we arrived at the hall, everyone noticed my mother's black eye. The word quickly spread that my father had struck her.

Paul and I were called on stage to recite our poem. I felt so nervous in the beginning. I could feel my legs going from under me and I tried to control the tension I felt. Eventually I started to relax.

There was a man at the front of the stage using a

camera. As we recited the poem, I began to smile when I spotted Father Keane in the front of the audience. I'd really liked him since the night we hosted the Stations of the Cross.

Father Keane smiled back at me, which was really encouraging because I knew I had to sing on my own next. I could feel my heart thumping at a mile a minute. However, after a few lines, I began to improve. Paul told me later that he was surprised that I had the courage to stand in front of a camera and sing at the top of my voice. It was nice to get a compliment out of him.

I really enjoyed the night, especially the singing. I had a passion for music. It put my mind at rest for a while and I couldn't go a day without listening to it. I wrote songs in a little red notebook that I had. I then sang the songs and taped them onto a blank tape.

Whenever I mentioned to my family that I wanted to be a singer when I grew up, the usual responses were: 'You don't have the talent to be a professional' and 'It's impossible to make a living out of singing'.

As ever, my parents were very supportive!

A few weeks after the concert, my brothers and I were walking down the hill on the way to school one morning. Paul and I were nattering on about what we'd do if we had some money. Patrick was walking a bit ahead of us. Suddenly, we spotted a plastic bag in the hedge at the side of the road.

Paul opened it and exclaimed: 'Jesus, it's amazing what you can find at the side of the road!' He opened the bag and several coins spilled out.

We picked up the coins and began counting. I was amazed and smiled as I shook the bag to ensure it was real money that was in it. Paul was also overjoyed and he began to count the money in the bag with me.

Patrick looked at us in shock: 'How did you two know that bag was there? Why were ye talking about money coming up the road?'

We looked at each other in bewilderment and then kept on counting.

Patrick said: 'Isn't that very strange? It must be a miracle or did Paul have a magic wand? There are so many kids walking up and down this street every day and none of them ever mentioned finding money at the side of the road.'

I told him: 'We've no idea where it came from and we certainly didn't steal it.'

Patrick looked at us, laughed and told us: 'Well, I think you should leave the money there and come and get it on the way home from school.'

We did just that and as we continued on our way to school, Patrick warned us: 'You had better come up with a good reason for having this money because if you told Dad you didn't know where it came from, he'd kick you.'

That afternoon, on our way home from school, we retrieved the money from the hedge. As soon as we reached home, Patrick told my mother and father about our good fortune. He explained how Paul and I had discovered the money. As soon as he was finished speaking, my father said: 'Well, the Lord save us, I noticed there was money missing from the wardrobe the other day.'

We were confused and wondered what was happening, as Mam reached over to take the bag of coins. My parents told us to forget about the incident. While I had no idea who was the actual owner of the money, I instinctively knew that it wasn't my parents.

My father concocted a story about losing money

from his wardrobe while Mam made up a story about having won the money at bingo. My brother and I knew that both my parents were lying.

My mother took the bag of coins and began counting them at the kitchen table. As soon as my mother began counting the coins, my father winked at me and said: 'Well, I hope it's all there. I'm sure that I had some money in my wallet. I'm certain that I had a jar of coins under my bed.'

We were disgusted that they weren't going to give us one penny of the money. We decided to do something about it. A few nights later, our next-door neighbour Delia visited us. My mother sent us to bed early so that we would be up on time for school the following morning. We lay in bed straining our ears to see if Delia was still chatting to Mam. When we heard their voices, Paul and I knew it was safe to get out of bed. We'd already planned to search our mother's wardrobe to steal the coins and buy sweets.

We crept into our parents' room and opened Mam's wardrobe. There before us was a jar full of coins. She had put in some of the ones from the bag we'd found in the hedge.

I looked at Paul. We both started giggling with happiness. Our dream had been answered!

'I bet you she doesn't know how much is in the jar. It's full of coins and she wouldn't have the time to count all that,' Paul said.

A soon as Paul popped the lid open, we both caught sight of lots of 2ps and some silver coins. We must've made some noise because Mam shouted up from the sitting room: 'Go to sleep.'

But we were going on an adventure.

We opened the window in my parents' bedroom and managed to sneak out. I was glad we lived in a bungalow. Paul and I were nervous in case my mother opened the sitting-room door and caught us going out. I have no idea what time it was but it was late at night. We both hurried down the hill, encouraging each other all the way.

We were heading towards the local shop to stock up on sweets. At the time, our parents seldom bought sweets for us. My mother told us that they would damage our teeth. We imagined that the shop would be open late. However, when we reached the shop at the bottom of the hill, it was closed.

The two of us stood outside banging on the door.

'Keep knocking there, Barbara. The people running the place are ancient; it'll take them a while to get to the door.'

We kept on knocking, but no one replied so we had to admit defeat and head home. As we were coming out the gate of the shop, we ran into our Aunt Anne, my father's sister, coming from her neighbour's house.

We got the shock of our lives and so did she. Her eyes widened when she saw us.

She asked: 'Where the hell are you going?'

We were speechless.

Eventually, we told her: 'We just dropped down to the shop.'

She laughed and said: 'Sure the shop's closed. Wait 'til I see your mother tomorrow.'

We started to trudge back up the hill towards our house. The two of us had been hoping that she wouldn't tell on us. We managed to get back in the window without any difficulties but it was hard to get to sleep. All that night, Paul and I worried about what our aunt was going to say to our parents.

In the morning Paul said: 'We can tell Mam that our Aunt Anne imagined that she spotted us. Who is going to believe that kids our age go out at that time of the night? Mam will tell her that she put us to bed and that our aunt was imagining it all.'

We sat on the sitting-room couch as the sun shone through the window. We heard my mother going out to water the flowers.

'Oh the Lord save us. Please ensure that she doesn't go near the geraniums near the wall or she'll be facing Granny's house. Our aunt might come out and tell her about last night,' Paul said.

I rushed out, but before I got the opportunity to stop my mother, my Aunt Anne had called her over.

As usual, my aunt spoke at the top of her voice and I could hear her telling Mam about meeting us the previous night. I ran into the house and told Paul what had happened. As we sat there, we wondered if it would be easier to stay indoors or go out to our mother and face the music.

Before we had reached a decision, my mother rushed back into the house and asked us what we had been doing outside of the house at that hour of the night.

'We didn't go out at all. Maybe she's imagin…' We'd only started trying to explain ourselves when she grabbed the little brush and started hitting us with it on the legs.

My brother put many curses on my aunt that day but none of them worked.

It was difficult for my parents to find a babysitter for us and my aunt used to babysit us as well sometimes. Mam would also ask other people in the area. Beartle's daughter, one of our neighbours, came to mind us one night soon afterwards.

She asked him: 'Would one of your girls mind looking after the children tonight? It's just we have a friend's party to go to and we're really stuck.'

The man replied: 'Of course, one of my girls would love to do it.'

Later that night, when the babysitter arrived and my parents were still in the house, she looked a bit concerned and was obviously wondering why we weren't saying anything. We were all sitting like dummies in our chairs. We all knew if we opened our mouths, our father would go on and on about it after the visitor had left. It was easier in the long run to keep our mouths shut. However, as soon as he left for the night, we wouldn't stop talking.

The day after the party, some of my father's relations called in and started to complain to my mother. They claimed she had insulted them in front of the babysitter. Angered, my mother rang the babysitter.

'Did I make any comment about my husband's family?' she demanded to know.

The babysitter replied: 'No, you said nothing about them.'

My mother told me that she was mortified about how my father's family had spoken to her. I thought to myself that the poor babysitter was dragged into the middle of this family squabble. I heard later that the girl had been very upset over it all. I could understand why she never came back to babysit us again.

As Easter approached I was helping Mam around the house more, hoping that it would stop my father coming near me. One day after school, I was sitting in our kitchen, working away and asking Mam questions. I can't remember what the questions were about but I must have been asking too many as my mother became angry. I was standing beside her at the table as she was chopping some bread and suddenly she snapped. She lost control and accidentally prodded me with the knife.

Mam got a shock when she saw the open cut on my arm and said it was an accident.

I began to cry: 'Look, I'm bleeding.'

'Shhhh!' she said. 'Put a bandage on it, quickly, so the rest won't come in and see it.' She opened the first-aid box and pulled out a bandage and scissors along with some white tape. 'I didn't know the bread knife could cut like that, it's not sharp at all,' she said. Later that evening it was still painful. The following day at school, some of my classmates noticed I was pale and asked: 'What's wrong with you? You look really white.'

I told them that I was feeling sick because I'd hurt my arm.

On our way home from school that afternoon, my brothers and I met our mother who asked us if we would like to go to the circus in Carraroe. I thought she was probably trying to make up for my arm. It was a lovely idea.

None of us had ever been to a circus before. As we jumped into the car, we were so excited. It didn't take us long to get there and I spotted a few kids from my school there already. When I first saw the stage, the first thing I thought was that there were so many colours. I could see beautiful rainbow patterns. Some of the clowns were brilliant performers and it was great to see all the different animals.

I could hear people around me laughing but despite all the clowns' antics, I found it difficult to laugh. When one of the clowns drove an old bonnet-less car into the ring, it reminded me of a car my father had. It made me feel sad. I tried to put it out of my mind and just enjoy the show, which went on for two hours.

We got home and at dinner that evening, a row erupted between my mother and father about the church.

'Stop criticising the church in front of the children, it's not right,' my mother said to him. 'It's Easter time.'

'Sure the church and all those who work in it are crazy people and that includes the priest,' my father replied. 'The church is just a money-making racket, sure look at those priests, living in nice big houses and they don't do a day's work. Where do they get all that money?'

My mother ignored him and left the kitchen.

The following morning as we were heading out to Mass, my father started on my mother again: 'Why are you wasting petrol by going to Mass?'

My mother replied: 'Don't put the children against religion just because you don't believe in anything.'

As we followed her out the door, my father said: 'There's a war going on in this house. Rushing to Mass because of the priest, he's not forcing anybody to hurry there.'

My mother shouted: 'Jesus, Mary and Joseph, what kind of belief is that? Keep your voice down and don't have them listening to that kind of talk.'

He shouted at my mother as we made our way out to the car: 'If the church is so good to you, why do you have so many problems?'

As I sat in the car, I was glad that I didn't have to remain in the house with my father that morning. Mass was like a sanctuary.

A few weeks after Easter, I woke up one morning with really bad pains in my tummy. I called my mother into my bedroom.

'Don't worry, I'll call for the doctor right now,' she told me and rushed out of my room to look for the doctor's number in the phonebook. My father walked around the place with a guilty look on his face. While my mother was searching for the phonebook, my father pulled up my top and said: 'Look, she has no breasts. She is so flat-chested.'

I felt so terrible when he did that – really awful.

My mother turned on him and asked: 'What are you doing? You're acting like a maniac, pulling Barbara's top up like that.'

He got very annoyed and gave the impression that he was within his rights to be pulling my clothes up and commenting on my body.

Eventually they stopped arguing and my mother found the doctor's number: 'I'll just head down the road to Delia's to ring the doctor.'

As she went out the door, I heard my father say to my mother: 'Don't let Delia know what the calls are about. It's none of her business.'

Thankfully, he didn't come near me while we were waiting. When the doctor arrived he gave me some tablets. He didn't ask many questions and seemed to think I'd get over it quickly. I hoped I would because I was always terrified of being sick as it meant I was left with my father.

Just as I'd feared, a few days later, I was still sick and it was just the two of us in the house.

I was in the kitchen when I heard him shout out: 'Come here to me, Barbara, I'm in my bedroom. Come in and lie down beside me.'

I felt shivers running through me with disgust. The thought of stabbing him kept running through my mind. All I could think about was the knife.

Suddenly, I heard a knock on the front door. Seeing this as my chance to get away, I ran to answer it. It was an elderly man from the neighbourhood who had dropped in for a social visit.

'Is none of your family around?' the man asked me.

My father had told me to pretend that he wasn't at home so I replied: 'No, I'm on my own.'

At the same time though, my father began to make silly whistling sounds and called to me from his bedroom: 'Get rid of whoever it is quickly and don't be offering them any tea.'

He could be heard clearly at the front door. I knew very well the elderly man had heard everything my father had said. My father was cruel. I was really embarrassed as the old man came in.

We chatted for a while but eventually he said that he had to leave as he had a few things to do. I dreaded him leaving as I knew my father would try and hurt me again. I tried to bring up new topics of conversations hoping to keep him engaged. I thought if I could keep him there long enough, my father might lose interest and change his mind or the rest of the family would have arrived back. But he had to go. I felt so depressed as I said goodbye to him at the door.

Once he had gone, my father called to me: 'Come on into my room here, Barbara.'

I shouted in at him: 'No, I don't want to go into your room.'

He kept insisting and shouted: 'I'm dumb and deaf and I can't hear what you're saying. You're mumbling out there in the hall at the heater. Nobody can hear you with your big ugly mouth.'

I didn't want to take on board what he had said but it was upsetting me.

He called me again and kept insulting me: 'You're ugly, disgusting-looking. That's why I was abusing you all along. It's good enough for you...'

I ground my teeth and clenched my fists with anger. I felt such uncontrollable rage when he made these hurtful remarks.

It felt like being raped again. He made me believe that the reason he was hurting me was because I was so ugly and deserved to be treated like that.

The words he used against me scarred me. I've never forgotten them.

When I was just getting the courage to run out of the house, my brothers arrived home. He told Paul to hit me, which he did. It hurt but not as much as what my father would have done to me. This was his idea of sport, getting Paul to start a fight with me.

It pleased him to poison us all and to try to turn us against one another. He created a terrible feeling in the house when he was in one of his moods. It was bad sometimes when he came back from the pub late as well. We'd hear him and Mam fighting.

A week later, my father beat my mother so badly that she was admitted to Galway Hospital. The night before I had heard my father hitting my mother and then I listened to her crying in the bedroom. The following morning, I saw her walking crippled and she left for the hospital.

It was horrible when she was gone.

My father used to go on the drink and I'd see him coming home intoxicated. He used to come into my room after he got back from the pub.

I missed Mam and I felt awful looking at my father running the house. I thought to myself that he was some clown to be left in charge of us.

While she was gone, my father made me wear a pair of dungarees to school that had holes in them. I felt ashamed walking in the school gates. I spent the day seated on my chair hoping that my classmates wouldn't notice the holes in my trousers. When school finished for the day, I waited for everybody to leave before I got up and went home.

After a few days, Mam returned from hospital and

everybody asked where she had been. My father told them that she had been visiting her uncle in Galway.

I told Mam that my father had made me wear the dungarees with holes in them to school. Her eyes widened and she placed her hand over her mouth and said: 'Jesus, Mary and Joseph.' She then discovered that Paul wore the same shirt to school every day without changing and she gave him a slap. Between us all she was probably sorry to be home.

That evening I heard my father shouting at his parents next door. When I walked out, I saw him grabbing a rock as my grandfather shouted over the wall: 'Go on, throw it.'

My father threw the stone with all his might. My grandfather jumped back and it barely missed his feet.

My father continued arguing. Some of his siblings then shouted over the wall at Mam: 'Your husband is a cheat and very dishonest and you need to know.' One of them then said that she saw my father trying to rape another woman.

My mother went red in the face.

Deep down something inside me hoped that Mam would believe it. I looked at my mother's face and tried to give her a sign. I pointed at my father but she wasn't looking at me.

Mam asked what was meant by that and got the reply that she ought to know at this stage what he was like.

My father began to shout hysterically and I thought they were all going to start brawling when my mother suddenly pointed at a car that had pulled up outside the gate. It was one of my father's friends and he was transfixed, watching the whole family screaming at each other.

The row ended after my father cursed his own father

at the wall. The neighbours across the road could hear
him roaring, there was so much noise. I ran into the
house in fear.

When I looked out minutes later, I saw my father
sitting outside the gate in his friend's car, talking very
intently to him.

My mother was in the sitting room, looking shocked.
I went in and sat down beside her.

Shortly afterwards, my father got out of the car. He
rushed in to my mother and his face was still red with
anger.

'Your man told me that I shouldn't bother wasting
my tongue rowing with that lot. He said that I should
wait until darkness,' he ranted.

'What do you mean?' Mam asked.

'I want to set the family home on fire!' he laughed.
'I'm going to organise to get a few jars of petrol and to
end it all for them.'

'What did they mean about the rape? What was that
about?' Mam asked.

'Oh, they're capable of contriving any stories and
everything they say begins and ends with rape. They're
dangerous and they make up stories to try to get me in
trouble. My blood pressure is going sky high from all
their lies and I know that they've caused the blood
pressure all along. I'm going to get them all with that
fire,' he raged on and on.

Mam gave me a look to tell me to leave and I gladly
edged out of the room.

Later that day, Mam and I were in the sitting room
watching television when my father's sister walked
into the house with one of her brothers.

'I want to speak with your mam, Barbara,' she said.

I got up to go but Mam told me to stay.

Then my aunt said, straight out while I was there:

'Patsie tried to seduce my friend last night in her apartment in town. I thought you should know.'

I looked at Mam.

'Go and put the kettle on, Barbara,' she said.

I was sorry to miss out on the information that Mam was getting about my father's behaviour. I tried to make the tea as quickly as possible.

When I came back in, my mother was pale and asking if the story was true.

My uncle whispered something to his sister. I couldn't hear what he'd said. My aunt turned to him quickly and said: 'If you don't shut your mouth, I'll tell everyone all the things that you've got up to.'

I couldn't believe it. He looked so embarrassed. What surprised me is he did shut his mouth with fear.

After they left I felt happy thinking that my mother might leave my father this time. I waited for her to say something but sadly she didn't react much.

'That crowd would say anything,' she said finally.

She didn't want to listen to what other people had to say about my father.

I remember a few times after my father had hurt my mother wishing that she would leave him. Sadly, she lacked the courage.

Just before the summer holidays began, a social worker came to visit Mam because of the beatings my father was giving her. My mother put myself and my brothers out of the sitting room while the social worker was having a chat with her. When the lady had gone, Mam called us back into the room. We were all feeling nervous. She told us that the social worker had suggested that my mother might be better off if she were to leave my father. We were going to move to a new home in Galway City.

I was elated when I heard this news. I looked at my brothers with joy. Paul said he was really happy as well. I could feel my heart thumping I was so excited at the prospect of putting as much space as I possibly could between me and my father.

I felt that my mother was unsure about wanting to leave him so I said everything I could to encourage her. I told her that he wasn't treating us nicely and I also reminded her about the night that I had found her on the cold floor after my father had hit her so hard she passed out. I was really hoping that my mother would stay in the mindset of leaving my father. I almost told her about the abuse but was afraid she'd think I was lying.

My mother didn't respond to any of my comments but just said that she was going to have to wait until she got the house in Galway City before we could do anything.

I had to be satisfied with that for the time being but I couldn't stop feeling excited whenever I thought about it.

The next morning, I walked to school with my two brothers and Aunt Sally. I couldn't help telling her that there was a possibility that we might be moving away. She wasn't too happy and said that she would miss me. At that stage, I was too happy at the thought of getting away from my father to feel sad even though I knew I'd miss her too.

When I returned home from school that afternoon, my mother was there. She told me that my father was out for the day. We sat down to have some food and she started to tell me about how she had run away, years ago, to be safe from my father.

'I took you and your two brothers to your granny's house in Lettermore,' she said.

'Why did you come back to my father?' I asked.

'He showed up at Granny's house with a Pioneer badge and promised that he would quit drinking and things would be different from then on,' she replied. 'I believed him.'

'I don't remember much about that time,' I said.

'Sure how would you? You were only a young child,' she told me.

My only memory was sitting on the floor with my brothers, with a bowl and spoon in my hand, looking at Granny's candle on the table.

When I heard this old story I was hopeful that my mother would still leave my father but I began to question it as well. Deep down I felt that there was a chance she would stay.

Over the next few days I was very up and down. I'd feel excited one minute and then depressed the next.

As time dragged on, and a few weeks passed, Mam seemed to be sticking to the plan. I began to honestly believe that my mother was going to take us away from my horrible father. I used to daydream about the new life we'd have. I was looking forward to it so much. Paul was as well. I think Patrick was the only one who wanted things to stay the way they were. My sisters were too young to know what was going on. I couldn't wait to leave the tense atmosphere in the house behind.

But as more and more days went by and nothing happened, it gradually began to dawn on me that I wasn't going to escape.

Then one day, when I arrived home from school, my mother dropped the bombshell.

'We won't be leaving after all, Barbara,' she said.

She didn't give any reasons.

I was devastated.

'We're all staying put,' she added.

I began to cry when my mother told me that we were staying. I couldn't believe it.

I told her that I'd thought we were moving to a nicer and safer place. I had been under the impression that I was going to have a happy, normal life, away from my father.

Days later, I was still trying to deal with the realisation that I was stuck in the house with my father – the monster – and I had no hope of getting out. There had been an eerie silence in the house for a while but suddenly my parents began talking again. They were acting as if nothing had happened.

I couldn't join in and pretend.

I felt so sad and low in myself.

I knew that things were going to be as miserable as ever and that I wouldn't be able to escape my father's clutches.

SIX

Summertime

The summer holidays arrived and I tried to get over my disappointment about staying with my father. It wasn't easy as he was still abusing me whenever he got the chance. The holidays always made me nervous as I had to spend time working in the house. It was almost better when we had to work on the bog for hours.

On the last day of school, we ran home, knowing that my parents were out and we had the house to ourselves. I felt really happy, thinking I'd be free to play my favourite music to celebrate the holidays. As soon as we got into the house, however, Paul found a letter on the table.

'Jesus,' he said.

'What is it?' I asked.

'Well, I won't be sitting around watching the TV in peace as I thought.'

He was annoyed when he read the letter out loud to us. 'They've asked me to bring in a few bags of turf for the night, wash the driveway and to bring out the ashes from the fire. Your name is on the list too.'

I took the piece of paper off him and read my list of chores, which included washing the dishes and the windows, mopping the hall and the back kitchen and putting the clothes out on the line when they were ready.

I should have known that an afternoon off was too good to be true. There was so much work to do. It was hard, especially having to wash the windows. This entailed bringing a chair outside, climbing on it and scrubbing hard. Even with the chair, I couldn't reach the top of the window. I got angry and stormed over to Patrick whose name wasn't even on the list. All he was supposed to do was look after us and report to our parents. Instead, he got the spare set of car keys, went outside and started up the blue Massey Ferguson tractor that my father had parked in front of the house. Patrick was no saint.

When I arrived over to complain about the windows, he had no interest in helping me.

I was so upset and angry, I grabbed the bucket and threw the water on the window and it went all over the place.

Paul got angry then because he'd been given the job of cleaning the driveway and now he had to go back and do it again.

I left the window wet, knowing it would dry quickly as the sun was shining. I did the same job to every window in the house. We made sure we had everything done quickly before our parents returned as otherwise my father would hit us. As we worked, Patrick reversed the tractor back and forth in the garden, speeding about, delighted with himself but half concerned that the relations next door would tell on him. For once, they didn't.

When our parents got back later that afternoon, my father looked around the house to see if anything was out of place. He told Paul to lift the barrel of gas out of the back of the boot. I pulled the remainder of the shopping bags out with Mam.

A couple of weeks later, we came home off the bog to a similar note. I picked it up this time. I had to wash out the fridge and mop the house. All the work was given to Paul and me, excluding Patrick again.

Patrick got the keys from the jug and started driving

the car. He began reversing it back and forth, which burnt up a lot of fuel. My Uncle Tommy saw him doing it and had a good laugh.

I was a bit nervous in case he would tell our parents but Patrick said he wouldn't. Then he had a problem when the car got stuck on the hill. We helped him out because I didn't want to hear my father causing trouble over it. One of us had to keep an eye on the road for our parents' return so they didn't discover that Patrick was messing with one of the cars.

Thankfully he got it going again and we could relax.

The next day, my father dropped my brothers at the place where we were supposed to work on the bog. I started to get out as well but he pulled me back and told me I was staying with him for the day.

I began to get scared as he drove up the road towards another lake, in the opposite direction from home.

'I've more turf down here and I need you to turn it,' he said.

I didn't really expect anything to happen to me in the car but I didn't know where he was taking me. He arrived at the lake and parked the car.

I began to get nervous.

He said: 'I'm going to tell you something about one of my family members. I sold my car to him the other day. Well, he had to go and set fire to it last night because the police were chasing him.'

I wondered if my father was talking about himself and trying to shift the blame to one of his brothers.

'He'd been exposing his private parts to children in the park when someone saw him doing it. They rang the police and made complaints against him.'

I just nodded and hoped that would be the end of it.

When he finished telling the story, he started the car and we drove off.

I can still remember how relieved I felt.

Eventually, he drove off the main road and stopped at the end of a lane. He looked everywhere to see if anyone was around. When he was satisfied that we were alone, he turned the ignition off and proceeded to rape me.

I was taken completely by surprise. I'd thought I was safe in the car.

As he raped me, I cried. It was extremely painful. I will never understand how my father could inflict such pain on me. Had he forgotten that I had a soul? How could he hurt his own child?

When he finished, he tried to console me.

But it didn't console me to hear that I was beautiful and that he no longer had any interest in my mother. He told me: 'You should never let any man come near you.'

That made me cry even more, I felt so bad. I knew that he was trying to keep me to himself. I felt sick to my stomach listening to him. I wanted the ground to open and swallow me.

I hated him being around me and I never understood why he was called my father or why I was his daughter, after all he had done to me.

On our way home, my father dropped into the shop at the bottom of the hill and bought me some liquorice sweets. As we drove up the hill, he said: 'Cheer up, you look really sad.'

There was no way I could act normally or pretend to be happy after this incident. A packet of sweets did not make me feel better. I felt like I could explode with anger.

I went to bed when we got home and tried to sleep.

When I joined my siblings in the sitting room later that evening, I told Patrick what my father had said about the car. At the time, I felt that I could confide in my brother – I was wrong. He told the story back to my father and he hit me.

'And don't think you'll be coming to Dublin with me tomorrow because that's off,' he raged. He was due to get the train at six o'clock the following morning. He said: 'I'm going to take Patrick with me instead.'

I was relieved. I'd never wanted to go with him anyway. He'd tricked me by saying that Mam was coming as well and we could go off shopping while he took care of some business. Then suddenly, he had said that we were going on our own.

He spent time on his own chatting to Patrick. I overheard him saying: 'That Barbara should never be trusted, she's a dangerous liar.'

I was disgusted. I knew he was manipulating my brother by saying things to him behind my back. I felt sad when I realised that Patrick seemed to believe him.

Just before my father left the next day, he came into my bedroom and woke me up. He said: 'You're going to miss the trip because of your big mouth.'

When they left, I thought he and Patrick were good company for one another.

They only spent a few days in Dublin and were back all too soon. My father returned home from the bog early a few days later, in a panic. 'There's a TV licence inspector in the area checking to see if everybody has a TV licence,' he yelled as he came in the door.

My father, of course, had 'forgotten' to get a licence for the TV. As soon as he came into the house, he went straight to the sitting room and disconnected it. He carried it into his bedroom and placed it in the wardrobe, with a cushion over it.

When he returned to the sitting room, he told us: 'Go outside to the garden and play; let me know as soon as you see a stranger approaching the house.'

We filed out to the garden and did as we were told. Shortly afterwards, Paul spotted a man in a suit walking up the hill. Paul turned and ran into the house, with my sisters and me following behind him.

My mother was a little nervous. 'Will you go out the gate and speak to the man?' she asked my father.

'Don't worry about it,' he replied.

Seconds later, the inspector walked in our gate. Before he reached the front door, my father stuck his head out the sitting-room window.

'Excuse me, can I help you there?' he called over to the man. The man told my father that he was a TV inspector and was checking that households in the area had a current licence. My father told him: 'Ah well, you're wasting your time here, we don't have a TV.'

'How do you manage without a TV?' the inspector asked him.

'Sure people did without television for years.'

I laughed when I spotted the TV aerial sticking out of the wardrobe. I was standing at my parents' bedroom window that was wide open and I could hear word for word what was said.

'Sure there's never anything good on the TV anyway. The last time we had one was before we built this house. Do you want to come into the house and check?'

The inspector was quick to reply: 'No, no, I believe you, there's no need.' With that, the inspector turned and walked away.

My father laughed, delighted with himself, as the inspector strolled down the hill.

Another time, soon after this, a man we didn't recognise walked up to our gate. When he introduced himself as a representative from the ESB who had arrived to check our meter, my father panicked. We never received a high electricity bill at home because my father used to put a lead on the wall, from our meter box to the white box outside our home. I think the lead prevented the numbers from rising in some way. My father was afraid someone would find out. One time, Gemma had spotted the cable on the wall as she was passing our house.

'Thankfully that lady wouldn't have a clue what the cable is for,' my father said to me later but he always kept a close eye on her when she walked by after that.

Anytime I wanted to have a shower, I had to let him know.

'You're not to go near the bath until I've put the lead up to stop the meter from working,' he would warn us.

He also warned my mother not to cook and use electricity until he had the lead fixed to the meter box.

When the ESB man arrived, my father managed to tell him to go around the back of the house. Then my father jumped out of the chair that was beside the window and yanked the grey cable out of the meter box on the wall. I could see sparks flying out from it. He rushed out to the back and took the lead out of the white box. He was sweating nervously but he had the man well timed. He knew he could get everything covered up before he came around the house to check the meter.

Luckily for my father, the ESB man didn't notice and he didn't get caught.

As I got older my birthday seemed to bring out the worst in my father. The year I turned 12, he put Paul and I outside the house for the night. He told Mam: 'I'm putting them out because I hate having them in the house.'

My father had made a wooden circle in the centre of the garden.

'Get out and sleep outside in that wooden circle,' he said.

'Don't make them sleep outside,' my mother pleaded but he would not be dictated to.

In the beginning, we were afraid of the dark. However, after a while we became accustomed to the dark and began to tune into all sorts of noises.

'It's more peaceful outside than in the house listening to him going on,' Paul told me.

I remember looking at the stars that night.

A few hours later, while my father was asleep, Mam managed to bring us back into the house.

The following morning, my father noticed we were in bed and told us he wanted us as quiet as mice in the house from then on. Whenever he was there, we tried to live by that rule.

I don't remember him putting us outside again but a few days later he got his revenge for my disobedience. While my mother was visiting a relation, my father brought me out to a field and raped me in view of my granny's house.

We were so near the house I hoped that one of his family would see him. I felt sick and so numb, almost as if my soul left my body while he was abusing me.

My father never cared when I begged him to stop.

I got home finally and went straight to my brothers' room.

'Where have you been? You've missed the best part of the film,' they said, looking at me.

I couldn't sit still in the room. I felt miserable.

I went to my bedroom and slept – sleep was my only way out of the misery.

A little later, my father came into my room and woke me up.

'Get up out of the bed and wash your face,' he told me.

I didn't want to get up. Everything felt like it was getting on top of me.

As he left my room, he warned: 'You'd better have a smile on your face when I see you next or there'll be trouble.'

That evening, when my mother returned, she noticed that I was pale. I said I was fine and went out to take the clothes off the line. I wanted to get out of the house. As I was getting the clothes, I spotted my uncle removing a window frame from his sister's mobile home. It was parked across from Granny's house. He then got in the window and I heard noises as if he was searching for something in the mobile home. I wondered what on earth he was doing.

My father was standing at the wall watching him and I knew that he was somehow involved. A few minutes later, my uncle emerged from the mobile home. He then replaced the window and started to walk towards my father.

With the clothes basket in my arms, I walked slowly towards the house, hoping to overhear what my father and my uncle were saying. I heard my uncle telling my father that his brother-in-law was stupid and all that he had in the house were anti-depressants and prescriptions. He said: 'It's no wonder he doesn't have a job, he spends most of his time running to the doctor.'

My father joined in: 'He's always going on about having a black belt in karate. I swear to God, if he says that one more time...'

In the pub the following Sunday afternoon, things came to a head between my father and his brother-in-law. My father told us afterwards that while they were both in the toilet, he grabbed his sister's husband by the neck and said: 'You mention your bloody black belt one more time and I'm going to stab you with this knife right here.'

A stranger, who happened to be in the toilet at the

time, ran for it when he saw my father pulling out a pocket knife.

My mother asked him: 'Why did you challenge him? What had he done?'

'My sister's married a waster and he needed to be taken down a peg or two,' my father replied.

An hour later, a police car pulled up outside the house. We were in shock looking out the window. Three police officers emerged from the car and approached the front door. My father met them there and they all climbed into the back seat of the police car.

We all knew he was telling them that his brother-in-law was lying and was on all sorts of medication. Inside the house, I was hoping and praying that my father would be arrested and sent to jail. As soon as he came in the door, I heard him say to my mother: 'Everything's fine, sure there's no policeman in the world that would listen to the madman next door.'

I was stunned. He had gotten away with it.

'Have the police dropped the investigation?' Mam asked.

'I told them she married a tinker,' he replied.

My mother was very shocked.

'You don't know whether or not he's a tinker. You shouldn't be saying that,' she said.

'What do you mean? I made a very powerful point to the police about him and they won't be taking any further action. I explained that he was going around trying to intimidate us with his black belt,' he raged.

My mother had to keep her mouth shut after that because my father was getting angry.

She sat there and nodded. We all knew that whatever she said wouldn't matter anyway.

Before school started again that year Paul and I talked a

lot about running away. We used to discuss plans all the time. We'd try to figure out who would go out the window first that night, where we'd go, how we'd get some money and how much food we'd need to bring with us. We got so engrossed one night that we didn't notice that Patrick was listening to our conversation until it was too late.

I knew he'd tell our father.

Later that evening, he told both our parents what we were planning to do. He told them that we were saying that we felt unloved and that we were always picked on.

My parents were furious and from that moment on, we were watched like hawks.

Our plans had been foiled.

SEVEN

My Father

We got ready to go back to school that September. I was going into sixth class and it would be my last year of primary school. We'd given up on the idea of running away because Paul and I both knew that our father was not a man to cross. Other people in the area came to realise this as well when his boat was damaged a few weeks later.

My father had some money left over from the robberies so he bought a wooden boat that needed some repairs. He was going to use it for fishing. When he finally had the curragh repaired, he tied it to the top of the car and drove to the 'cave', a place nearby where people moored their boats. He left the boat there and returned home. He announced to my mother: 'I'm going to take the curragh out for her maiden voyage tomorrow. I'll do a bit of fishing.'

But the following morning, when he drove back to the cave, the boat was nowhere to be seen. He began to panic and started to search everywhere for the missing boat. He told us later that when he reached the little bridge down from the cave, he noticed that the green van that belonged to some lodgers who were staying with one of our neighbours had been pushed into the little river. He initially thought that an accident had taken place and went down to investigate. When he approached the van, he spotted his boat submerged under it.

He screamed so loudly that people came out to see what was wrong. He said that nobody had sympathy for him even though he'd spent the whole summer working on that boat.

When he returned home, he dropped over to Delia's house and phoned the police. My father rushed over to them when they arrived. He explained the situation to them and showed them the remains of his boat.

'How long is it going to take you to find out who destroyed my boat?' he demanded to know.

They tried to reassure him: 'We'll do everything we can, Mr Naughton, but we can't say exactly when we'll know something.'

'Well, I actually have a few suspects already,' my father told them and proceeded to give the police the names of the people he suspected. 'I'm convinced my own brother was involved in this somehow.'

As soon as the police left, my father's temper erupted and he started cursing them.

'Sure they're no good. I'm going to have to take charge of this thing myself. I'll find out who did this.'

'Would you not just wait and see if the police find out who was involved?' my mother asked him.

He started mocking the police and he shouted at her: 'I'll find out quicker myself. I'll carry out my own investigation and leave no stone unturned. Sure the police only go easy on people when they question them. But watch what I'll do.'

My father then went on to tell us his plan to catch the culprits who destroyed his boat.

'I'm going to question one of my suspects. I'm going to tell him that the other people involved in the incident had confessed and that there's no point in denying their involvement.'

'You shouldn't be going around accusing people,' my mother replied.

'Ah, wait till you see, I'll sort this out,' he replied. 'I'll bring Patrick along as a witness too.'

My father and Patrick then drove off in the car. Patrick told us all about what happened next when they got back. As soon as my father spotted one of his suspects, he called him over. He was a 14-year-old local lad.

My father hurled questions at the miscreant and the young lad sounded nervous. But he denied any involvement, so my father threatened him: 'If you don't give me the names of those involved, I'll stop you from going to college in the future.'

The lad continued to deny having any involvement so my father decided to give up on him and go to question another teenage suspect. My father was hell-bent on catching him before anyone else spoke to him. He drove like a lunatic and spotted the second suspect standing at a shed.

My father whistled at him and beckoned him to come over. He told him: 'The rest of the lads have admitted their guilt and have agreed to pay the price of the boat.'

The young lad blushed; he didn't know what to say.

'Well, are you prepared to pay your part of the damages?' my father asked.

The young man nodded: 'Yeah I'll pay my share.' My father smiled as he began to explain what had happened: 'It was an accident. We pushed the van over the bridge but we didn't know your boat was in the cave at the time.'

Patrick told me later that the teenager innocently told my father the names of all the people involved. Before my father left, he warned the young man: 'If you don't want your name splashed all over the papers, you'll pay the damages as quickly as possible.'

'Oh, I'll pay my share as quickly as I can and I'll tell the others to do the same,' the lad replied. He was very apologetic about the whole episode.

My father was very excited and rushed to the third suspect's house before anybody had a chance to talk to him. When the young lad opened the door, my father told him that he knew exactly what had happened and who was involved. My father related the whole story and the young man was surprised to hear how accurate all the details were.

The young man had the same reaction as the previous one; he apologised and promised to pay his part of the damages as quickly as possible.

When my father returned home, he triumphantly related his exploits to my mother. 'I single-handedly resolved the whole matter. Wait till you see – the damages for the boat will be paid very quickly indeed.'

He was right. They paid almost immediately and must have regretted pushing the old green van down the hill.

My father didn't have any time for the neighbours. I remember I came home one afternoon before Hallowe'en and my parents were listening to the local news on the radio. Mam gasped when she heard that a lady she knew well from our village was very ill. She turned to my father and said: 'I'll have to keep a close ear to the radio in case Mary passes away.'

'Why would you spend the day listening to a radio waiting for someone to die? Why are people in the area so fascinated with other people's misery?' my father asked.

'I know the woman very well. I'm hoping she recovers,' my mother replied.

'Why do you care whether she lives or not? Jesus

Christ, that's their problem, not yours. If she dies, so what? Her time was up. What's the big deal? She's old. It's time she passed on. She would only be taking up space for the new generation. She had enough time spent here. Jesus, it would be worse if a young person was dying. An old person, Jesus, that's to be expected.'

As I listened, I realised that he didn't care about anything or anyone, except maybe his own family. Even though they used to fight all the time, he'd still help them if they needed it. I remember one night as I looked over the wall, I spotted my father and some of his five brothers working on a car in my grandfather's shed. I watched my father single-handedly lift an engine from one car and place it into another. He was really strong. They were drinking *poitín* and spent the entire night working on the engines. At some point my Uncle Michael cut his head and had to be rushed to Galway Hospital. When my mother visited him the following day, he told her that he was sick of his life and would have been happy if he had died. He had been unemployed for several years and the strain had taken its toll. Finding work in the west of Galway at that time was extremely difficult.

Although my father had a talent for mechanics and could do anything with cars, he refused to look for permanent employment. He never seemed to use his talents in a productive manner. Instead he misused his skills. It was exactly the way he was with the accordion. Sometimes my mother would say to him: 'Why don't you travel to England? There would be much more work for you over there.'

My father would reply: 'I never want to work as an employee ever again, having somebody telling me to do this and do that all day.'

On another occasion, my mother suggested to him that he should consider opening his own business. As usual, he agreed and did nothing about it. I think he was easily bored. When he couldn't think of anything else to do, he used to sit in his car and spin the tyres, hoping that someone would come out of the house and pay him some attention. Mam used to say: 'What the hell has gotten into him?'

He used to spin the chips and speed down the road. My brothers and I would rush out to the wall and watch him speeding off.

I'd be glad to see him go.

He had a terrible sense of humour as well and was only happy if the joke made somebody feel bad. Just after Hallowe'en he returned from the pub delighted with himself.

'I dropped into one of the neighbour's gardens on the way home and took some of their underwear off their clothes line and put it on one of their donkeys.' He was laughing loudly and thought it was extremely funny.

Patrick was in stitches laughing too. My mother shook her head and walked out.

The following morning, the minibus arrived to collect the elderly ladies for Mass. My next-door neighbour, who was on the bus, later told my mother: 'Everyone on the bus roared with laughter when they spotted a bra on the donkey.'

The two elderly ladies who recognised their underclothes were extremely embarrassed and asked: 'How could anybody be so wicked as to put our underclothes on a poor animal?'

The entire conversation on the bus to Mass was about who would be so wicked as to take the elderly ladies' underwear and place it on the donkey. While other people on the bus couldn't stop laughing about the situation, the elderly ladies were upset and I felt so sorry for them.

He didn't have much time for most of the old people in the area and seemed to enjoy shocking them. A few weeks before Christmas, two other ladies from our neighbourhood asked my father if he would drive them to Carraroe to do some shopping.

'We'll pay you for your time,' they said, probably knowing my father wouldn't do it otherwise. He agreed and my sister and I went along for the drive. When we arrived in Carraroe, the two ladies headed off.

My father headed to the pub and left my sister and me in the back seat with the warning: 'No messing now, the pair of ye are to stay in the car.'

As soon as our father entered the pub, we jumped out of the car and walked around the town. We knew our father would be in no rush to leave the pub. When we got back to the car an hour later, the two elderly ladies were sitting in the back seat. They asked us: 'Where's your father?'

'He's in the pub,' we told them, pointing across the road.

'Would the pair of ye drop into the pub and ask your father how long he'll be?' one of the ladies asked us.

So we walked into the pub and immediately spotted our father sitting on a bar stool, chatting to an elderly man.

'The ladies are waiting in the car and want to know how much longer you'll be,' I said.

He got annoyed as he didn't like being rushed and said: 'I'll be out in five minutes.'

We went back to the car and told them he was nearly ready. We then waited ... and waited. An hour passed and my father had still not appeared.

'Would ye drop into the pub again to see what's keeping your father?'

We entered the pub again and told our father that the ladies were complaining. He gulped down the last of his pint, slammed it on the bar and returned to the car with us.

When we reached the car, one of them said: 'We've been waiting in this car for two hours. What kept you?'

'Nobody fuckin' asked ye to wait. Why didn't ye make your own way home? All ye women are the same, not happy unless ye are complaining or gossiping,' my father shouted.

The elderly women looked at him in shock.

'Go on, get your arses out of the car. Go and make your own way home.' He told them that it would teach them a lesson and that maybe in future they wouldn't be complaining all the time.

When the ladies left, my father brought the two of us back into the pub.

I was mortified as the two ladies were lovely. They wouldn't harm a fly. I thought my father was a real pig doing that to them. He laughed at them when they left.

We had to stay in the pub for another hour.

My father talked a lot about how to handle people, as well as teaching them a lesson. He was always worrying about people getting one over on him, especially the neighbours. Shortly after the New Year's celebrations, my mother went to Galway shopping. My father was sitting on his bed writing letters. I knew that there was little chance that my father was sitting down and doing something productive so I asked him what he was doing.

He replied: 'Well, I was going to call you and show you the technique for handling people that you hate;

how to take revenge and bring them down to their knees where they belong.'

He continued: 'Your woman, there down the road, makes me sick. She's always in here blabbing away about things and never has a good word to say about me to your mother. Well, she has lodgers in her other house; the one that's in her son's name. I'll stop that happening very quickly. I know she's also on the dole. However, she'll find out the pen is mightier than the sword.'

I asked him: 'So what are you going to do?'

He replied: 'I'm writing a letter to the Inspector of Taxes. This is his address in case you need to contact him in Galway. Do you see now what I mean?'

'The inspector might have more important matters to deal with,' I told him.

He shouted: 'He will listen. He has a boss over him. I will go to the highest mark to nail him if he fails to do his duty. This woman needs to be straightened out and I am the man who will straighten her.'

I couldn't believe what I was hearing. I was standing there trying to make sense of it all. I wondered why my father spoke nicely to the woman whenever she came to visit us and did all this behind her back. He used to be nice to her husband too.

'What's the purpose in doing all of this?' I asked him. None of it made much sense.

He got very annoyed with me and replied: 'Are you stupid or something? A person is not allowed to be signing on the dole and working – especially that lunatic who lets out one of her houses and gets the dole. That's illegal.'

His face was red with rage and he shouted: 'It's not fair for the innocent people out there to be suffering.'

My father only ever seemed to concentrate on anything or do any work when he could cause trouble for people. A few days later, I walked past my father's bedroom door and I spotted him writing another letter. He said it was to the inspector again. My father was complaining about a man who was supposed to be his friend.

'He has an awful cheek coming over to Kinnvarra cutting seaweed in our patch. There's plenty of seaweed near his own place, but he's so greedy he comes down to my patch. All the seaweed in this vicinity is mine. I don't like it when other people cut seaweed from my patch. That man needs to be taught a lesson,' he ranted.

I thought to myself that he should have been a private investigator as he had such a methodical approach to his work. If he made an error while writing, he would rip up the page and start again. At least he should have been getting paid for reporting people, as it seemed to be his new job.

'I know how to deal with people like him. This is the man you write to whenever you have a stone in your sleeve for somebody.'

He used to read some of the letters out to me. He told the inspector that this man had an awful cheek coming over to Kinnvarra cutting seaweed and that he should cut seaweed in his own area in Camus. He also mentioned that this man was drawing the dole as well and that he shouldn't be working in Kinnvarra. He said that it was the inspector's duty to put a stop to it.

He read out the letter to me a few times before he placed it in a brown envelope.

'I'll post this letter later today and the inspector will receive it by tomorrow morning.' He continued: 'Don't you realise I'm doing the inspector a favour? As a matter of fact, I'm doing his job for him. He should be doing this himself.'

He was really excited when he finished the letter and rushed off to post it.

A week later when I came home from school, my father was in great form. He told me that I missed one of our neighbours that had come around to our house to have a chat with my mother.

'I sat in the bedroom and listened to her telling your mam all about the inspector showing up at her relative's door in Camus. My blessings are working,' he said, winking at me. 'She was very unhappy about it.'

My father was also always on the look-out for slights and reasons to fight with people. The following day he brought Alison and me into Spiddal. On the way he dropped into our local petrol station and, as ever, he put £5 worth of petrol in the car. As my father was paying, the man asked him: 'Why do you only ever put £5 worth of petrol in your car?'

My father replied: 'I'm not getting this petrol for nothing; I don't see why I should answer your stupid questions. I think you should keep them to yourself in future.'

We could hear all this clearly.

When my father got back into the car he said to us: 'Always check and make sure that no one takes advantage of you.'

That wasn't enough for my father. He mimicked and cursed the garage man all the way home in the car. He complained about him asking stupid questions and repeated the same story to Mam. She agreed with the garage man and they ended up having a row about it.

Another time, my father went to the garage and had a plastic jar and asked the garage man to put £5 worth of petrol in it. He wanted to see how far the car would go before the last dregs of petrol were used up. I remember the car conked out on him on the main road and he got a plastic container and ran a hose from it into his car to get the car going again.

It was a wonder he didn't write a letter to the garage complaining about their petrol.

He was very conscious of his appearance and was as concerned about people laughing at the way he looked as he was about people trying to take him for a fool. It was just before Easter that year when a boy approached Paul in school and asked him: 'Does your father think that everybody is thick?'

Paul looked at him quizzically and asked: 'What are you talking about?'

'Your dad wears a wig and whenever there's a strong breeze, the wig flies off his head. I saw him chasing the wig along the road one day.'

Paul got embarrassed. 'Mind your own business,' he shouted.

That afternoon, Paul rushed home from school. He'd barely come in the door and taken a breath before he told my father what the young boy had said.

My father lost the head immediately: 'That little runt must have overheard his parents gossiping.' He studied himself in the mirror and then turned to my mother. He asked: 'Does this look straight on my head? Does it look like a wig?'

'Yes, it does look like a wig. I wouldn't be seen dead in one,' she replied.

He started kicking things and shouted: 'I paid 300 fucking pounds for this. I was told that it suited me.'

Several days later, my mother said to my father: 'I saw an ad on TV for a new product coming on the market that helps hair grow back. Look, here's the free number you can ring to order some.' My father phoned them immediately and ordered some sprays.

A week later, two bottles arrived in the post. He

sprayed it on his scalp religiously and after a couple of weeks his scalp turned brown to match the few strands of hair he still had on the side of his head. It looked a little odd.

My mother said to him about how silly it looked on a few occasions when they were fighting. This might be why he then decided to start wearing a green cap with holes in it. He believed that the holes would allow air to circulate around his scalp and encourage hair growth. Over a period of time, he used all sorts of home remedies, such as soaking his head in a bath full of freshly picked nettles or even seaweed to try and get his hair to grow back. The bath was always black after he had boiled nettles or seaweed in it.

It felt good to be able to laugh at him. I couldn't understand why he was so self-conscious about his image. As a married man with five children he should have been more concerned about other things.

Sometimes I thought my father never seemed to have a good word about anyone. One day as my father and I walked down the road towards the local shop, he spotted a man in the distance walking towards us.

My father told me: 'That man there was a patient in the psychiatric ward in Galway Hospital. If that man ever commits a crime, he won't be prosecuted as he can claim that he was mentally unstable and unaware of what he was doing. Anybody who has attended a psychiatric ward is classed as not being the full shilling.'

When my father realised that the man was heading towards the shop, he grabbed me by the arm, turned and walked back towards our home.

'It's better not to have any contact with mental patients,' he told me.

I looked back at the man and wondered what wrong he had ever done on my father and why my father was the way he was – full of badness.

EIGHT

Trapped

I couldn't believe my time in primary school was nearly up. As the days flew by, a lot of our time was taken up preparing for our Confirmation which was taking place at the end of June. I was excited about it.

'Can we go to Galway City and pick out a dress?' I asked Mam.

'I don't have that much money at the moment, Barbara. Your Aunt Kelly in England has already sent over a lovely dress in the post,' she replied. It was navy blue with polka dots and she showed me a picture of a young girl wearing it.

I didn't really feel that the Confirmation dress was for me. I could picture myself in something different. I told my mother that the dress was special for my aunt's day, not mine. But there was no money for anything new.

A couple of days before the Confirmation, I still hadn't settled on the name I was going to take. I was going to choose when being confirmed by the Bishop. I discussed it with my granny and mother and in the end I picked Anna-Marie.

On the day of my Confirmation, I rose early to get ready and because I was too excited to sleep. As soon as I was dressed, I headed towards the kitchen for breakfast. As had happened at my Communion, my father said: 'I won't be standing with you at the altar.' I was glad when he said he wasn't coming. He would have ruined my day. In my heart I was relieved that he wasn't going to be close to me as I was confirmed.

My mother looked at my father in dismay and tried to persuade him to change his mind, but he was not to be swayed.

My mother dropped into my granny's house next door. They decided to ask my godfather Peadar Hopkins if he would stand for me at the Confirmation. My mother knew his parents so she'd thought he'd be a good choice as godfather. Thankfully, he agreed. My cousin, the hairdresser, had arrived at our house to do my hair.

'You should stop cutting Barbara's hair so short and let her curls grow,' she said to my father as she was styling my hair.

He ignored her.

When three o'clock arrived, we headed off to the church. As soon as we got there, I spotted my headmaster. He walked over to me and told me that I looked beautiful in my dress. It made me feel happy and more confident in myself when he said that.

During the Mass, my headmaster sat next to me. When I looked in the choir's direction, I could see the teacher busy organising them.

Halfway through the Mass, I turned my head and spotted my father standing at the back of the church. I was surprised to see him. I didn't know why my father had shown up but I felt uncomfortable with him there.

I nudged Patrick. 'Look, Dad's in the church,' I said and gestured in my father's direction.

Patrick looked at me in disbelief but changed his expression when he looked back and saw my father. I turned to my mother and told her that my father was actually in the church. She looked back, saw him and smiled.

Towards the end of the Mass, Bishop Eamon Casey,

who performed it, called all the children who were to be confirmed to the altar.

I walked up to take my place on the altar with my mother and godfather at my side.

The Bishop confirmed me and on the way back to my seat, I noticed that my father was nowhere to be seen. I tried to get him out of my mind and concentrate on what the Bishop was saying.

When the Mass was over, my Aunt Barbara took lots of photos of me outside the church. I felt happy to be confirmed and was smiling. My father was hovering in the background and my mother called him over: 'Come on over and stand beside Barbara there and we'll take a few photos.'

Eventually, he joined me. When he put his arm around me, I felt sick. At this stage, my father's touch repulsed me. I couldn't wait for my aunt to finish taking the photos. We stood there posing for photos like any other father and daughter, with no one realising how sick to the stomach I felt and how I wanted his disgusting hands off me.

When she finished, we headed home.

Later that night, my whole family dropped down to the local pub where a band played music all night long.

Most of my Confirmation Day was great. I felt a bit flat after it. I was glad the summer camp was starting a few days later.

My brother Paul and I had decided we wanted to join the camp the minute we heard about it. As always, it was difficult for us to get permission to go. We begged and begged and eventually my father relented. 'Keep a close eye on Barbara,' he told Paul.

There was a bus organised to bring us to the camp, where we would stay for two nights, and my parents had given us some money. I was happy to be away from my father. We were all so excited, we sang all the way there. There were four boys from my class on the bus.

I was chatting away to them. They all began to sing on the bus and I decided to sit at the back and join in. I was happy to go away. The feeling of being out of the house filled the flesh on my bones with excitement and freedom.

Our days at camp were packed full of activities. On our first day, we learned how to play basketball. I loved it and quickly got the hang of it. We also had art classes and learned how to make little puppets. We had a different tutor for each activity. Two of our tutors were from my mother's village and were very kind to us.

That afternoon, we climbed Croagh Patrick. It was hard work. My feet were slipping off the rocks. I tried to rush up Croagh Patrick as I felt it was an infliction. I must have used up a lot of my angry energy to make it to the top of the mountain.

When we reached the summit, some of the group entered the little church and took confession but I didn't go in.

I found it much easier on the way down and managed not to fall once.

For the first night, I shared a tent with two other girls. I slept well that first night but on the second night the weather worsened and our tent was damaged. We jumped up and ran over to where the tutors were sleeping. One of them came over and had the tent fixed in a matter of minutes.

When I awoke the following morning, I felt sad that I couldn't remain longer at the camp. All the people I'd met were lovely and the tutors had been very helpful. There was one boy in particular who I was going to miss. His name was Joe and he had gorgeous blue eyes. I hoped that someone like him would someday take me away from my miserable life. Whenever my brother mentioned his name, my eyes always lit up. The boy lived next door to my granny in Lettermore and he knew I visited my granny every now and again. He used to visit my Uncle Padraig in Lettermore all the time. I thought how lucky my uncle was to see him every day.

I felt very broken going home. As soon as I saw the house again, I wished I could turn and run away. Paul seemed as upset as I was. We sang all the way home on the bus, trying not to think about it.

When we arrived home, one of the tutors had an announcement: 'You're all going to be invited to a reunion party in about two weeks' time. We hope to see you all there.'

I was happy when I learned that I might see Joe again. I just hoped my parents would let us go.

Just as the camp ended, my father received a call from the secretary in the National School asking him if he would be interested in painting some of the classrooms and fitting some new windows. As it was paid work, my father jumped at the chance.

On the first morning that my father started painting the school, he told my mother: 'Send Barbara down with my lunch at lunchtime. She's always complaining that she's bored and the walk will do her the world of good.'

When my mother had his sandwiches made, she gave them to me and told me to go down to the school and give them to him.

On my way to the school, I spotted a stray dog on the side of the road. He looked lonely and his eyes were sad. He reminded me of how I felt inside. I gave the poor animal a couple of my father's sandwiches, which he wolfed down hungrily.

When I arrived at the school, my father was painting a ceiling in one of the classrooms. I called out to him, placed his lunch on a table and turned to go as I wanted to get away from him as quickly as I could.

He called out: 'Hang on a sec, Barbara, I haven't spoken to a soul all day, other than yer man from the shop.' When he approached me, however, he spotted I didn't have a flask and his mood changed. He began cursing and shouting: 'Where's the fucking flask? Does she think I'm a fucking monkey and can eat sandwiches without a drink?'

I was afraid.

'Did you eat some of the sandwiches on the way here?'

I didn't know what to say.

As his ranting continued, I became more frightened. 'Take off your clothes and lean on that table.'

I refused.

He grabbed hold of me and started undressing me. I attempted to push his hand away but he was stronger than I was. He then placed his arms around my body and raped me.

I found it so hard to breathe. I think I was in shock. It was horrible that he was raping me in my school, where I'd had so many happy days away from him.

When he was finished, he told me to dress. I wanted to leave but he insisted on telling me stories he thought were funny to try to make me laugh.

He made me sick and I didn't find his stories funny.

A few minutes later, the door opened and the old man from the shop entered. My father looked at him nervously and said: 'I'm just having my lunch at the moment, why don't you drop back later for a chat?'

When the old man had gone, my father said to me:

'You'd better put a smile on your face before going home.'

When I reached home, I went straight to my bedroom and stared out of the window at the trees and clouds. I wondered why my father was hurting me.

What had I done?

What could I do to make him stop?

For the remainder of the afternoon, I listened to the birds singing outside.

That evening, I was in my bedroom when Mam called me into the sitting room.

My brothers were already there.

'Sit down here and watch this documentary, it's very interesting,' she said.

The documentary revolved around a father who had been sexually abusing his daughter. All the people in it spoke with strong Dublin accents.

I was disgusted and it made me want to cry when I saw how the father was punishing his children. I knew exactly how they felt.

Mam wanted all of us to watch the documentary as she thought it would educate us and open our eyes about what goes on in the world. She told us that this type of behaviour went on throughout the country but was seldom reported.

My father was sitting on the small coffee table, picking his nails nervously.

'You shouldn't be telling them things like that,' he said suddenly. He started making movements on the table and whistling to distract Mam from talking about the programme.

I kept my head down and found it all very upsetting. I was afraid to say anything to Mam even though that would have been the perfect time for me to confide in her.

My father was always in the way.

Over the next few weeks, I became a big Tina Turner fan. She had a wonderful voice and was a very powerful singer. Years later, I discovered that she had had a difficult marriage and had suffered physical abuse. While I didn't know that at the time, her music consoled me during a difficult period of my life.

I started to feel a bit better when my mother received a letter with an invitation for Paul and myself to the summer camp reunion party. Thankfully, we were allowed to go.

I was nervous getting dressed up for the dance. When we arrived, they were playing good songs from the 70s and 80s. I noticed Joe looking in my direction. I pretended not to see him. A bit later, I watched him walking in and out of the club. I was hoping he would ask me up for a slow dance but sadly he never did. Perhaps he was too shy. I was probably being a bit too nervous around him. I was afraid to chat in case Paul told my father.

I felt sad when the party was over as I never got the chance to talk to him.

Later that week, my father received another call from the secretary of the National School. The secretary told him that someone had broken the windows again and that this was sadly becoming a regular occurrence. She asked him to put in some more new windows. When my father received the news, he turned to my mother with a big smile.

'I've great news,' he said and explained about the job.

My father started work in the school the following morning. He never collected his wages for the work he did in person but always sent Paul to get it.

My father didn't have the neck to go himself.

* * * *

The summer rushed by and I was getting nervous about starting secondary school. One weekend, just before my 13th birthday, my mother brought me into Galway City and bought me a lovely long red jacket. When we got back, Paul was not happy to see me sporting a new coat.

'Why are you always buying her new clothes? I never get anything new,' he gave out. He continued complaining to her about the matter all day. When my mother ignored his whining, he went to my father and started to complain.

My father checked my wardrobe and came back out to my mother.

'You're buying that girl too many clothes,' I heard him say. I knew that Paul had sparked my father off. My father continued on at Mam: 'The clothes she had should've done for another while yet.'

Paul's mood changed when he heard my father complaining to my mother about the new jacket. He felt guilty and realised the trouble that he'd caused.

My mother told my father: 'She needed a jacket with a hood on it for the autumn when she starts in the secondary school.'

That seemed to shut him up.

My father made my first teenage birthday one to remember. I was due to start secondary school about a week later. My father celebrated by cutting my hair so short that I looked like a boy. At the time, I was extremely self-conscious of my appearance and very sensitive about the negative comments I knew I was going to get. I was dreading starting school.

Secondary school was as bad as I'd thought it would be. I hated it. The first couple of months I was in the lowest grade classroom. I had the same teacher for English and History. I wasn't able to concentrate on a word he was saying.

One day, he called me outside the class and asked me in an angry voice what on earth was wrong with me. I broke down in tears. I couldn't communicate with him as he had an unnerving manner just like my father. I couldn't talk to him and I felt like he was bullying me. I used to hate whenever I had to go to school to face him.

With everything else that was happening, I found it difficult to progress in school, but some of the new things I learned over the next few months were great. One afternoon, when I got home, I told my brothers: 'I learned how to make queen cakes in school today. I'll make some for ye this evening.'

While I was baking, my father returned home and came into the kitchen.

'Follow me down the road on your bike,' he told me.

My brothers could hear him from the sitting room. They came back into the kitchen and Paul said the brakes weren't too good on the bike but was told to shut up. Patrick looked at me and realised that I wasn't a bit happy about leaving the baking but what could any of us do.

I was really angry and I hated the fact that my father was ruining any possibility of happiness I had for the evening. All I'd wanted to do was show my brothers something good I'd learnt in school.

The boys went back into the sitting room and I tried to say that I was baking but my father said I had to do what I was told. On his way out the door, he told me that I would suffer again if I failed to follow him down on the bike.

I left the house, grabbed my bike and set off to meet him.

I was so angry. I was in my first year of secondary school and I just wanted it all to end.

I wondered to myself, 'What is the reason for living with all of this?' Deep down, I believed my life would always be miserable.

I decided I wanted to end my life completely.

I'd thought that going to secondary school would be a mind-opening experience for me and would somehow put me on the right path but I felt trapped there as well.

I stopped at the top of the hill, just a few yards away from my home.

At 13 years of age I decided I'd had enough.

I was going to end my life.

I raced the bike down the hill as fast as I could, knowing I wouldn't be able to stop it.

I heard my father's voice in the background calling after me.

When I reached the road at the bottom of the hill, at high speed, sadly there were no cars passing.

The bike careered across the road and crashed into a small wall. I was thrown over the handlebars. When I hit the ground, I could feel pain all over. A couple of girls from our neighbourhood ran over to me and asked: 'Are you OK?'

Cathy, from the shop, came over as well.

'I'm going in to ring for an ambulance,' she told me.

My father then arrived on the scene. He said: 'Don't worry, I'll look after her.'

He lifted me off the ground and carried me back to the house.

I was very sick. I felt extremely weak and helpless. I couldn't believe that I was still alive and my father was carrying me up the road. I knew he wouldn't call an ambulance.

I was furious that I'd lived. I was so sorry it hadn't worked.

I repeated to him that I was very sick and that I felt like throwing up. I showed him the cuts on my knees and arm.

My father didn't care and told me to be quiet. Suddenly, before I knew it, I found myself lying on wet ground behind an old house. I was so upset and angry. I told him that my arm was hurting and that I couldn't move. It didn't matter to him and he proceeded to rape me.

The pain was excruciating. He gave me more injuries on top of the ones I already had from the bike.

Afterwards, he said: 'Now, you're to tell your mother you only scratched yourself.'

When we returned home, my father attached a stick to my arm with a blue roll and wrapped a bandage around my hand.

'The stick will keep your bone straight until the morning,' he explained to me.

I hated him.

He disgusted me. I knew that he was afraid I would be taken to hospital and all my injuries would go on record.

My mother, who had been visiting a neighbour's house, arrived home an hour later.

'What happened to your arm?' she asked me. She turned to my father: 'You'll have to bring her to casualty to have her arm X-rayed. She's in a lot of pain.'

'We'll wait till the morning and if she hasn't improved by then, I'll bring her to casualty,' he told her.

The following morning, I woke up to find that my hand was swollen. My mother came into my room to see how I was.

'It's really sore when I try and move my hand,' I told her.

My mother immediately went to my father.

'You're taking Barbara to casualty right away.'

My father had no choice but to bring me to the hospital. We had to wait a while but the doctor finally examined my hand. It was throbbing with pain.

'I'm afraid she has a chipped bone in her wrist. Her hand will be in a cast for the next few weeks. She needs complete rest and shouldn't be doing anything physically demanding around the house.'

My father was wandering around in circles, impatiently asking the doctors to hurry up so that he could bring me home. I was annoyed as he was making me feel worse.

When I returned home, I spent the next few days in bed. I had a cast on my hand and all I could do was read magazines. I didn't enjoy it. I was feeling very low and trapped. I was bored at home waiting to recover but I didn't want to go to school either. I didn't seem to fit in anywhere.

I spent a lot of the time chatting to my Uncle Tommy. I remember my father telling me around the same time: 'Sure you could quit school now if you wanted, it wouldn't make any difference. I quit school at your age. And look at Joe over in England.'

Joe was my father's brother who left school at 13. He had his own successful business in England.

I didn't believe that leaving school at 13 would mean I'd get away from him so I tried to ignore him.

A few mornings later, I received a letter from one of my classmates, Judy. She was concerned that I hadn't been in school for a couple of weeks. It was so nice to get the letter.

I wrote back to her and said that I had broken my wrist and could only write with my left hand. As I sat re-reading her letter, my father appeared.

'What are you doing?' he asked me.

'I'm reading a letter I got from one of the girls in school.'

'Let me have a look at it,' he said and put out his hand to take it.

I stood up and said: 'It's nothing you haven't read already.'

The letter had been opened before I'd received it.

He took the letter off me and questioned me about a boy in school Judy had mentioned in the note. She'd called me by his name. When I realised how angry my father was, I looked at him in shock. I told him that Judy was only teasing me and it was just a joke.

He went to Patrick for confirmation and seemed even angrier when he got it. He threw the letter back at me and stomped off.

I felt so angry because he was behaving like a husband. He was a sick monster.

It was a relief when I recovered enough to go back to school around the middle of November. I found it very hard because there was so much to catch up on. I was still afraid of the bullying teacher and he used to speak very quickly in English which I found difficult to follow. At the same time, I was under a lot of stress from my father at home. I didn't seem to be able to cope with him any more. I found it really difficult to concentrate on anything and I couldn't even have a conversation with my friends. I was at such a low ebb. All my natural chattiness and life was gone. I spent too much time thinking about what would happen next at home and how I could avoid it.

There were two boys in my class who ridiculed me all the time as well. They called me 'dogface' and used to bark like a dog in the class when I walked in. I didn't have the strength to say anything back to them.

I began to hate myself and I thought that they could

be right. I thought maybe that was the reason my father was sexually abusing me at home, because I was so ugly he wanted to hurt me.

My brother told my father about the young boys in my class bullying me. This gave him the perfect explanation for why I looked so depressed all the time.

He used to say to Mam: 'That's why she's so sad; the bullying at school is too much for her to take.'

I felt so angry at him when I heard him say that, I wanted to scream. As he had the perfect explanation of why I was so down all the time, I felt I had no avenue left to talk to anybody about what was happening. I knew he'd blame the bullying if I told anyone.

Several of the girls from my class constantly chatted about the local youth club. I listened to them talking about what boy they had kissed or wanted to kiss. I envied them but said nothing. My father had given me permission to attend the local youth club on one occasion, chaperoned by Patrick. It hadn't been much fun.

As Christmas approached, the day of our holidays from school finally arrived. The class was dispersing when one of my friends asked me: 'Are you coming to the youth club tonight, Barbara? It's a special occasion to mark the start of our Christmas holidays; you should try and make it along.'

'I'll have to ask my parents,' I replied. As soon as I got home from school, I immediately asked my mother if I could go.

'Please, Mam, everyone's going! It's to celebrate the Christmas holidays.'

'You'll have to ask your father,' she replied.

My heart sank. I knew what his answer would most likely be.

When my father arrived home later that evening, I asked him if I could go.

When he said no, I started to cry. I was so disappointed. I knew everyone from school would be at the youth club and I'd be missing out. I begged and pleaded but both my parents ignored me.

As I sat on the settee watching TV later that night, my father came into the room and sat down beside me.

'You're to tell your mother you want to come down to the pub with me,' he told me.

I felt really anxious when he said this. He'd never asked me to go to the pub before. I was worried. I didn't know why my father wanted me to go with him.

As I spoke to my mother in the kitchen, I could hear my father at the door listening to every word I said. My mother had no problem with her 13-year-old daughter going to the pub with her father. I felt so trapped when she said yes. I think she thought my father was trying to make it up to me because they wouldn't let me go to the youth club with my friends.

We drove off in the car and my father started to discuss his past, as usual: 'I shouldn't have married your mother. If I could only live my life over...'

He would always ask my opinion and used to look at me for my reaction. When he said that my mother wasn't doing anything for him, I think I was supposed to look happy. He'd then say that I was bubbly and extroverted which I wasn't really anymore. He'd usually mention that he couldn't have a normal conversation with his own family, as they were all too stupid and didn't understand anything.

I'd never say much in these conversations. Most of the time I just nodded along, trying to humour him.

This time he told me that marriage had trapped him and that a person should stay single. 'If I had the knowledge then that I have now, I would never have made a fool of myself and married your mother,' he said. 'I thought I was marrying one person but I ended up married to the whole family. It's taken me years to get them out of my life.'

We stopped at a pub and my father put a glass of whisky in front of me.

'Now drink that, it'll warm you up.'

I sniffed the drink and didn't like the smell.

He kept cajoling me to drink it so I took a sip. It was horrible and I nearly got sick.

I told him: 'I'm too young to be drinking. I want a glass of orange.'

As there were people in the pub, he didn't want to make a scene.

After he had a couple of drinks, he decided that we were going to head off to another pub. This time, he drove many miles away from where we lived, to a pub where nobody recognised him or me.

Again, he tried to make me drink whisky and I refused.

His mood changed the more he drank. First, he was grovelling and apologising about his behaviour towards me. Then he got angry and started cursing my mother's family. It was like a seesaw, one side, then the other. When we were finished in the second pub, my father drove towards our home.

On the way, he told me that he had been sexually abused as a child. At this stage, I never believed anything he said. He started to cry and apologised for hurting me again.

'I'm sorry, I'm sorry, I really am. I'll never do it to you again. I promise.'

I knew better than to believe his promises.

'I swear, I'll never do it to you again.'

He then asked me: 'Do you remember when I started interfering with you?'

I was caught off-guard by the question: 'No, I can't remember.'

'Well, it only started a few months ago,' he said.

Although my mind was addled at this stage of my life, I knew the abuse had started years earlier. I had no idea why he was saying this to me. I merely nodded in agreement and hoped that he would drive directly home and leave me alone.

He then looked at me and said: 'I suppose you'll turn around sooner or later and tell people what I did to you. I know you'll always have a mark in your mind, but remember I can always put you in a place where nobody will ever find your body... so keep your mouth shut...'

We were still a good few miles from the house when my father turned the car off a by-road. I knew what was coming and tried to think about something else as he started to rape me.

When he was finished, he slumped over and fell asleep.

I sat in the car for the next three hours, waiting for him to wake up and bring me home. I kept thinking about getting out and walking home but I was too afraid of the dark. I didn't know what would happen to me in the middle of nowhere on my own. I was also tense in case I woke my father up when I opened the car door. I knew that nothing got by him.

Instead, I thought again about telling people what was happening. I was wondering if I could tell a teacher at my new school.

Looking outside at total darkness, I decided I just couldn't do it. I didn't think they'd listen to me. By now I was sure everyone would think I was crazy.

*   *   *   *

When I returned to school after Christmas, I was moved to a different classroom. I'd managed to pass my exams in the middle of everything and I went to a better class. I don't know how I did it. At least it got me away from the two bullies.

My favourite teacher was a nun who taught me French and Religion. I remember one time, when the nun gave out the results of the French exams, she stood in front of the class and said: 'Everyone in the class has failed except Barbara Naughton.'

Oh my goodness, it felt like my heart would explode with excitement. I was so excited and I felt such a sense of achievement. I found it easy to learn from Sister Kaitlin, the teaching nun. After that exam, my mind would wander into daydreams, imagining that I could go further with French studies, become fluent and get as far away from my own language as possible.

One afternoon, Sister Kaitlin said to me: 'Tell your parents that I'll be dropping around to your house later in the week to discuss how you're progressing in school with them.'

I felt I was doing well in school so I wasn't too worried. I sensed that she was being kind and that I had nothing to fear.

True to her word, the following Saturday morning, she called round. Mam met her at the gate and invited her into the house. As they were chatting, I made the tea. From the kitchen, I could hear Sister Kaitlin explaining to Mam how well Patrick was getting on in second year.

'He's able to concentrate well and picks things up easily,' I heard her say.

'As regards Barbara,' she continued, 'she seems to have difficulties concentrating and her mind appears to be elsewhere.'

'Barbara, come in here to the living room,' Mam called out to me.

The nun asked me directly: 'Is there something bothering you? You spend so much time looking out the window in class.'

I didn't know what to say. I was so surprised. I thought she was happy with my progress in school. I hadn't expected this.

I went red and started crying.

I couldn't stop myself shaking.

'Well, it must be something very bad because of the way you just reacted,' she said, looking me straight in the face.

Mam stared at the carpet.

I sighed and looked at my mother. I would have preferred if she hadn't been there when Sister Kaitlin asked the question.

I looked at her and then stared at the floor. I didn't want to say that there was nothing wrong as I knew I would be lying. So I took a long, deep sigh and said there is something wrong. My mother raised her eyes and looked angry. The impression I got from her look was to keep my mouth shut in front of the nun.

I looked at Sister Kaitlin's curious face.

'There is something bothering me but I don't know how to say it,' I told her.

The nun had a concerned look on her face. She looked at my mother and said: 'It must be something very serious the way she looks sad all the time and finds it very difficult to talk about.'

'I really don't know anything about it,' Mam replied.

'I've noticed her leaving the classroom and getting sick a lot. This isn't normal for a young girl. It appears something is distracting her.'

Her approach was very nice to me in front of my

mother. She appeared to be extremely professional but I couldn't get the words out and she left soon afterwards.

Sometimes I used to think about catching the nun alone in school and telling her but I never got the chance.

I no longer really thought about telling my mother. As I'd got older, my instinct told me that there would be no satisfaction in doing that. She reported everything back to my father, including anything that might have made the doctors suspicious.

My mother didn't ask me anything when Sister Kaitlin left. I knew my mother would leave those questions to my father.

Later that evening when my father returned home, my mother told him everything the nun had said.

'She's having trouble with those bullies in school, that must be what the problem is,' he told her afterwards.

The matter was closed.

I remember feeling that my life should end somehow. I said to myself, 'No, not yet, the time is not right.' Something was holding me back. I was disgusted with myself and felt ugly and unloved. I was very angry.

I began to question myself inside. Why was this still happening to me? Why was my father hurting me like this?

I began to question myself inside. Why was this still happening to me? Why was my father hurting me like this? I'd thought it might get a bit better as I got older but I was wrong. The only thing my age changed was that my father was afraid I might get pregnant. Now before he raped me he'd work on himself first, to make sure there was nothing left that might get into my system. It was so embarrassing watching him.

If he'd been drinking he used to grab me and question me the next morning because he wouldn't remember if he'd come near me or not the night before. He'd force me to have boiling hot baths, telling Mam it was for my health, or he'd send me out jogging with Patrick. My father was convinced that a lot of exercise would make sure nothing happened. He used to make me carry very heavy objects as well to stop anything sticking.

I remember around this time my periods stopped and my father was nearly frantic. He put me into the car and drove me 40 miles to a doctor I'd never seen before. He didn't want our family GP asking awkward questions. When I was called, my father insisted on coming into the surgery with me and demanded that the doctor explain what was happening.

The doctor looked at him in amazement and told him that I was anaemic, which was what had affected my periods.

My father calmed down after that but he was still paranoid enough to want to double-check the doctor's opinion.

He drove me to another doctor in Spiddal a few weeks later.

'Don't tell him I brought you here,' my father ordered.

I nodded but when I went in to see the doctor I blurted it out and asked about a pregnancy test.

'Why would you want that?' he asked me. 'You're too young to be worrying about having a baby.'

I started crying so he gave me some forms to fill in and told me to come back with a urine sample in two weeks' time.

I took the forms and walked back out to my father's car.

He went mad: 'There's no way you're putting any details on a form. Give me that stuff.'

As we were driving home, he threw them out the window like he did to the rubbish bags.

From then on he was more careful whenever he came near me.

My life began to change at school. I started fighting with some of the girls. We used to fight over silly things but I guess that was part of growing up. I used to listen to some of my friends saying that they were going on holidays with their parents and talking about everything they would do during the summer.

I had little in common with them.

They told me about the lovely gifts their parents used to buy for them. I'd sit there and look at them and think that they were so lucky having wonderful parents.

I began to spend a lot of time on my own, sitting on the stairway, away from my fellow classmates. I kind of liked that in a way, as I could spend time thinking.

I spent a lot of time daydreaming about suicide. I felt trapped in my own body. I had no one to turn to. I believed that if I said anything, it would be questioned and people would think I was making it up. If anyone asked about me, my family used to say that I was fine. Nobody ever seemed to notice that anything was wrong. They all thought I was a normal teenage girl.

I remember one afternoon a few weeks later, my godfather, Peadar Hopkins, who lived next door to us, dropped in for a chat. He spotted me at the back of the hall standing on the mop bucket. He started laughing and asked my mother how I managed to keep balance on both sides of the bucket. My mother told him that I got up to every sort of devilment.

As the year progressed, the abuse continued.

When I finished my first-year summer exams, it was time for my brothers and me to return to the bog. We had to help our father gathering turf. He would generally cut the turf from the ground and then my brothers and I would lift two pieces and stand them against each other to help them dry out. I found it very difficult to work for more than a couple of hours.

After having a long day on the bog I used to go home at night and feel weak. I had trouble with my tummy and I was getting constant headaches. I used to bang my head on the chair at night in my bedroom with the headaches I was getting. My breathing was out of control.

My brother Patrick heard me one night: 'You'd be better staying in the dark. Do you remember that helped me get over those migraines I used to have?'

Sadly, it didn't work.

I began to cry in my bedroom. I felt so depressed. I wanted to get myself back to normal but the bog made me physically ill.

However, my father threatened: 'If you don't stay on the bog until we're finished, then I won't let you sit beside the fire when the winter comes.'

I was mentally trapped. As we worked with the turf all day, I couldn't stop thinking about everything bad in my life.

I thought about running away again but I knew I'd suffer if I was caught and brought home.

One afternoon, my father and I were working on the bog alone when he suddenly asked me: 'Do you know what the word "rape" means?'

Before I could reply, he began to relate incidents of rape he had read about in the newspapers.

'Rape is when a man forces a woman to have sex with him at knifepoint. Quite often, the man cuts the clothes from the woman's body with a knife. I'm going to keep using you as I've been doing. If you tell anybody, I'm going to hurt you.'

I was so angry that I wanted to throw something at him.

He saw that my temperature was rising. 'Do you feel like telling your mother that I raped you?' he asked.

'I always want to tell my mother,' I replied.

I didn't tell him that I'd decided there was no point. I wanted to see what he'd say.

'You better keep your big mouth shut. She'd have a heart attack if you ever told her.'

We didn't speak to each other for the rest of the day, which was a blessing.

When we returned to the house that evening, I went straight to my bedroom and cried. I realised that my father had no intention of stopping.

The words he used had been glued into my mind. I couldn't stop thinking about what he had said to me.

I hated myself.

I finally went to bed to try to sleep through another headache. All I seemed to want to do was sleep my life away.

Over the following months I worked on and off with my two brothers, cutting and storing turf with my father.

It was a horrible summer.

NINE

Crocodile Tears

Shortly before my 14th birthday my mother decided to bring all of us to the shrine at Knock. My father wasn't too keen on the idea, but eventually relented. It was a beautiful day when we arrived in Knock, the sun was out and there was a clear blue sky. There were lots of stalls selling crosses, religious pictures and religious ornaments. My mother bought crosses for all of us.

My father approached one stall and began speaking to an elderly woman. After a couple of moments, I spotted him praying. At the time, I found the episode very confusing and wondered how my father could constantly criticise the church on the one hand and then pray on the other.

The Sunday afternoon after we got back, my father brought Patrick who was just about to turn 15 out in the car for driving lessons. At the time, my father was driving an automatic BMW. My brother was under the impression that he was a professional driver like his father.

'There's no way I'd ever crash; Dad's too good a teacher,' Patrick once told me.

While my father was giving Patrick instructions, my sisters and I were in the back seat. Suddenly Patrick turned the steering wheel a sharp right; the car went into a drain and kept moving.

My father grabbed the steering wheel and tried to control it. However it was too late and the car banged straight into a rock.

My sisters started screaming. I just smiled. I thought

it was funny that my brother had managed to crash the car despite my father being such a 'good teacher'. This would cost my father a packet. I was glad he'd have less money to spend in Galway pubs.

I held my breath and waited for the tirade of abuse to follow.

But my father told Patrick: 'Don't worry, I can fix the car.'

If Paul or I had crashed the car we would have been on death row.

My father got the car out of the drain and then said to him: 'We'll give Barbara a go now to drive. I know she'll be a mad driver like I was.'

I wasn't a bit nervous when I sat behind the wheel of the big car and drove fast down the lane.

'Barbara drives like I did when I was her age,' he told my siblings. He was laughing his head off; he thought it was so funny.

Patrick once told me: 'If Dad was doing 100mph in the car, I wouldn't be afraid to sit in the passenger seat.' My mother was the same. She never feared sitting beside my father in the car when he was driving at speed.

There were nights I lay awake wondering how my father managed to drive home in his car, considering the amount of pints he had taken. Many nights, God forgive me for thinking it, but I wished my mother would get the news that my father had crashed and died. It's a terrible thought but that's how I felt at the time.

When most people were afraid to take their cars out at Christmas because the roads were icy, he kept driving. My father didn't care about road conditions.

A few days later, we received word that my father's cousin in Toureen, near Lettermore, had died. My father asked me to attend the funeral with him. I was surprised he wanted to go at all because he usually wouldn't bother but he was so twisted. He changed from one minute to the next.

I said I'd go because I knew he was nervous facing people on his own and I thought if I did something to help him he might leave me alone for a while. I also knew that he was going to pick a friend of his up in Spiddal and he wouldn't be able to touch me.

We drove to Spiddal first where my father met his Uncle Paddy in one of the local pubs. Paddy told my father: 'I hate funerals, I dread going to the house for the removal.'

'Don't worry, it'll all be over in a few hours,' my father reassured him. We left the pub and headed towards Toureen.

When we arrived at the house, the remains were laid out in the coffin in the front room.

I couldn't take my eyes off him. It gave me the shivers.

I recognised several of my father's family in the room and they all began chatting. As I stared at the dead person, my father leaned down and whispered in my ear: 'That could be you. Remember the lake.'

I was frozen to the spot as he went back to chatting with his uncle.

He walked over to the deceased man's wife and paid his respects. He looked back at me and I followed him out the front door.

That September I started second year and I realised that it was possible to become involved in music classes. I began to learn how to play the keyboard. I had always loved music but classes helped me to develop a real passion for it.

As we could only use the school equipment during school hours, I asked my mother if she would buy me a keyboard to practise on at home for my birthday just gone. There hadn't been time for me to get a present with going to Knock and then all the preparations of getting the five of us ready for the new school year. I was delighted when she said yes. We arranged to go into Galway City that weekend to get one.

I tried not to care when my father insisted on coming with us. On the way in, he beeped the horn at several female drivers. He enjoyed insulting them and giving out about them to my mother, saying 'Women shouldn't be allowed on the roads.'

As soon as we went into the music store, my father spotted an accordion and brought us over to look at it. The assistant approached us.

'How much is this accordion?' my father asked.

He nearly keeled over when he heard the price.

Mam just looked at him and said: 'We're here to buy a keyboard.'

At the time, I knew my mother had little money so I made sure that I chose a relatively inexpensive one. I wanted to get out of the shop before either of them changed their minds. When my father heard the price he said it was too expensive.

I felt my heart starting to pound. I was so angry because I thought he was going to take the keyboard money. I knew that my father hated me getting anything new and was against even the possibility of me progressing in life.

Luckily my mother said it looked like a good one and she'd thought it would cost a bit more. She brought it over, paid for it and handed it to me.

I was so happy to have my own keyboard.

Mam did her shopping in the city centre before we

left. On our way home, my father stopped at a pub in Galway for a few drinks. When Mam complained, he asked: 'Well, why don't you join me?'

I didn't go in because I was only interested in going home and practising on my new keyboard. Mam went in for a short period but got sick sitting in the pub and came back to wait in the car.

We got home eventually and I practised with the keyboard for the rest of the night.

Having my own keyboard made a big difference to the lessons and I was soon getting the hang of how to play it. Eoin, one of the boys from the neighbourhood who went to these classes, was an excellent guitarist. I really enjoyed listening to him as he had such talent. He loved playing Garth Brooks songs and after several weeks, I was able to play a couple of songs as well. I was glad I'd learnt them but what I really loved was putting my own twist to the music and writing a few songs. I always felt best singing my own songs.

Our teacher took a keen interest in our development and constantly encouraged us. I often wished that my father could be more like my music teacher.

One afternoon, after finishing a music class, I met up with my two brothers. As we walked home, I told them about how good Eoin was on the guitar. They were both huge Garth Brooks fans and were excited when they discovered that a boy in school was playing his tunes. As we arrived at our front door, Patrick was singing a Garth Brooks song.

We let ourselves into the house as no one appeared to be at home.

Paul said, 'I'd love to be able to play the guitar and sing Garth Brooks songs.'

As I was dropping my school bag to my bedroom, I called back to him: 'Put the kettle on!'

When I reached my bedroom door and tried to open it, I realised that it was locked.

'Did either of you lock my bedroom door?'

They both shook their heads.

I dropped my bag against the door and returned to the kitchen. My brothers and I continued to discuss Eoin and his talent.

Suddenly, my bedroom door opened and my father emerged.

We turned around and looked at him in surprise. He had been eavesdropping on our conversation. We all thought it was very strange and we felt uneasy.

'Who are ye talking about?'

We told him that we were discussing a young boy from the neighbourhood who played Garth Brooks songs really well on the guitar in school.

My father replied: 'No true musician copies another musician's work. To be deemed a real musician you have to compose your own songs.'

Our father was quite musical himself and only ever played his own tunes. He'd brought us to a funfair in Carraroe village one time and when Patrick and I went to find him he'd been sitting beside a man playing an accordion. My father had asked for a go playing both rows. The man had agreed and my father had begun to play, trying to find a tune he liked. I remember Patrick said to me: 'He'll be happy as soon as he gets the chance to express himself in public.'

People had been surprised that he played so well and the man who owned the accordion had asked my father: 'What's the name of that tune you were playing? Who's the artist?'

I always remember my father had replied, 'I prefer to compose my own tunes. I don't like copying other artists' works.'

It stuck in my memory because it was one of the few times I agreed with him.

My father continued complaining about Eoin: 'No one in that boy's family has ever been able to play any musical instrument. He'll never succeed as there's no history of music in his family.'

Patrick, Paul and I looked at our father and wondered why he had developed such spite for a young boy he barely knew. We thought he was jealous of him but were afraid to say anything.

I wanted to get away from my father. I stood up and went to my bedroom to put my school bag away. As soon I walked into my room, I stopped dead.

My room looked as if it had been burgled.

My earrings were on the floor and my nightclothes were all over the place. My teddies were strewn across the floor. Someone had cut the tail and whiskers off my tiger teddy bear. I was crying as I loved the gorgeous tiger. I knew my father had done it.

Several minutes later, my mother arrived home. My father ignored her and left the house.

She then asked me what had happened. I told her about my room but she didn't say anything.

I spent most of the following day in my bedroom, practising on my keyboard. I had got the sheet music for several songs with it and I was gradually learning how to play some of the tunes.

As I played, I sang.

After a while, my father began shouting at me: 'You'll never make a living out of singing. Just give it up now.'

As ever, there was absolutely no encouragement for anything. When my father continued complaining about the noise I was making, my mother came into my bedroom.

'Wait until your father's gone out before you play again. Maybe you should leave music altogether for the moment. If you still feel the same way about it when you're older then you should take it up again.'

I felt awful when she said that. I was convinced that music was the reason I'd come into the world. It was through music that I could really express myself and I hated my parents for never supporting me. When they bought me the keyboard I thought that had changed, but it hadn't.

To let things calm down, I began to practise on an accordion Patrick had borrowed from our Uncle Peter next door instead. Patrick was doing well on the accordion and I used to learn from him at home. He had sheet music and used to practise tunes. Some of the neighbours used to visit now and again. They thoroughly enjoyed our playing.

When Patrick asked my father to help him with the accordion, my father replied: 'I can't read sheet music, I only play by ear.'

After a while, my younger sister Suzanne also began playing the accordion. Nearly everyone in our house knew how to play it.

I couldn't understand why my father was so against the keyboard when he didn't seem to mind us all playing the accordion. I started playing the keyboard again after Christmas.

In school, I had to join in various new sports that year, which I found hard. At this time, like all teenage girls, I was very conscious of my appearance but for different reasons. The abuse was still affecting my ability to make friends in class. I was slowly becoming an introvert. My natural buzz was gone. I felt that my father's behaviour had taken its toll on me and that I couldn't chat to people as I once used to.

One day, my cousin Colm asked me if I would like to join his soccer team. Initially, I declined. However, he was adamant and eventually convinced me to join.

I was glad I did. Our team was very successful and managed to win various school trophies during the year. This provided me with an opportunity to block out what was happening at home.

Over the following few weeks, my father began going for long walks around the area. It was cold that March and there was a lot of rain but he had become concerned about his weight. He was doing everything possible (other than giving up the drink) to reduce it. Several times he told me to accompany him on these long walks. He would generally bring me to the most remote areas in the locality and rape me. The ground was often soaking wet and I remember how cold I'd get. On every occasion, he threatened to hurt or drown me if I told anybody what he was doing.

The incidents of abuse were not restricted to the outdoors. One afternoon, while I was ironing clothes for my mother, my father returned from the pub and told me to follow him into my bedroom. My two brothers were in the sitting room watching TV, oblivious to what was going on.

I followed my father into my bedroom and he pushed me onto the bed and raped me.

When he was finished, as usual he began telling me simplistic stories trying to comfort me. When he looked at my face and realised my complexion was very pale, he said: 'Go on out for a cycle and come back in an hour when you've perked up.'

When I returned home an hour later, my mother asked me: 'Where've you been?'

I was afraid my father was right and I'd give her a heart attack if I told her the truth. I didn't think she could help me anyway.

'I was playing with the neighbours,' I replied.

At this stage, I was so afraid of my father, after all the years of abuse, that I'd no fight left in me. I remember another night when he was driving me home from the shop, he pulled in to the side of the road.

I got an awful feeling but he was focused on something else.

He parked outside a house and turned the car lights off. My father had spotted a pink bike and said: 'I have to get that bike over there. It's Alison's birthday tomorrow.'

He jumped out of the car and ran towards the bike. He grabbed it and threw it into the boot. He rushed back into the car and started driving away, keeping his eye on both mirrors to make sure that he hadn't been spotted. He was very careful in what he was doing.

As soon as he got out of bed the next morning, he told Alison: 'I've got a lovely present for you.'

She was jumping with excitement.

'What is it? What is it?' she immediately asked.

'Let me put it like this to you, it's something that you have always wanted. I bought it in Galway yesterday. Before I give it to you, though, you have to promise to take care of it. You'll have to wait a little bit longer for it because I have to do some work on it.'

He then called Paul and told him to get a knife and bring it to the shed. I thought they were probably scraping the existing code off the bike and re-painting it.

After an hour, my father emerged and called out: 'Alison! Come here and see your present.'

Alison ran out to the shed and squealed with happiness as soon as she saw her new bike.

She jumped on it and flew down the hill.

When he was still a few months short of his 14th birthday, Paul started working part-time in a pub in Maamcross for the summer. He was also turning turf at the weekends and he gradually began to lose interest in school.

After a while, Paul asked me if I would like to help him with the turf at the weekends. I was delighted as this provided me with the opportunity to get away from the family home.

I enjoyed my time with Paul on the bog as there was no one there telling us what to do all day. After we'd finished, I found it difficult to go home. It was harder than ever to even talk to my father. I understood now that he didn't care that what he was doing was hurting me. He wasn't worried about that.

I thought if I got some money together maybe I could get away from him. Unfortunately we didn't earn that much.

One evening, Paul returned from work and came into the sitting room where we were all watching TV.

'Dad dropped into the pub this evening. He gave a bunch of young girls a lift from one pub to another,' he told us.

Nobody asked Paul any questions but the following morning at breakfast, my mother asked my father: 'So who did you give a lift to last night?'

My father didn't look up.

'No one,' he replied.

'Well, why did Paul tell me you gave a group of young girls a lift?'

'Paul must've been mistaken.'

Later that evening, when Paul returned from work,

my mother brought up the subject again. As she questioned Paul about the matter, my father winked at
him.

Paul looked confused and repeated what he had said
the night before.

Anger crossed my father's face.

My mother wasn't put off. She asked: 'So what
exactly went on? Who were the girls in the car?'

My father had to change his original story: 'I just
gave a lift to a few girls that work with Paul.'

My father gave Paul a threatening look and he
agreed with him.

I knew Paul was too frightened to tell the truth and
Mam let the subject drop.

That weekend my father barged into my bedroom on
the Friday night.

'You're coming to the pub with me. Go in and tell
your mother you want to come to the pub.'

He warned me if I didn't go with him that I would
pay for it the next day. So I did what I was told, asking:
'Mam, can I go to the pub with Dad?'

Every bit of me was hoping she'd say no.

'Yeah, that's grand. Tell him not to be keeping you
out too late though.'

My father's plan had worked. This was gradually to
become a common occurrence.

That night, my father planned to bring me to a pub
in Galway City.

In the car on the way to the pub, he said to me: 'I'll
never do that thing to you again.'

With tears in his eyes, he went on: 'I'm really sorry
about all that stuff. I promise I won't do it again.'

When we got inside, my father was trying to
force alcohol on me. When I refused he gave out to

me. He got me another drink and said it wasn't alcoholic.

I felt merry after drinking a bit of it and he admitted there was some alcohol in it.

On our way home from the pub a few hours later, he pulled up in a lane near Forbaigh. With all his earlier promises forgotten, he raped me in the car.

He'd actually made me believe his crocodile tears and his promises that he would never do this again.

I felt so angry and ugly in myself.

When he'd finished he told me strange stories about when he was a child. He told me that he had an aunt who touched his private parts. I didn't know whether to believe him or not but it still didn't give him the right to abuse me.

I remember one thing in particular he told me: 'There's no point for you to be looking forward to your 18th birthday as you'll still be under my control. You might not even be alive then if you don't keep your mouth shut. I could get rid of you, put you in a place where nobody would ever find you. I could do it without leaving any trace behind.'

My health, and to some degree my sanity, gradually began to give way. My stomach always seemed to be painful and I regularly had severe pains. One evening I lay in bed hoping that it would pass. My parents weren't in the house and I didn't think my brothers and sisters could help me.

The pain didn't go away. I lay there for ages and finally decided I no longer wanted to suffer.

I felt I had no reason to live and every reason not to bother going on. Whenever I showed an interest in anything, I was constantly mocked. There was nothing good in my life.

At the time, the answer was quite obvious.

I grabbed a bottle of pills that were on my dressing table.

I opened the bottle and swallowed the entire contents with the help of a glass of water. As I lay in bed, I began to shiver. Soon the pain eased and I felt numb.

'Finally,' I thought, 'I'm escaping this nightmare.'

However, fate was to intervene. I began to vomit uncontrollably. The entire contents of my stomach spewed forth.

My two brothers, who had been watching TV in the sitting room, heard me getting sick and rushed into my bedroom.

'What's wrong?' Patrick shouted.

I told him that I could have taken too many pills. They were in shock, standing beside me staring at me. Then they panicked, ran out, and returned carrying buckets for me to get sick in.

Patrick was practically crying and obviously concerned. He was only 15 and had no idea how to respond to such a situation.

As I continued to get sick they were arguing about whether or not to go over to Delia's and call an ambulance. They were afraid that our father would go mad if they did it without his permission.

I kept retching. The pills obviously hadn't done the job. I wasn't sure whether I was relieved or not.

At least the throbbing pain in my stomach had eased.

When my parents returned home later that night, my two brothers told them that I had spent the entire night vomiting. They came into my bedroom and were taken aback by my sickly pallor. None of us told them that I'd taken too many pills.

The following day, my mother brought me to the doctor.

The doctor asked me: 'So what happened?'

'I just don't feel well.'

I didn't mention taking the tablets.

The doctor spoke to my parents: 'I'm going to have her admitted to University College Hospital Galway for tests and observation.'

I spent three weeks in Galway Hospital the first time. I was in a ward with two elderly ladies and one young girl like myself.

My father was more concerned than my mother was in case I would open my mouth. He used to come in to visit at night, all dressed up, on his way to the pub. He used to ask me how I felt and would tell me to walk in the corridor with him. If I said no he'd order me out of bed, saying that the nurse was giving him dirty looks.

'I've a bad pain in my side and I can't get up,' I said the second night.

'I need to tell you something important. I can't talk while the other people here are looking at me. Get up and come for a walk with me. You need a break from that bed and I need a smoke.'

I knew he wouldn't go away so I followed him into the corridor.

The nurse looked at my father and said I walked like an old lady and that wasn't on for my age. She told him it was his job to find out why I wasn't happy.

My father just smiled with embarrassment and walked by her quickly.

'What are the nurses and doctors saying about your condition?' he asked.

'They're asking about the pain I have.'

When he reached the smokers' room it was empty. He cursed the nurse and told me that she had a man's face, with her hair cut tight short.

'She's really nice to me and I like her,' I said back.

'Did you say something to her? Is that why she's giving me dirty looks?'

'I didn't say anything. I don't know why she's giving you odd looks.'

'I told your mother I was coming to visit you,' he said, changing the subject.

I asked him: 'When is she coming in to see me?'

He got annoyed with me. 'Why? Am I not good enough for you? She'll come in when she has some shopping to do in the city and not before,' he said.

I felt bad as I'd wanted to see her. I told him I had to go back to bed.

As he was leaving, he spotted the nurse walking up the corridor. He turned and loudly asked me if there was anything I needed from the shop.

I knew very well that this was a manipulation exercise so the nurses would think that he was a normal father. I kept my head down and shook my head to say no.

My father then said that he would come and visit me the following night.

The next day, the doctors came in to do their rounds. They told the elderly lady across from me that all her results were clear and that she was due to go home.

I was next and the doctor asked: 'The stomach tests we conducted all came out clear.'

'I still feel sick,' I told him. 'I've a pain there all the time and I'm still getting headaches.'

'We'll keep you in and try a few more tests.'

I was glad not to have to go home.

After he left, the elderly lady's family walked in. I began to tune into the conversation she was having with her daughters. I couldn't believe it when she said that the doctor told her that she had TB.

One daughter panicked and was really shocked. She asked her sister to call the doctor again.

'We need to talk to him about how the condition can be dealt with,' she said, as her eyes became watery.

I covered my mouth with the blanket and laughed, looking at the elderly lady. I'd heard the doctor telling her that all tests was clear. The family had to wait another 30 minutes before the doctor was free again. In the meantime the daughter, who was also a nurse, was arguing with the ward nurse about whether or not her mother had TB.

It was very funny to listen to and I had to pretend I was looking at the television to explain why I was laughing. I thought it was entertainment when the doctor then walked into the room and told the daughter that all her mother's tests were clear. The daughter repeated that her mother had told her she had TB but he reassured her there was no sign of it.

Her daughter was mortified and obviously didn't know what to say.

'What about the gallstone she was initially referred for?' she asked.

'It may have disappeared as we couldn't see it in the ultrasound test,' he replied. The elderly lady touched her tummy and moaned with pain. 'We'll conduct a few more tests on her,' he said, leaving the room.

'You had no such thing as TB,' the daughter said, glaring at her mother.

'I heard the student doctors saying it,' she argued back.

The daughters sighed with relief and got up to leave. I was trying not to laugh too much because the elderly lady had given me a nod but it was very funny.

I felt safe in hospital with other people in the same ward. It was a relief knowing that I would be able to sleep there at night. I wasn't afraid and tightening up my body, praying that my father wouldn't come near me. I was able to breathe freely knowing there were other people in the room.

I was prescribed various types of medication, including tablets for ulcer symptoms. Sadly, none of the medical experts who examined me realised what was causing my illness.

I was disappointed when I was sent home a few days later but, in a sense, this incident proved to be a very significant moment in my life. My father had obviously realised that neither my body nor mind could tolerate any further abuse.

He made no attempt to come near me when I got back.

About a week later, as I lay in bed trying to relax, I was playing with my favourite teddy Vefin.

I was surprised when Patrick came into my room.

'I read a story,' he told me. 'It was about a girl who couldn't sleep at night without a teddy bear. Playing with a teddy at your age is a sign of insecurity or that something has happened to you.'

I felt confused as I wondered why I really had such a deep affinity with teddies. I began to think about the question, looking at him.

'Do you have the bears for support?' he asked me.

'Yeah, yeah I do,' I told him.

I was very upset when I found out that he repeated everything back to my father. He admitted it a week later when I spotted some of my bears hanging on the trees at the back of our house. One of them was wearing a little nightdress which was soaking wet by the time I got to it.

When I lifted one of the bears off the tree, I noticed a very deep hole in its neck. I knew immediately that it was my father who had damaged my bear. It was a warning.

When I came into the kitchen, I showed my mother the poor teddy and said: 'It's a good thing the teddies aren't alive to feel the pain of my father tearing their tails off and putting holes in their necks or hanging them on the trees.'

She used to get angry whenever I mentioned the teddies to her. She thought I was being childish. There were other times when I was younger he would hide my bears and I would never find them. When I asked him for them back, he would say: 'Not until you take that face off...'

I hoped that my father would leave me and my teddies alone.

A few nights later, as I sat watching TV, my father commented on my complexion.

'Your skin is looking great. That medication the doctor has you on is doing wonders for your looks.'

As ever, I was stunned by my father's insensitivity.

He went into my bedroom and returned with all my packets of medication.

'Which one of these has the doctor most recently prescribed?'

I pointed to the tablets and wondered why my father was so interested.

That evening I told my mother about the conversation I had with my father. She told me to ignore my father's comments and that I was a naturally pretty young girl.

The following morning, my father went to the doctor's surgery and told him that he was suffering from the same symptoms as I was.

'So if you just prescribe the same medication I'm sure I'll get better, just like Barbara did.'

Bizarrely, the doctor believed him and prescribed the same tablets.

When my father returned home and told me what he did, I was speechless. I was glad to see my father's complexion didn't improve over the next few weeks.

More weeks passed and my father still didn't approach me.

I began to hope it might finally be over.

When my mother then convinced my father to sell our house in Kinnvarra I thought I might be able to leave it all behind me. She wanted to move away from his family as she was tired of living next door to them. We were all very surprised when we first spotted the FOR SALE sign outside our house.

When we started back at school, I announced to my friends: 'My parents are selling our house.' They were all interested in where we were going but I didn't know.

Later that afternoon, during a break in classes, I began to vomit.

When my English teacher entered the classroom, she realised I wasn't well and brought me to the bathroom where I continued to get sick. She helped me to the teachers' room.

'Take a seat there beside the window, get some fresh air. I'm going to ring your neighbour's phone and get them to run over to your parents to let them know what's happened,' she told me.

We still didn't have a phone in our house.

As I sat in the teachers' room, my English teacher asked me: 'So is this the first time this has happened?'

'No it isn't, I've been having problems with my tummy,' I replied.

She sat and chatted with me until my parents arrived in the car. They took me to the local doctor who prescribed further medication and talked about sending me back to hospital but my father said I'd be fine.

A few nights later, as I lay in bed, I began to have difficulties with my breathing. I couldn't stop focussing on all that had happened to me and my breathing went out of control. With all the ongoing problems I was having with my health, I was quite frail at the time. I suffered from asthma attacks and I also had menstrual problems.

When my mother heard me coughing in the bedroom, she rushed in. She noticed that I was very pale and called out to my father.

'You'll have to bring her to the hospital in Galway City immediately.'

'Don't worry,' he replied. 'I'll bring her as soon as I've had my shower.'

When he was finished showering, he asked his Uncle Paddy who was visiting at the time to help him carry me out to the car.

While driving to Galway, my father and mother were stopped by the police for speeding.

'Can you tell me why you were speeding?' the policeman asked my father.

My mother pointed to me in the back of the car: 'She's terribly ill. We're taking her to Galway Hospital.'

The police officer looked at me, lying in the back of the car, and realised that my mother was telling the truth.

'Would you like me to call you an ambulance?'

'No, no need at all. We'll be at the hospital in ten minutes,' my father replied.

When we arrived, I was immediately examined by a doctor.

'We'll need to do some blood tests to determine what the problem is,' he told us.

Once the doctor left, my father told my mother that

he was dropping out for a quick pint. He said that he'd return within an hour.

My mother sat at my bedside as we waited for the test results.

When my father returned two hours later, he asked my mother: 'So has the doctor come back with the blood test results?'

When my mother told him that he hadn't, my father stormed down the hallway towards the doctor's office. We heard him barge in and demand to know why the test results were taking so long.

My mother and I could hear my father shouting.

When my father returned to my bedside, he told us: 'The doctor will be here in a few minutes with the results.'

He arrived back to say that the tests were clear and that I could be suffering from panic attacks. He also mentioned that there may have been something else that could have given me a shock that resulted in shallow breathing.

I didn't say anything.

'The pain you're having in your stomach is connected to acid and possibly a bowel problem. You have the tablets to control the ulcer symptoms but you need to increase the amount of fibre going into your system as it's not sufficient,' he continued.

I was discharged from the hospital at 4am, with some medication.

The panic attacks continued. I couldn't seem to stop thinking about all the horrible things that had happened to me.

There were many nights when I wished that the pills had worked.

TEN

The Psychiatrist

My health continued to deteriorate that winter. My father was still leaving me alone but it was as if all the years of abuse were finally catching up with me. I was experiencing tightness in the neck area and tummy pains, along with weakness and shortness of breath. I was admitted to University Hospital Galway. I spent three weeks there and several tests were conducted on me. It was quite a frightening experience for a 15-year-old girl as nobody knew what was wrong with me.

The nurses were surprised when they saw the amount of visitors who came in to see me. My mother's family were very good and my neighbours from Kinnvarra, Camus, also came in. Some of them began to think that I was a diabetic when they saw all the sweets and fizzy drinks in my cupboard.

I remember one day the doctor tried to get me to say what was wrong. I kept looking out the window and wasn't really talking to anybody.

I told him that there was something bothering me and sighed. I wanted to say it was a physical thing that triggered my problems but I couldn't get the words out.

He said the test showed there was nothing wrong with me.

I was annoyed when the doctor told me this; I knew I had an underlying medical problem.

I ached all over.

While I was in hospital, my father visited me in between going to the Galway City pubs. He'd tell me to walk along the hospital corridors with him. He wanted to create the impression that we had a very loving relationship. He got angry when I refused.

My father was trying to spin the same yarn as before so that we could be seen as a happy family. I thought to myself that he had another thing coming.

I was finally allowed to go home after all the tests had come back negative.

Over the next few months I was getting sick all the time. I began to drift away from eating. I was deliberately starving myself because I thought it might make me feel better. When I tried to eat a little food in the mornings, it hurt to swallow it. I couldn't even eat Mam's Christmas dinner. I lost about two stone.

I just couldn't seem to make myself eat.

I never felt hungry.

My mother noticed that my health wasn't improving. She panicked and started giving out to the local doctor.

'This is ridiculous. Something has to be done. She's only drinking tea in the morning with a piece of toast. It's not psychological, there's something medically wrong with her.'

The doctor replied: 'All the results came out clear. I've liaised with several specialists in Galway to find out what's wrong. They all told me she's as clear as a doll inside. However, they did suggest that stress or anxiety may be contributing to Barbara's unexplained medical condition.'

My father ignored that and decided to seek advice from our neighbours instead.

'When you have a toothache you know the problem is in your mouth. It's the same thing with Barbara's tummy, no doubt,' one neighbour said to him.

Patrick told me: 'Sure there's nothing wrong with you, other than stress.'

'I'll prove to you there's something medically wrong with me, something that the doctors haven't seen yet,' I replied.

My mother took me to a specialist in Galway and begged him to do something: 'Please can you do something for her? I'm fed up of running in and out of casualty in Galway Hospital and watching Barbara sitting on a trolley all night.'

'I'll send her back to hospital and carry out a scope test,' the doctor replied.

Days later, I was admitted to hospital again and the same examinations were carried out on me. They finally discovered that there was acid leaking from my tummy but they didn't know where it was coming from. They told my mother that they didn't have the appropriate facilities to carry out the relevant tests on me so I would have to go to Beaumont Hospital in Dublin for further tests.

I was angry as I felt this was all my father's fault. At least he kept away from me.

Two weeks later, I received a letter asking me to attend an examination in Dublin. I immediately asked my mother if she would bring me.

'I can't, I have to look after the students,' she replied. 'Your father will bring you.'

At the time, we had students who were attending Irish College staying in our house.

When the ordained morning arrived, my father and I took the morning train from Galway to Dublin. The whole way to Dublin, he constantly warned me not to say anything to the doctors.

I burst out crying and several other passengers became concerned.

'Is she OK?'

'Do you need anything?'

My father became worried. 'Ah, she's just frightened because she's getting some medical tests done in Dublin,' he told them.

Shortly afterwards, my father headed to the bar area. He returned half an hour later and gave me a bottle of orange and a bar of chocolate. The train was approaching Dublin and his mood had changed. He was trying to comfort me, telling me everything would be fine.

We walked out of Heuston Station and took a taxi to Beaumont Hospital. We found the right department and after a while, the doctor brought me into a room and conducted several tests on me. The worst one was when he placed two thin wires through my nostrils. It was really uncomfortable and felt very strange. He said that I would have to leave them in my nose until the following day. He also placed a 24-hour monitor on my body.

We went back out to my father who was sitting waiting, looking bored. The minute he saw us he jumped up and tried to put his arm around me.

He looked nervously at the doctor and smiled at me.

The doctor thought my father was worried about me and explained: 'Barbara will have to come back in tomorrow to remove the wires and the monitor. We'll have the results of the tests by then. We'll arrange a bed and breakfast for you both, one that's very close to the hospital.'

While the doctor was speaking, my father didn't know where to put his hands. He began to fiddle with them nervously.

When the B&B was being arranged, they asked: 'Would you like to share the same bedroom with your father for the night?'

'I'd prefer to have my own separate room.'

I was glad when two rooms were booked for us.

As we were leaving the hospital, my father's concerned mood changed and he became angry.

'Why did you ask for a separate room?' he shouted at me.

'I just wanted to sleep in a room on my own.'

He glared at me.

That afternoon, we went shopping around Dublin. My father was with me in the beginning but thankfully he soon left the shopping centre and went to the pub. I waited until every shop had shut before joining him.

My father took me into a bar that evening. I still had the wires in my nose and I wasn't in the humour for sitting in a pub. I finally said: 'I'm not feeling well. I want to go back to the B&B.'

He took me back without a fuss, which was a surprise.

The doctor had asked me to fast from midnight but it was no problem as I was in bed before then.

The following morning, as the doctor removed the cables from my nose, my father sat outside the door. The doctor asked me questions about how I had been getting on and then he noticed the test results had arrived.

He called my father in to show him the results. He told him that I had a huge amount of acid emanating from my tummy and that if it had been left any longer then it would have inflamed the walls around the chest. He said that there was 80-85% of acid emanating from the stomach and it needed to be dealt with immediately.

Oh gosh, my father's whole face lit up with excitement when he heard that. He got the opportunity to curse the hospital in Galway in front of the doctor. He called them crazy lunatics and thanked the Dublin doctor for finally finding out what was wrong.

The doctor then said that reflux, in reality, isn't all

that bad and that there must have been something else that led to acid build-up.

There was a silence after that. I was looking at the floor because I knew the doctor and my father were looking at me. I didn't say anything.

My father's demeanour changed. He went a lot quieter and said: 'Is it any wonder because of the length of time she was left?'

'I'm going to remove the cables if you'd like to wait outside,' the doctor then said.

It was a huge relief that my condition was finally diagnosed. I was afraid that everyone had thought I was pretending to be sick.

The doctor continued: 'You look sad, is there something else bothering you?'

'Yes, there is,' I replied.

'Are you sure you don't want to tell me what it is?' he asked me.

I felt comfortable with the elderly doctor. He seemed to be a nice man. I tried to open up.

'There's something hurting me.'

He watched my face as I spoke and replied: 'It must be something very bad if you have such difficulty speaking about it.'

I couldn't really talk as I was sure my father was listening so I pointed in the direction of the door.

The doctor rose quickly and opened it. He spotted my father rushing back to his seat outside the room. I was very frightened when I looked around and saw my father in case he had overheard something. It made me panic. I couldn't say any more.

The doctor looked surprised and said to my father: 'She'll be out in a couple of minutes.' He closed the door and went back to his seat.

The doctor knew that I'd paused when I saw my father and didn't ask me any more questions.

He wrote something on the report and said: 'You'll be meeting some nice doctors in Galway shortly.'

I thanked him for his help and left.

As soon as we arrived back in Galway, my father told my mother about the results. The next day, Delia came in.

'We've had a phone call from Galway Hospital. They're looking for Barbara to attend an appointment tomorrow,' she told us.

The following morning, my parents drove me to the hospital.

Once we arrived, the doctor spoke to my mother: 'If you'd just like to take a seat with your daughter in here. We're just waiting for the specialist to arrive.'

My father had gone across the road for a pint.

When the specialist arrived, he stepped into the room with the nurses by his side. He pulled the curtains and looked at me sitting up on the bed. He turned and asked the nurse: 'Is this the girl who's having trouble at home?'

My mother immediately jumped off the chair and approached the doctor.

'What do you mean by "having trouble at home"?' she asked him.

He looked at her and apologised: 'I'm very sorry. I've mixed her up with another patient.'

I thought the doctor who had examined me in Beaumont had probably forwarded comments to the Galway doctors but I didn't say anything. My mother was looking angry enough already.

The specialist then told her that they had to do something about the level of acid in my stomach.

I was admitted soon afterwards and they operated

on a valve in my tummy that was leaking acid into my chest. I was kept in hospital for three weeks and I couldn't walk for days after the operation. I felt very weak and sore all over.

I still had difficulties eating, which surprised the doctors. They couldn't understand why I wouldn't eat now that the reflux was dealt with.

A dietician visited me and asked me what was wrong.

I hadn't even noticed myself fading away. It seemed to have happened so quickly.

She told me I was anorexic. I just lay in the bed, listlessly, as she talked to me about my eating habits. Before she left, she mentioned trying to organise psychiatric sessions. I knew my father wouldn't agree to that.

My granny, auntie and uncle on my mother's side visited me. They were very supportive and I loved to see them coming in. When I got out of bed to go to the bathroom my granny saw how thin I had become. She had to leave the room because she was in floods of tears.

Several days later she returned and said to my mother: 'I wouldn't be surprised if one of Barbara's ribs has collapsed because of the length of time she hasn't been eating. It can't go on much longer. Is it OK if I bring Barbara to a spiritual healer? He has a special gift with sick people; I really think it could help.'

My mother agreed and my granny told the nurses that she needed to bring me out for a couple of hours.

When we arrived at the cottage where the old man lived, I believed that he had a gift. I could sense it. He confirmed to my mother: 'Part of her rib has collapsed. That's why she's always short of breath and won't eat.'

He placed his hands between my ribs and slowly

worked down to the one that was affected. I felt him doing something that relieved the pain.

My mother offered him some money as we were leaving but he told her: 'Don't insult the gift of healing by offering money. I do accept tobacco though.'

She rushed out and bought him that.

He was very nice to me and I felt much better when I left his home.

We drove back to the hospital and I was very grateful for Granny's intervention.

I felt like I had been in hospital for a long time when I eventually returned home.

I was very thin. I was eating again but it was taking me time to put the weight back on.

My mother asked me if I wanted to sit my Junior Cert examinations. It was mid-March at this stage and I wasn't sure what to do.

'Maybe you'd be better off to defer them until next year as you've missed so much school,' she said.

I decided I didn't want to repeat the year. I went back to school and completed the last two months of third year. It was hard to get used to being back at first but I was feeling a good bit better. I concentrated on catching up on all the schoolwork I'd missed and started studying like mad for the exams.

When the day of the first exam arrived, I was very nervous. That morning I sat at the mirror and told myself that it would be a happy day for me and that I would pass all of them.

I got through them but it was a stressful time. I was still having trouble eating and vomited every now and again.

My parents made an appointment for me to see the local doctor a few days after I finished the exams. He told them: 'Barbara's symptoms are more to do with the mind than the body. I highly recommend that she attends a psychiatrist in Galway City.'

A look of concern crossed my father's face the instant the doctor suggested the possibility of a psychiatrist.

The doctor continued: 'I can go ahead and arrange one. I'll just need both parents' consent.'

I held my breath and waited for my father's response.

There were a lot of arguments at home over the psychiatrist but my father finally agreed. Three weeks later, we received a letter in the post from the doctor with details of my appointment. I was supposed to attend the following week.

'You'll have to take her to Galway for the appointment, I have the students to look after,' my mother told my father.

I was upset as I could just imagine what the car journey would be like.

The day before my appointment, my father pulled me aside in the kitchen. He leaned in towards me: 'You're to tell that psychiatrist about the bullying you're getting in school. Tell him that's what's causing your stress symptoms.'

While my jacket had been ripped in school, this was normal fare and had little impact on me. I hadn't had any real problems in secondary school since the two boys had bullied me in first year.

The following morning, my father and I headed off early. My father spent most of the drive repeating his instructions. He ranted: 'And under no circumstances are you to mention that I've interfered with you, if you know what's good for you.'

When we arrived at the psychiatrist's office, my father sat in the car while I went in.

I felt confused at the time as I wasn't sure what a psychiatrist was for and I didn't have anyone to ask. The psychiatrist was a young woman in her mid-20s. She introduced herself and asked me to take a seat. I was wondering if I could open up to her.

She started by asking me several questions about myself.

'What year in school are you in?

How many brothers and sisters do you have?

Do you make sure to eat breakfast in the morning?

What do you do for fun?

Do you have many friends?'

She was writing down every word I said. I felt I didn't have her attention in the beginning as she was so busy recording everything.

She apologised about that and said: 'I need to make a note of everything as it's your first appointment.'

I felt a bit nervous then. I was lost and didn't know where to start. I wasn't sure if I could feel comfortable with her.

Then she asked me: 'How do you feel about yourself?'

'I hate my image,' I finally replied.

'Why?'

She was looking straight at me.

I was unable to respond; I didn't know what to say.

She next asked me about my clothes and whether the blouse I was wearing was a pyjama top.

I immediately felt that she thought my clothes looked strange. At the time, I was highly sensitive about remarks like that and began to feel embarrassed.

The idea of opening up to her vanished. I felt that she was trying to say there was something wrong with the way I dressed.

'Why do you dress like that? Is it because of the way you feel?'

I began to get confused as I felt that talking about my clothes was moving away from why I was really there.

I didn't reply.

She then told me that she saw that I'd been given medication for a possible ulcer the year before.

'I think that's cleared up now,' I said.

'I'm concerned that you might have some problems due to stress,' she replied. 'The notes from the hospital say that you had trouble eating after your surgery.'

'I just didn't feel hungry,' I replied. I told her about the spiritual healer my granny had taken me to and how much it had helped.

I was trying to sound positive but I was worried. I couldn't stop tormenting myself because of my father hurting me.

I didn't really want to talk after that and she said: 'I'm arranging another appointment for next week.'

I thanked her as I left, still feeling confused.

When I returned to the car, my father appeared very anxious.

'What did you say to her?' he questioned me.

'The conversation is private. The psychiatrist told me not to speak to anybody about it. She's booked me in for another appointment next week,' I replied.

My father's demeanour and approach changed as we drove off. He no longer threatened me. He tried to ask me probing questions about the conversation I'd just had with the psychiatrist.

When he realised that I had no intention of discussing the matter with him, he changed the subject. I was surprised when he agreed to drop me in the following week.

All my family began to ask me questions about the session when I arrived home but I refused to respond.

A few days later my father asked me: 'Is the abuse weighing heavily on your mind?'

'Yes, it's bothering me,' I told him.

He asked me more questions about how I was feeling and I finally said: 'Why are you asking me all this?'

'I went to a doctor in Galway City and told him that I was sexually abusing you,' he replied.

I was shocked.

'I had to go to a doctor that was further away from home so that it would make things easier.'

'What did the doctor say?' I asked.

'He asked me if my daughter was pretty and I said that you were a beautiful teenager, with reddish brown hair. The doctor told me to continue on abusing you if you were a nice girl and I wasn't bothering anyone else,' he claimed.

'What a sick liar,' I thought to myself. I couldn't believe what I was hearing and before he could say anything else, I walked off in disgust.

I had my second appointment with the psychiatrist a few days after that. This time my father accompanied me into the office and said he wanted to sit in on my counselling session.

The psychiatrist seemed to accept him being there.

As soon as we began, my father started to interrupt and answer questions for me. He totally dominated the session and I sat there silently, saying nothing.

'She's being bullied in school, did she tell you that?'

'Well, actually, she told me she was happy in school.'

This angered my father and he started to rant: 'Her expensive leather jacket was slashed with a knife and three separate schoolbags were ripped last year. Two boys in her class are constantly calling her names like "dogface".'

He was growing red with anger. I tried to say that all that happened years ago but he glared at me so I kept quiet.

'I've complained to the school principal on three separate occasions regarding these students' behaviour towards her. Nothing's been done.'

At this stage she was directing questions at him.

'Is everything OK at home? How does she get along with her mother and her siblings?'

My father looked in my direction and replied: 'Everything's fine at home.'

'Is she having any difficulties with her diet? I read the report from Galway Hospital which indicated that she's having some difficulties.'

He looked at me again.

'No, she's not having any such problems. Her eating habits are fine now.'

When we were nearing the end of the session, the psychiatrist asked my father: 'Is Barbara able to come to next week's session?'

'I'm concerned that some of her friends might discover she's coming here and they might think she's not the full shilling.'

'All our sessions are treated with the utmost confidentiality,' the psychiatrist replied.

'I'm just afraid that if her friends found out, they'd mock her even more and life would become unbearable for her.'

I sat and listened as he lied.

Although my father had few other talents, he was, without a doubt, the greatest and most plausible liar I have ever come across in my entire life.

'I feel it would be better for her to end the sessions now. Thank you very much for all your help,' he said.

With that, he led me out the door.

As soon as we returned to the car, my father smiled at me and said: 'That's how you handle smart people.'

We drove back home in silence after that.

My counselling sessions had ended before they had begun.

ELEVEN

Carraroe

My parents found a buyer for our house a couple of weeks later. I was happy to leave Kinnvarra. The place held too many painful memories for me.

We moved to Muicineach, where some friends of my parents offered us the use of a house until we found one to buy. Muicineach is a small village not too far from Kinnvarra.

One of our new neighbours, Mrs Hogan, soon visited my mother on a regular basis.

She had two daughters who were around my age. When my father discovered that I spent a lot of time with her daughters, I overheard him telling Mrs Hogan: 'That Barbara's a liar. You shouldn't believe a word out of her mouth.'

I was so angry hearing him tell this woman I was a liar.

One evening as my mother chatted to Mrs Hogan in the sitting room, my father came in.

'I'm heading out for the evening,' he told my mother.

'Will you bring me out to the Country and Western night that's on in Carraroe?' she asked him.

'Sure I've no interest in that type of music. You'll have to make your own way there if you want to go.'

My mother blushed.

Mrs Hogan stood up and said: 'I'd better go.' She was obviously embarrassed.

My mother, defeated as ever, just accepted my father's behaviour and returned to watching the TV.

My father headed out the door.

I turned to my mother and asked her: 'So are you going to drop down to Carraroe for the music?'

She looked at me blankly.

'No, I'm not in the mood for going out anymore.'

I was disgusted and wondered why she still allowed my father to speak to her like that. I thought to myself, 'If that is what married life is about, to control someone's interests, I don't want to try it.'

The next Sunday, my mother and Patrick went shopping in Carraroe. They drove towards Doilin Beach and she stopped the car. Mam had spotted her father who she hadn't seen for years and had decided to approach him.

They came home two hours later and Patrick immediately told my father what had happened.

My father got a shock.

'Say that again,' he said to Patrick.

'I was sitting in the car while Mam chatted to her father on Doilin Beach,' my brother repeated.

'That's ridiculous. I can't believe you approached that man again after he told us himself, six or seven years ago, that there was no evidence that he was your biological father,' he raged at Mam.

'That's not the case,' my mother replied.

'It is the case,' my father shouted. 'Remember when we went to Hotel Carraroe a couple of years ago and you saw him and called his name. He turned and said that there was no proof that he was your dad.'

'Is that true, Mam?' I asked.

Patrick was standing there looking blankly at them. He might have been wishing he'd kept his mouth shut for once.

'Go on, tell her about that night at Hotel Carraroe, when he told you not to call him father.'

I was stunned and confused. We didn't know what

to think and our parents were still at each other's throats.

Suddenly Mam said: 'I've told my father that I'll meet him for drinks tonight to catch up.'

My father stormed off but Mam looked happy.

Later they were both getting ready to go out and Mam told him that her father was picking her up. This seemed to really annoy him. My father wasn't a bit happy that she was in contact with her dad again.

It was great being home alone with my brothers and sisters that evening. I was able to sing and we had the radio and TV up loud.

The following morning, a row erupted at breakfast. My father was annoyed that my mother had stayed out till the early hours with her dad in the pub.

My mother told him: 'I've no option. You never take me out. I had a great night with my dad.'

My father, bitter as ever, said to her: 'What about the time you met him and he showed no interest in you? Sure there's not even evidence he's your biological father.'

I was totally confused by all this. We hadn't even realised our granddad on Mam's side was her stepfather.

'I'm delighted I've met my father again, nothing you say can change that,' she replied. 'I know he's my dad.'

However, my father continued tormenting my mother until she eventually left the kitchen in tears.

I followed Mam into her bedroom and tried to console her. 'Don't listen to what he says; he's only trying to be spiteful,' I said.

When I returned to the kitchen, I overheard my father saying to Paul: 'She could be having an affair with her own father.'

I knew my father was a sick individual but this was a new departure, even for him.

Moments later, my mother returned to the kitchen. She announced: 'If you say one more bad word about my dad, then I'll spend the rest of the day in the pub with him.'

For the first time in my mother's life, she no longer felt alone. Even though her mother lived in Lettermore and many of her brothers and sisters lived nearby, for some reason Mam wasn't that close to them. I don't think she got on very well with her stepfather growing up. She said that he didn't like her because she wasn't his daughter.

Later that afternoon, when my grandfather arrived at the house, my father kept his mouth shut. He was accustomed to bullying women, not men who were several inches taller than him.

My new grandfather was not remotely afraid of my father.

My father realised that he was going to lose this battle and would never be able to touch my mother again.

As soon as Mam left, my father started insulting him. Of course, he would never insult this man to his face.

Weeks went by and my father began to rant about everything. He moaned about Mam's father and also the new neighbours: 'There's no privacy in this place. That Hogan one is never out of the house.'

'Well, what about moving to Carraroe?' my mother suggested.

They'd started speaking to each other again at this stage but my father was still bitter. He said: 'Ah, I know what your plan is. You just want to move closer to your father. Well, it's not happening. I've no intention of moving closer to him.'

He pressurised my mother into asking her friend in

Ballinahowen to lease one of his houses to us. His plan was that we could all live there until my parents decided where to buy a house.

Weeks later, my father got his wish and we moved to a town called Rosamhil which was near Tully.

A few days after the move, my mother's father visited us at the house. He handed my sisters and me a couple of boxes of chocolates and took a seat in the sitting room. He'd just started chatting with us when my father walked in. This was the first time that I had ever seen these two men sitting down under the same roof. My father said a few words to him about the weather and then walked into the kitchen with Patrick.

I was sure my father was in the kitchen speaking with Patrick, making uncomplimentary comments about my grandfather. This trait seemed to be an idiosyncrasy that ran in my father's family. They enjoyed talking about people behind their backs.

I thought my grandfather seemed very thoughtful and that he couldn't be as bad as my father was painting him to be. My mother and grandfather went off for a drive and he was a regular visitor after that.

I couldn't believe it when I received my Junior Cert results that September. I had passed most of the exams. My friends were surprised when I showed them. They were good results considering I had spent most of the school year in hospital.

When I returned home, I asked my parents: 'Can I go to the youth club tonight to celebrate the Junior Cert results? Everyone from my class is going.'

I'd turned 16 a few weeks before so my father couldn't really say no.

'I'll only let you go if Patrick chaperones you for the night. Be careful of who you speak to,' my father replied.

I agreed to that as I thought it would cause less trouble. Patrick was going anyway and I knew he'd be doing his usual spying act.

When I arrived at the youth club, most of my classmates were already there and it was quite full. I started chatting to my friends and noticed a girl my own age who looked like she was feeling left out. She was from a different school, so I began to chat to her to ease her loneliness and I introduced her to some of my friends. I could see a bit of myself in her. She was gazing into space and standing on her own.

It made me think of my father but he hadn't come near me since all my health problems began.

During the night, a boy approached me: 'Would you like to come up for a dance?'

I didn't know what to do; it was the slow-set.

I hesitantly agreed and I was practically shaking on the floor.

The young boy sensed my anxiety. 'Don't worry, it's only a dance,' he told me.

This relaxed me for a minute but then I panicked in case Patrick saw me.

When the song finished, I rushed off the dance floor. The young boy looked quite surprised by my behaviour but he didn't follow me.

I spent the rest of the night chatting to my friends under my brother's ever-watchful eye. The following morning at breakfast, my father asked me: 'What were you doing dancing with strangers?'

Patrick had reported back.

'It was only one dance,' I replied.

'Well, you'd better be careful in future, especially of

married men who are constantly looking to take advantage of young naive girls.'

I nodded and tried to concentrate on eating my breakfast.

Several weeks later, Paul managed to get me a job in the evenings. We were working in a local factory. The manager collected me and Paul and dropped us in. I was a machine operator and the work was enjoyable. For the first time in my life, I had a bit of real money to spend. Buying my own clothes gave me a sense of freedom.

I dropped out of school around the same time as I wanted to start earning money. I enrolled in a business course with my friend Judy. It was supposed to prepare us for getting work in an office and would run for a few months. In the meantime, I kept working at the factory.

One evening, as the manager was driving us to work, Paul asked him: 'Do you know if they'd have a job for my dad?'

I got a shock as I hadn't realised my father had told him to do this.

'Tell your father to drop in tomorrow evening and I'll see what I can do,' the manager replied.

I really hoped my father didn't get a job. I knew he wanted to check up on us to see what we were doing.

The following evening, our father drove us to the job as he was going for an interview.

It went well and the manager told him: 'You can start immediately.'

He directed him to the back of the building and showed him his work area.

After a couple of weeks, my father began complaining about the money he was earning. He thought he was entitled to the same amount of money

as I was earning. He didn't seem to understand the
bonus system operating in the factory, that anyone who
reached a certain target would receive the bonus. My
father became angry when he discovered that I had
been well paid on two consecutive weeks. He sent Paul
to the boss to complain about his wages.

The boss replied: 'Why didn't your father come and
complain to me himself?'

Paul had nothing to say. He was only doing what he
was told.

When my father finally mustered enough courage to
approach the boss, he told him: 'What I got last week,
£75, wouldn't feed an alien on a wet day.'

'Well, maybe you should leave if you aren't happy
with the pay and conditions,' the boss suggested.

My father took him up on his suggestion and duly
left the factory. He had managed to hold down a job for
three entire weeks, practically a record.

It was a relief that my father was gone.

A few weeks later, Paul and I were invited to attend
a social night with our work colleagues.

Just before we were about to leave that night, my
father said: 'I'm going to come along.'

I was totally disgusted. Now I'd have to spend all
evening trying to stay out of his sight. I decided to try
to ignore him.

I was wearing a long black velvet dress and Paul and
I spent most of the night jiving. We hadn't realised there
was a jiving competition and we were delighted when
we actually ended up winning a prize.

Every time I looked at the bar, I noticed my father
standing in the corner, watching me like a hawk. He
wanted to ensure that no lad was talking to me.

A young man I knew walked up to me at one stage.

'Your father has a nice job,' he said.

'What do you mean?'

'Well, he appears to be watching you all the time.'

I was surprised that somebody had noticed.

'I'll have to leave you alone now as your father's giving me dirty looks.'

At the end of the night my father asked me: 'What did that young fella say to you?'

'He was just asking after Patrick.'

I wished he would just leave me alone. Whenever he could he tried to stop me going out with my friends over Christmas. Luckily he was in the pub himself most nights and I made sure I was back before him.

One weekend in January, however, I returned home late after spending the night in a pub with one of my friends. It was 1am when I knocked on the front door. My father wouldn't give me my own key.

No one answered so I kept knocking. I was just about to give up when eventually the door opened.

My parents immediately attacked me. I know my father encouraged Mam to do this. She was so afraid of him that she would do what he said most of the time. I'd had a few smacks from her before, across the legs and on the face, but nothing like this. They dragged me into their bedroom and kept hitting me over the head with the soles of their shoes. They pulled my hair and nearly suffocated me on their bed.

When Patrick heard the commotion, he came in and was astounded by the sight before his eyes. He roared at my parents: 'Stop hitting her, stop!'

My father kept hitting me and told my mother: 'Slap her across the face.'

She obeyed and slapped me hard across the face, with the slipper, which seemed to be the end of it.

I staggered off to bed with Patrick's help.

The following morning at breakfast, I didn't speak. I

ignored my father when he walked into the room. Mam stayed in her bedroom.

I was thinking about my course. It was due to end a few months later and I was trying to work out how quickly I could get a job and save enough money to move out. I was dying to get away from them. If I couldn't get a job in Galway, I was thinking about running away to Dublin.

My father started lecturing me.

'You shouldn't be palling around with that girl. She has a dysfunctional family history. You shouldn't be associating with her.'

I didn't respond to him.

When he wasn't getting a reaction from me, he turned to my brother.

'Sure that one's probably only using Barbara to attract men.'

I was angry when I heard this. Whenever he saw my friend he spoke nicely to her.

Patrick joined in and said that his friends thought she was cheap and that she wore leather pants.

I looked at my brother and couldn't believe how old-fashioned he was. I knew that for some people in the area, if you wore leather pants or a low-cut top it was enough to brand you as cheap forever. I didn't think he was like that.

Even if they really thought my friend was using me, it didn't give my parents the right to hit me. I felt that my father was just grabbing that excuse to pretend to my brothers that he cared about me. He wanted an excuse to explain the beating himself and Mam had given me.

I'd no choice but to stay for the time being. I knew my father had put Mam up to hitting me so we just carried on as before.

Weeks later, my father gave out to me for going around in a car with some friends. I heard him telling my mother: 'She's not obeying the house rules. We'll have to become stricter with her.'

He went out drinking that afternoon and came home intoxicated at 10pm.

It was unusual for my father to come home that early from the pub. I presumed there was a thunderstorm on the way.

Patrick sat in the kitchen, chatting to him.

I walked into the kitchen to put the kettle on and my father began to talk about some man from Carraroe who apparently fancied me.

He said to me as he opened his cigarettes: 'I was drinking with the young man's uncle so I assume he could be a nice man but that doesn't give you the right or the permission to go near him. Patrick will keep a close eye on you in the pubs. He'll tell you who to associate with. Stay away from that girl.'

I tried not to listen to him.

That night, I heard him tell my mother: 'The best thing we could do is move away. The owners of this house are constantly calling in, so we have absolutely no privacy. I'm sorry we ever sold the house in Kinnvarra, you know. We didn't have any visitors there. I could do what I wanted without any interference.'

That was true enough as he hadn't come near me in the new house.

Eventually, my parents decided to leave Rosamhil and lease a house in Carraroe. My mother had persuaded my father that Carraroe would be closer to shops and the local amenities. Although my father had misgivings about the move, my mother was happy to be moving nearer her father's house.

As soon as we moved, my father began talking to me about my behaviour. He'd say things like:

'Don't be spending too much time with the young people in the area. And don't get involved with any of the young men from the village. That young lad's father is an alcoholic. Don't have anything to do with him as they have a family background of cheating and they don't know what the word honesty means.'

At this stage, I had developed a sense of selective hearing when it came to my father's comments. I zoned him out when he started talking like this.

He realised that I wasn't listening and became angry. He called my mother into the room: 'Would you speak some sense to the girl? She shouldn't be associating with any young lads in the locality.'

She repeated my father's comments.

I looked at her and let on that I was listening for a bit of peace.

After a couple of weeks, my mother managed to redecorate our new home. My father made changes with the fireplace and soon our new home seemed cosier than anywhere we had ever lived. My father still used to complain and talk about moving because of the lack of privacy but we stayed put.

We all started to relax and feel settled for the first time in years. It wasn't long, however, before my father sourced a problem – the electric meter. The meter required constant feeding (cash only) but my father was unaccustomed to paying for this service. It didn't take him long to decide enough was enough.

He devised a scheme where he punctured a hole in a coin, ran a string through it and simply used the same coin all the time for topping up the electricity.

Weeks later, when the landlord visited, he opened

the meter and was surprised at the scarcity of coins there.

My father had been out of the house when the landlord had called but when he returned that evening, my mother told him about it.

'I was mortified when he opened the meter and only a few coins fell out,' she said.

My father laughed, delighted with himself, and said: 'At least he knows that he won't be getting much money from us anyways, so he'll have to make a profit elsewhere.'

The following day, my sister Alison and I went for a walk into town after dinner. As we approached a shop, my father's car stopped in front of us.

'Where are ye going?' my father yelled out of the car.

'We're going for a walk,' we replied.

My father then sped off in the car.

As we continued walking, Alison turned towards me.

'Why has Dad been asking me such peculiar questions?' she asked.

'What do you mean? What kind of questions?' I asked her.

'Well, he's started asking me questions about the conversations I have with you. I told him that we talked about nothing in particular, perhaps music more than anything else.'

At the time, I would have loved to explain to Alison what had happened to me. It would have been such a relief to tell someone. It would also have explained exactly why my father was asking such questions. I looked at her and wondered if I should warn her to watch my father. I didn't really want to because I thought it would scare her. I knew he'd noticed that I always kept an eye on my sisters and I hoped that would be enough. He would also always sneak around when I was chatting to them in the house to see what I was saying.

In the end, I just kept on walking. I didn't want to start putting ideas into Alison's head as she was too young. A part of me also knew that Alison would ask my family what I meant.

Shortly afterwards, a letter arrived in the house for Patrick. My mother picked it up and said: 'I think it's from a university.'

My father took it from her and threw it into the fire.

'Patrick doesn't need to go to any university,' he said.

My mother stood there, flabbergasted.

'But Patrick was waiting for that letter,' she told him.

I was disgusted with him for destroying Patrick's letter. He had no business to even open it, let alone burn it.

Patrick never made it to college. They thought he had no interest when he didn't show up for the interview and never responded to the letter.

I finished my course and started looking for work. I quickly ran into a big problem. Many of the people I spoke to asked me if I was related to my father's family. When I answered yes, they refused to employ me. I'd no choice but to keep looking and hope to find somebody who'd never heard of them.

I was looking everywhere for work as I no longer had the factory job. Paul had managed to get a job in a pub in Maamcross and lived there during the week. I thought he was so lucky. I wanted a job like that. I dreamt about getting out of the house for good. My mother was working part-time with her friend Maggy, minding students in her house. I think that was her way of dealing with my father – getting out of the house as often as possible.

Over the next few months, I kept going to interviews but I wasn't getting anywhere. To get a bit of money, I worked turning turf whenever I got the opportunity. I tried to save some money but it was difficult as I didn't earn much. I thought about going to Dublin but I didn't know anybody there.

When I turned 18 I thought it might be easier but I still couldn't seem to get a steady job. I was giving up hope when I finally managed to get full-time work in a restaurant in Spiddal. I was earning a decent wage but had to pay half the rent at home. I'd thought about moving out but I wanted to get money together to go to the States and I could save more living at home. I wanted to get out of the area altogether.

I was looking forward to getting away from my father.

TWELVE

Mind Games

At the beginning of June 1997, my father arrived outside my workplace and offered me a lift home one evening when I finished work. Although I would have preferred to share a minibus home with some of my work colleagues, I decided I better accompany him in the car. He hadn't touched me in a long time at this stage but I was still wary of crossing him. He had a violent temper.

As soon as I got into the car, I could smell the alcohol wafting from his direction.

'I was around the Spiddal area so I waited to collect you,' he told me, as he drove off. 'I had to have a couple of pints in Spiddal to unwind after a hard day working on the bog.'

He drove down Rosamhil Road and took the opposite turn from home. He was driving me towards the beach.

'Why aren't you driving straight home? Mam probably has the dinner on,' I said to him.

'I want to talk to you about my interfering with you,' he said, as he stopped the car on the beach.

I panicked when he reminded me of the sexual abuse. I'd really tried to block it out over the last three years. I'd done my best to forget about it.

'What do you want to know about it?' I asked him.

'I need to know if you remember every time I abused you. I mean, it only happened a few times, can you remember those times?'

I knew what he wanted to hear.

'I don't remember any abuse,' I told him.

He kept pestering me in the car.

'Well, I bet you, after all my efforts not to do this to you for the past couple of years, that it's still on your mind,' he said.

'I don't remember. I don't want to talk about it.'

'Promise me you won't tell anybody,' he said.

'Why are you bringing this up again? I thought we'd put all this behind us,' I said.

'It doesn't make any difference to you. Either way, you go around looking moody and depressed. What's the point in stopping when you're showing all the signs that something has been done to you?'

He insisted that I take off my clothes.

'Take off your clothes and put the seat back.'

When I kept refusing, he eventually relented and gave up.

We arrived home just after 6pm.

'We got held up talking to that Gallagher one from Kinnvarra,' he told my mother.

When he looked in my direction for agreement, I nodded.

The following morning, I went to work as usual.

People noticed that I wasn't my usual talkative self and that I seemed to be a bit distant. I didn't know what to tell them. I couldn't believe my father was bringing all this up again. I'd thought it was all over.

When I finished work, one of my workmates told me that my father was outside again. I felt shivers running down my spine. I was frightened but knew that if I didn't go in the car with him there would be trouble.

When I sat in the car, I again smelled alcohol from my father's breath.

'I was on my way out from Galway City after taking driving lessons in a truck,' he claimed.

I knew this was merely an excuse for his presence.

When he took a turn away from home, I asked him where we were going.

'I just want one drink. We'll head home after that.'

He parked outside a bar in Spiddal.

'I didn't want to park near the main road in case Patrick spotted the car on his way out of Galway on the bus,' he told me.

Patrick was studying to be a male nurse at this stage. Mam used to drop him to the bus stop every morning to go to his course in Galway City.

'I'm hungry, I just want to go home,' I said.

'Well, can't you come into the pub with me?' he asked.

'No, I'll sit here and listen to music,' I replied.

'Well, go off and get some food from the chipper while I'm in there,' he told me.

I was tempted to leave but I didn't have the confidence to do it. I felt so low, thinking about what might happen if I wasn't there when he came out. It made me feel sick and I was angry at myself. I was 18 years of age. I was an adult. I knew I should have been able to leave but I was too afraid.

In the car, I ate my chips and listened to my favourite tapes but I couldn't concentrate. I was getting really tense waiting for him. In the end I went into the pub to see if I could get him to leave.

'Just be patient and wait until I've finished my drink,' he replied and bought me a glass of mineral water.

After drinking his pint he told me that he was going to drive to Forbagh, a small town near Spiddal.

I refused to go with him. 'I want to go home,' I said.

He ignored me and brought me to another pub in Spiddal.

I was very tired and couldn't stop yawning.

After we left the second pub, he drove past my workplace. He then drove the car down a quiet lane and turned off the engine.

I became extremely frightened and my stomach was in knots.

I had a very bad feeling.

He pushed his seat back and pretended that he was tired.

My father kept reaching over and trying to touch me on the legs.

'I know I haven't been a good father to you but I don't want to see your body wasted on another man,' he said.

He started complaining about Mam. I think he was still feeling bitter that my mother was so happy going off to meet her father most nights.

He repeated what he had said the night before. He told me that he'd only abused me on a few occasions and that he would leave me alone in future. Then he pulled the car out.

'I'll have my last pint in Inverin,' he said.

I spent half an hour in the car waiting for him. Eventually, I went into the bar to find him. He insisted on getting another mineral water for me.

After I'd finished it, he started demanding I order an alcoholic drink from the barman. He was going on and on and in the end I just had to take a glass. I was so ashamed of his behaviour.

We left the pub before midnight and my father drove down towards the same beach that we'd gone to the previous evening.

'Undress, take off your clothes,' he kept telling me.

I told him to leave me alone.

'I will leave you alone so,' he replied and I was relieved when he drove back onto the main road.

After a few minutes' driving, however, he took a right turn down a laneway that was facing a lake. He stopped the car and turned on the lights. I realised that he looked more evil than usual. I knew he was going to try and harm me. He'd been building up to it all night.

'Are you going to keep refusing me?' he snarled.

'Just stop and bring me home. Please, just take me home,' I pleaded.

'You know, you've always talked about committing suicide. You should get out of the car and drown yourself in that lake,' he said to me.

This really upset me. I didn't want to die while he was hanging around pressurising me. I was so scared that I didn't know what planet I was on. I felt dizzy from shock.

'I wouldn't do it without saying goodbye to Mam,' I replied, 'and I wouldn't drown myself in such an isolated area.'

He immediately locked the doors.

I knew I was in the middle of nowhere, with nowhere to run and no one to hear me.

'Take off your clothes,' he demanded.

When I refused, he became very aggressive. He put his two hands around my neck and began choking me.

I couldn't breathe and started gagging.

I'd almost passed out when he took his hands off my neck and raped me.

When he was finished, I thought that was the end of it.

I felt totally numb. It was terrible. After all those years of nothing happening I was back to feeling like a little girl again. My soul had left my body. I couldn't cope with it. I hadn't stopped him.

He then put his hands around my neck again and started choking me.

When I looked at him, it appeared as if he was possessed.

I felt my neck tightening and I couldn't breathe. I was crying my eyes out and my face was boiling with heat.

He kept a tight grip on my neck. I began to feel a bit removed from what was happening. I could feel myself shutting down.

As my father continued to choke me, I looked at the sky and promised myself if I survived that night I would press charges.

Suddenly, out of nowhere, a light appeared outside and someone began knocking on the car door.

My father panicked and moved quickly back over to the driver's seat. He unlocked the car to open the door to see what the man wanted. As soon as he did, I immediately opened the passenger door and vomited.

A young man stood at the door.

'Do you have a cigarette lighter?' he asked.

My neck felt sore and tight.

My father searched for the ignition with his car keys.

'No, we don't have a lighter,' my father replied.

The young man stood there looking directly into my father's face.

My father's hands were shaking as he pulled the car out.

'Shut the passenger door,' he shouted across to me.

I kept looking behind, wondering where the man had come from.

As we drove towards home, I was absolutely terrified.

Although my father had threatened me in the past, this was the first occasion that he had actually tried to kill me.

I was so relieved when we pulled up to our house; I couldn't believe I'd reached home safe and alive.

My father sat in the car for a couple of minutes before he allowed me to go into the house. He told me that he would be happy if I could pretend that nothing had happened.

'Don't show any signs in the house that something has happened. Go in and tell your mam that we were delayed in the pub. Tell her we had a wonderful night there,' he ordered.

I nodded and he finally let me out of the car. As soon as I got into the house, I went upstairs to my bedroom. He could deal with Mam's questions.

Shortly afterwards, I heard him coming into the house. After a few minutes, he went into his bedroom.

I went downstairs and stepped into a cold shower.

I noticed I had been bleeding so I scrubbed my body with Dettol.

When I awoke the following morning, I heard my mother and brother talking downstairs. I didn't want to talk to anyone and waited until they'd left.

I crept downstairs, hoping that my father wouldn't hear me.

When I entered the kitchen, I didn't eat any breakfast. I felt cold and tired due to lack of sleep. I just wanted to get into the bathroom. Unfortunately, my father heard me and called me into his bedroom.

'Don't say anything at your work. I promise I'll never touch you again, I promise,' he told me.

I didn't listen to him. In my head, I was thinking of who I should contact. I was determined to report what had happened the previous night.

When he had finished threatening me, I left for work. When I arrived, one of my friends said that I looked very pale. I mumbled that I was fine.

At 10am I had a 15-minute break. I rushed down to the coin box across the road from my workplace, rang the operator and asked for the Galway Rape Crisis Centre number.

She accidentally put me through to the Cork Centre.

'I've been raped by my father and I'm afraid to go home,' I told the counsellor on the other end of the phone.

'I'm actually from the Cork Centre, you should ring the Galway Centre. Will you do that?' the counsellor asked me.

'Yeah, I will,' I replied and returned to work.

As I put my uniform on, a colleague grabbed me.

'Is there anything bothering you, Barbara?' she asked, looking concerned.

'No, no, there's nothing,' I told her.

'There is, I know there is. You're usually joking and laughing with everyone in here but over the past two days you've been very distant. Has your father got something to do with it? Has he hurt you in some way?' she questioned me.

Suddenly, I couldn't keep it in any longer.

'He has hurt me,' I said and burst into tears.

I ran into the toilet and got physically sick.

She followed me and said: 'Do you mind if I ask Karen what to do?'

I shook my head. She called her over and I told her everything that had happened. She was a great comfort.

When our supervisor spotted us, she couldn't understand why there were two girls around me in the cloakroom.

Before we returned to work, they said: 'Don't worry, Barbara, we're going to help you now.'

I felt a sense of relief that I had finally told somebody but I was also afraid. I thought I could get killed for opening my mouth. I knew my father would be more than capable of killing me.

I couldn't stop worrying about what my father might do to me. I got so wound up I could barely breathe. I started to feel dizzy and just before lunch, I collapsed.

When I came to, all my work colleagues were gathered around me in a circle. They told me they'd called the doctor.

She arrived soon afterwards and took me into a private room.

'You should contact your GP urgently as he has all your medical records. Have you eaten recently?' she asked.

'I didn't have any breakfast this morning,' I replied. 'I'm getting severe chest pains too.'

As soon as I came out of the room, the manager asked me how I was.

'The doctor suggested I go and see my own GP,' I told him.

'I'll take you myself,' he said.

'It's in Carna though,' I told him. Carna was nearly 50 miles away.

'Don't worry, sure I travel from Tipperary to work every day, I'm well used to it,' he said.

As soon as we arrived at the clinic in Carna, a young doctor came out and called me into his office. My own doctor was on holidays. The manager said he'd wait for me.

I told the doctor that I had collapsed in work and that I had severe chest pains. He noticed I was very anxious and took my blood pressure and temperature. I could barely keep still, I was so tense. I was half hoping he might notice the bruising around my neck but I was wearing a polo-neck so he didn't see it.

He didn't find anything but told me: 'Come back tomorrow if the symptoms persist.'

When I came out, the manager asked: 'How did you get on?'

'If I still have the same pain in the morning, the doctor told me to come back,' I replied.

We set off for my house but when we were only a few miles away from the clinic, the manager spotted a car speeding towards us.

He looked a bit surprised as he said: 'I think that's your father driving towards us. How did he find out we were at the surgery? He was terribly quick if he's come from Spiddal.'

I was stunned in the passenger seat.

'I've no idea how he found out,' I replied.

My father pulled up in the middle of the road.

'I'll just have a word with him and let him know you're OK,' my manager said, getting out of the car.

My father thanked him for bringing me to the doctor, as he helped me out of the car.

He was treating me very tenderly, acting very concerned.

'How did you get here so quickly?' the manager asked.

'I went to collect Barbara and the ladies told me she'd fainted and you'd taken her here. Thanks very much for all your help. I'll take her home now.'

I felt uncomfortable but I didn't want to create a situation that would put my boss in an embarrassing position.

'Thank you for all your help,' I said.

He smiled and said: 'It was no hassle. I hope you have a speedy recovery.'

My father drove me home in the car and tried to manipulate me into saying nothing had happened the night before. He repeated the old stories again saying that he would never hurt me and that he was awful sorry.

I looked over and saw the same crocodile tears streaming from my father's eyes.

I felt sickened.

I looked out the passenger window and thought to myself that I would no longer buy into this bullshit. I had my mind made up that this would be the end of his psychological torture games, as well as the sexual abuse.

He realised that I wasn't listening to him but he didn't get annoyed which surprised me. He kept chatting, trying to encourage me to talk. I could barely hear him. My eyes were on the trees and the mountains. I kept my mind focused on my plan. I'd decided to go back to the doctor in the morning and tell him everything.

When we arrived home, my father wouldn't let me out of the car. I could see my brothers standing looking at us. I finally managed to pull away but my father then tried to drag me across the road. He was behaving like a lunatic.

I sighed and told him I wanted to get into the house because I was tired.

He let me go then because Patrick and Paul were staring at us.

When I walked in my mother told me she had made dinner. I told her that I wasn't hungry and went straight to the bathroom. The water was freezing but I had a cold shower and scrubbed myself with disinfectant again.

I went straight to bed afterwards and pretended to be asleep when Mam came to check on me. My father must have told her what had happened.

When I woke up the following morning, I still had the chest pains. It made it easier to keep my resolution to go back to the GP.

'Mam, I still have the chest pains. Look at the colour of my lips,' I said.

My mother was shocked when she saw the purple colour of my lips. She drove me down to the village to a public phone where I rang the doctor in Carna.

'My symptoms seem to be getting worse,' I told him.

'Come straight to me here. If needs be, I'll come and get you in Carraroe and bring you to Carna,' he offered.

'No, that's OK, my mam can drive me,' I told him.

I hung up the phone and told my mother what had been said.

'Well, we'd better go home and get some clothes for you in case the doctor sends you to hospital,' my mother said.

'No, let's not bother going home,' I replied. I was afraid that my father would convince her not to travel to Carna. Also, I was hoping that I would be on my own with my mother. I thought I'd be able to tell her what had happened to me on the way over in the car. In the end, though, she insisted we go home to collect my clothes.

As soon as we walked in the door, my father immediately pounced on her.

'Well? What did the doctor say?'

'He said we should bring her to him straightaway,' my mother told him.

'Well, I'd be happy to drive all the way to Carna,' my father said.

I turned to my mother and asked: 'Mam, will you come with me?'

My father gave me a dirty look. He wasn't too pleased.

'Ah, not at all,' he said to my mother. 'The journey will only tire you out.'

Eventually, after a bit more argument, the three of us headed off in the car. My father kept trying his best to make me smile. He was cracking jokes the whole way over.

I felt uncomfortable going all the way to Carna in the car with him. He kept staring at me in the mirror. I tried to block him out.

Forty minutes later, we arrived at the clinic. I asked my parents to stay in the car and went in alone.

As the doctor called me into his office, I took a deep breath – I knew what I had to do.

THIRTEEN

Opening a Can of Worms

Connemara, Co Galway, June 1997

'Sit up on the couch there while I examine your stomach,' the doctor said.

While he was checking me, I said: 'The chest pains from yesterday got worse last night. Do you think I hurt myself when I collapsed? I'm still finding it hard to breathe.'

He didn't answer but seemed absorbed in continuing the examination.

I was trying to pick the right time to interrupt when he stopped and turned to me.

'Forgive me for saying this but you have the symptoms of somebody who has suffered some form of abuse,' he said.

I looked at him in shock. I couldn't believe what I'd just heard. For the first time since the abuse began, all those years before, a sense of relief engulfed me. It felt like a very heavy load had been lifted off my chest.

I broke down in tears as I started to release years of tension.

Someone had finally realised what was going on.

'I've been waiting for somebody to say that my whole life,' I said. 'I could never come out with the words.'

I will never forget how I felt when he said it. The feeling of relief was almost indescribable. I had keyed myself up to tell him but it was so much better that he had diagnosed it without me saying anything.

Finally, after waiting ten years and going into hospital on numerous occasions, I thought a doctor had realised what was wrong with me. I later found out that my work colleagues reported what I had told them to Social Services, and they'd tipped him off.

I sighed deeply with relief but I was also conscious of feeling tense. A sense of anxiety was creeping up my spine. I was nervous after telling him. I began to bite my nails as he explained that the next step would be informing the Social Services and the police.

I knew this would open up a can of worms for my family.

He was shocked when I began to tell him how my father had raped and tried to strangle me two nights before.

I took off my polo-neck jumper and he looked at my neck.

'It still looks slightly red and I can see marks on it,' he said.

He stood up, went over to the window and pulled up the blinds.

'Are both your parents in the car?' he asked me, as he peered out the window.

'Yes, both my parents brought me,' I replied. 'My father insisted on coming.'

The doctor finished examining me and then said: 'You need to go to hospital. Do you want us to organise someone to take you or are you prepared to let your parents drive you over?'

I thought about Mam. I didn't want her to know what had happened yet.

'I'll get them to drive me,' I replied. 'It'll be easier.'

Before I left, the doctor rang Galway Hospital and told them that I was to be admitted that evening.

My parents drove me over to the hospital. I just told

them that I needed to go in for observation. My father was giving me worried looks but he couldn't say anything with Mam there. I was careful to make sure I wasn't left alone with him.

When I was settled in the hospital and my parents had gone home, two agents from the Social Services arrived to interview me. One of them asked for my date of birth and other details. Then they began to ask me about the abuse. I told them as much as I could remember. Now that I'd finally told somebody about it, I couldn't seem to stop talking.

'We'll have to inform your mother of what happened to you,' one of them told me.

I agreed and gave them details of how to get in touch with her. It was then that one of them reminded me that she had dealt with my mother years ago.

'Your father beat your mother on more than one occasion and I suggested to her that she should move to Galway City. I tried to get her to leave him but she wouldn't do it.'

I felt horrible hearing that. It reminded me of how happy I'd felt when I was 11 and thought we were getting away from the monster. When it sank in that my mother had been offered a house, I got extremely angry. Especially when the officer said that I could have been saved if my mother had moved. If only Mam had had the courage to leave him then.

Before they left, they explained that they would tell my mother on Friday what had happened to me. I was worried about how my mother would react when she heard the news. My father had told me on more than one occasion that she would take it badly and probably end up having a heart attack. I asked them to be careful about telling her.

For the next two days, I was extremely anxious. I

kept wondering how things were going to pan out and
worrying that something would happen to my mother.
One of my friends from work came to visit me. She was
very kind but she couldn't tell me what was going on at
my house. She touched my hand and asked me where
the bruises came from and I explained that they'd
attached a drip and were moving it around my hand.
I'd also had an ultrasound to check for damage.

I found out later that on Friday morning, my mother
received a letter at home asking her to attend an
appointment in Carraroe Health Centre at 2pm. She
immediately told my father.

He obviously realised something had happened and
that the cat was probably out of the bag. He
immediately made an excuse to my mother to get out of
the house.

'I'm just heading out to collect Suzanne,' he told her.

'It's too early to collect her,' my mother replied.

'Well, I need to get some cigarettes on the way,' he
said and left the house.

Shortly afterwards, as I was being pushed in a
wheelchair towards the X-ray room, to have X-rays
taken of my chest and abdomen, a nurse approached
the porter.

'There's a phone call for Barbara, bring her to the
nurses' office,' she told him.

The porter wheeled me back and the call was
transferred to the corridor phone.

I'd a feeling of dread as I picked up the receiver and
put it to my ear. I thought something bad had happened
to Mam.

I barely had time to say hello before my father
started shouting at me.

'The Social Services contacted your mother. They
want to see her this afternoon in the local Health

Centre. Have you opened your big mouth?' he roared down the phone.

'Yes, I have,' I whispered.

I could barely speak because I was scared of what he would do.

He started making threats immediately.

'You'd better keep your mouth shut. If anything happens to me, I'll make sure you suffer. And you know I can make that happen,' he warned.

I wanted to be strong but it was all too much. I started crying. I recognised the demonic side of my father coming out again. At the same time, I felt extremely angry towards him and a part of me knew that this was his way of trying to keep me from freeing myself.

He mentioned some of the nastier things he had done over the years, specifically referring to one incident where he claimed to have blown up a police sergeant's house.

'If I hear you've been opening your mouth, I'll kill you. I'll kill you with my own hands,' he hissed down the phone at me.

I dropped it.

The porter saw how distressed I was and asked: 'Is everything OK?'

A few of the nurses approached to see what was happening.

'My father was on the phone, threatening me,' I told them.

I didn't understand why they'd gotten me to take the call. When I was leaving the clinic, my GP had told me that all the nurses on the ward would be made aware of my situation before I arrived at the hospital. This was why I didn't have to go through casualty but went straight to the ward.

The nurses told me not to worry and that they hadn't realised it was my father. They promised to make sure he didn't get through to me again.

'Don't worry about it, he can't hurt you now,' they reassured me.

As the porter wheeled me back down to the X-ray department, I tried to put the phone call behind me. I couldn't stop thinking about them telling my mother and what she would say. I hoped she'd believe me.

I phoned the Social Services officer later that afternoon and asked what had happened.

'Well, she was upset but she took the news as well as could be expected,' she told me. 'She's on your side.'

I didn't know if she'd come to see me that day. I waited nervously in my bedroom, hoping she'd arrive.

An hour or so later, I received a phone call from my sister. She explained that Mam had gone to work, minding the summer students for her aunt as per normal. She'd told my sisters that our father had done something horrible to me and that they shouldn't miss him wherever he'd gone.

'Before she went to that appointment I heard him telling Mam that you were a liar and not to listen to a word you said. What's going on, Barbara?'

I couldn't take it all in. I asked my sister to repeat where my mother had gone. I couldn't believe she was in work. And it sounded like my father had run off but nobody had told me.

I didn't tell her anything and ended the phone call.

I felt so depressed. I couldn't stop thinking that if my mother was truly affected, or touched, by what had happened to me she would never have gone to work that afternoon.

In the meantime, my father had disappeared. Paul

told me later that while Mam was with the social worker, my father had returned to the house. He stuffed some of his clothes and belongings into a bag. Before driving off in the car, he shook Paul's hand.

'I never did anything on you,' he told Paul.

Once my father had gone, Paul got on his bike and left the house. He knew something had happened. He was on his way down the road when he saw my mother approaching him in the car. 'What's going on?' he asked her.

'I hope your father has left the house. He's done something terrible,' she told him.

As all this was unfolding, I was waiting anxiously in my hospital room.

After my sister's phone call, I decided to get up and walk as far as the hospital church downstairs. I said a couple of prayers and returned to my room. There was no point trying to contact my mother as she didn't have a phone at the time. They used public phones to call from Carraroe.

Shortly afterwards, at about 7pm, the nurse rushed to my room to say that there was a phone call for me from my mother and that I could take it in their office.

I got out of bed and followed her. I grabbed the phone and I heard my mother's voice.

She told me that she'd found out what had happened. As Galway Hospital was a good few miles away from our home, she said she wouldn't be able to visit that evening but would come the following day.

'Don't worry about your father. He's left the house and I'd say he's taken the boat to England to stay with his brothers over there,' she said.

As she told me this, I wondered how he'd managed to leave for England in such a short space of time.

'Since he's left the country, I really don't think there's

much point in pressing charges. You'll never have to see him again,' my mother continued.

She reassured me that my father was gone for good and that we would have a fresh start.

I didn't know what to think as I said goodbye and hung up the phone.

Later that evening, as I walked down the hospital corridor, I suddenly saw my father. He was standing at a radiator in the hall, beside the nurses' office. He was unshaven and was wearing a long blue raincoat.

I was shocked to see him standing there.

I started shivering. All I could do was stand there and stare at him. I didn't say anything as he approached me and began to speak.

'If you've made any statements to the police, I'll kill you,' he snarled at me.

I was terrified and there didn't seem to be anybody around to call for help.

He told me that he wasn't leaving the country; he wasn't going anywhere.

I had got the courage to start moving away from him when I realised that Patrick and my cousin Michael were approaching. I greeted them with relief.

My cousin immediately sensed there was tension between my father and myself.

'Mam phoned me. She said you'd moved out, Dad, and it's something to do with Barbara. What's going on?' Patrick asked.

Patrick had been at his nursing course all day and had no idea what had taken place in the family home.

'Get in touch with Mam, she'll tell you what's going on. Don't listen to him,' I told him, gesturing to our father.

'But, what's th—' Patrick started.

'I really don't want to upset you, just ask Mam,' I told him.

He could see I wasn't going to say anything else so he dropped it. My father wouldn't go away and I didn't want to have to tell Patrick what had happened while he was there. I didn't want to create difficulties with Michael either.

As we walked back to my room I did manage to get Patrick alone for a minute. I told him that my father had done something serious to me. It was a very awkward situation but I wanted to at least say that much.

When we'd all chatted for a while, my father offered them a lift home. I was unhappy to see Patrick leaving with him but I couldn't do anything else. I was afraid he wouldn't believe me.

Before my father left, he seized his moment when Patrick had gone into the corridor and whispered to me: 'Think long and hard about what I've said.'

I knew my father would have little difficulty manipulating Patrick. I felt so upset and didn't know what to do after they'd left. I told the nurses that my father had been there but I wasn't sure about telling the police. I'd already spoken to a female police officer who had come into the hospital to see me. She'd told me there was nothing she could do about my father until I signed a statement. I'd always been told to avoid having any dealings with police officers and I didn't want to sign a statement.

The following day, my mother and Patrick, Paul, Suzanne and Alison all visited me in the hospital. My mother leaned over the bed and gave me a hug.

'I'm so sorry to hear what happened to you,' she said. She sensed that I was on edge and had learned from the Social Services that I was worried about returning home. I'd asked the women who interviewed me if they could find me alternative accommodation as

I didn't think staying with my family was a good idea. They'd advised me to give my family a chance as staying on my own could prove to be very hard.

'Don't worry, everything will go back to normal,' my mother said. 'Your father's gone off to England. He told Patrick he was leaving last night. You need to start thinking about coming back home.'

My family stood in front of me and promised that they would support me, no matter what. They said that they would stick by me and help me pull through it so that I could leave it all behind me.

My sisters hugged me as well and said they knew our father was a bad person.

They all left after a couple of hours and I felt much better.

Later that afternoon, however, I received an angry telephone call from Patrick. 'The story has spread around the whole of Carraroe,' he told me. 'The girl you confided in was upset and told some of your work friends why you fainted. Michael heard her and came back to me with the story. We can't have people thinking that about the family,' Patrick told me.

I was absolutely livid. He didn't seem to care about how I felt. He just seemed to want to ensure that the family name was protected.

It was obvious that his main priority was what people would say. I was totally disgusted with him and slammed the phone down.

As I lay helpless in a hospital bed, Patrick was not really behind me – so much for all his promises of support a few hours earlier. He was more concerned about public opinion or the shame involved than the hurt I had suffered.

I felt disgusted and realised that my instinct was right. I'd never wanted to discuss it in detail with Patrick because I'd always sensed he wouldn't understand. I was so angry with him when I went back to bed but I also felt so low that I thought about killing myself.

Later that day, I received another telephone call from my father. He pretended to be my cousin Michael and I was caught by surprise when he started threatening me. It made me feel really unsafe. Telling the nurses about him hadn't helped. His threats were making me feel terrible again and I was seriously tempted to make a statement, as the police officer had suggested.

I was very confused about what to do. I'd gone into hospital meaning to prosecute him but I'd ended up going along with my family's advice – to leave it all behind me and not to press charges. I'd believed my mother when she said my father had gone to England but it obviously wasn't true.

I hung up on him and went back to bed. I felt so trapped.

That evening, between 9pm and 10pm, I walked from my room towards the toilet with a drip hanging out of my arm.

Suddenly, my father appeared out of nowhere. He'd obviously been waiting for a moment to get me on my own. He grabbed me at the entrance to the toilet and pushed me violently inside.

He began to unbuckle his trouser belt, shouting: 'I'm going to rape you again. I might as well now the story is out.'

I started screaming hysterically. My screams appeared to unnerve him. He was probably worried somebody would come along to find out what was wrong.

He pulled his trousers up, fastened his belt and ran.

Despite my screams, nobody came to my assistance. As I walked out of the toilet, I spotted my father rushing down the corridor towards an exit door. I was surprised to see a man who had apparently suffered from high blood pressure for years move so quickly.

I approached the nurses' office but it was empty. I made it back to my room and immediately pressed the nurses' bell. I was frightened and felt unsafe. I was so disorientated I began searching under my bed and in the wardrobe to ensure my father wasn't hiding there. It was terrible to feel so anxious.

After what seemed like an age, a nurse appeared.

'Why did no one come to help me? Did no one hear me screaming? My father tried to rape me in the toilet,' I told her.

She apologised and a student nurse came in to sit with me afterwards, which made me feel better.

Later that evening, my mother phoned and I told her what had happened.

'I can't believe he tried to do this again,' she replied angrily.

'I don't feel safe in the hospital,' I told her, little realising I was about to feel a lot worse.

A few days later, Patrick rang me to tell me that my father had signed himself into a psychiatric ward in the same hospital.

I was shocked. I had to get him to repeat it before I could take it in.

'I'm downstairs calling from the ward. I feel sorry for him. The psychiatrist is giving him shit instead of helping him,' he said. 'The psychiatrist has no right to treat my father that way. You should go downstairs to see him. I'm worried because he's coughing up blood and the Samaritans approached him because he's so down.'

'How did the Samaritans know anything about him?' I asked.

'Oh, he said that they spotted him sitting by the sea while he was feeling suicidal,' he replied.

I was disgusted. I wasn't a bit surprised when Patrick then told me that he had moved into our uncle's apartment in Galway to be close by.

'I don't want to go anywhere near my father,' I said and hung up.

I felt so threatened after this phone call. I was at my wits end, knowing this man was intent on doing me harm and he was staying in the same building as me.

I immediately spoke to all the nursing staff and told them how nervous I was about the situation. They tried to reassure me and said they'd make sure my father didn't come near me but I felt terrible. I believed he'd had himself admitted in case I pressed charges. I thought he was going to pretend that he was mentally unstable.

My mother visited me that afternoon and told me that she had gone to see my father in the psychiatric ward.

'Why are you going near my father after hearing what he did to me?' I asked her. She explained that Patrick had given out to the staff in the psychiatric ward for not helping my father with his illness and asked her to sign him out. He'd been told that she was the only one who could do it, so he'd made her go down to the ward to talk to the staff.

Patrick later told me that the psychiatrist pleaded with Mam to leave our father there as it would teach him a lesson over what he had done. So she didn't sign him out.

I wished she had so he'd leave the country.

The next day, my father appeared on my ward dressed in pyjamas and accompanied by Patrick.

I felt nervous as I watched them approach and started looking for the bell.

I was disgusted with them. I realised that I couldn't trust them one bit. My father was well able to pretend that he was depressed in front of my brother. He knew how to manipulate Patrick and isolate him from the rest of the family.

'Don't ring the nurse's bell,' Patrick told me, as I pressed it down hard.

Before my father left, he threatened me again.

'You'd better go along with what I tell you to do and say, if you know what's good for you,' he hissed at me.

Later that week, my mother went to see him again.

It was the day she had come to bring me home. I asked: 'Why would you do that?'

'Patrick put a lot of pressure on me to do it. He said the doctors weren't being very sympathetic towards your father and that I needed to sign him out.'

I was very upset and shocked when she confirmed that she had done it. As I was going home I'd felt better knowing that my father would still be stuck in the hospital. I'd been told to ensure that I avoid stress so that my tummy problems would not come back. I thought my first instincts were right and I should have asked the social workers to get me away from the whole lot of them. After telling my family about the abuse, I knew nothing would ever be the same.

On the way home, Mam explained about the phone call she'd had from Patrick.

'I sympathise with him,' Patrick had told my mother. 'My father's told me he's considered suicide. Things are very hard on him. His high blood pressure is acting up and he's started coughing up blood.'

I was glad Patrick had moved out.

Two days later, my father and Patrick arrived outside our house. My father stopped the car at the front door.

Patrick got out and came inside. He started chatting to my mother.

'I miss living here, Mam. I miss your homemade bread,' he said to her. 'Is it OK if Dad comes in?'

'If that man approaches the hall door, I'll call the police,' I said.

'OK, OK, I won't let him in,' he replied.

After chatting to Mam for about half an hour, Patrick left. I said to my mother that I didn't want my father to be entering the property at all.

She reassured me that he wouldn't come in and that things would be different.

While I was trying to recover, I wasn't able to return to work. I missed it a lot as the people there were great fun. I really missed the stories they used to tell and the craic we had.

With my mother and I at home together all day, every day, tensions began to rise. We weren't getting on. I was really glad when she arranged for me to go with a group to Lourdes soon afterwards. I was looking forward to getting away.

We flew from Shannon Airport and arrived in France on a warm summer morning. A coach dropped us to our hotel and I walked to the grotto later that afternoon. The area was crowded with people. I found it hard to relax as the other people were a distraction and it was impossible to get near the statue. I decided the right time to go would be at night when I'd feel a deeper connection so I went back to my hotel and had a nap.

When I returned later that evening, there were far fewer people there. I felt it was a very spiritual place where a person could reflect. As I sat on a wall, I stared at the sparkling candles and for the first time in ages, I felt at peace with myself.

When I returned to my hotel room, I discovered that

an elderly lady was sharing it with me. At first, I felt uncomfortable. However, we began chatting and she told me that she was from Loughrea, a town 40 miles from where I lived in Galway.

'I come to Lourdes as often as I can,' she told me. 'I find the experience very uplifting.'

As I got into bed, I spotted her placing a navy nun's uniform on the chair beside her bed.

'I wonder what type of conversations I'll have with a nun,' I thought to myself. I decided that I would agree with anything she had to say on religious matters!

The following morning as we chatted over breakfast, I began to develop a sincere affection for my roommate. She was a very interesting human being and excellent company. We went to Mass together and then we walked to the grotto.

'It's very hard, living without my husband,' she told me as we walked.

I was shocked. 'I thought nuns weren't allowed to marry. I saw your nun's uniform last night,' I said.

She smiled. 'I only wear the uniform whenever I visit Lourdes,' she replied. 'When I was young I wanted to explore life so I left the nuns.'

'I'm not very fond of walking around the grotto during the day,' I explained as we reached it. 'I prefer it at night. I love sitting here looking up at the stars and watching the candles sparkle.'

We went our separate ways after that and I spent the day walking around, looking at souvenirs with some ladies from Kinnvarra.

The next day, I decided to go on a day trip to Paris which I enjoyed. I liked the French people, who were very friendly. When I returned to Lourdes, I spent the evening in the hotel. There was a singing competition that evening which was great fun. I sang with a group of people and then worked up the courage to sing a song on my own. There was a priest from Oughterard there who was very entertaining. Not only was he a talented singer but he was an excellent raconteur. He kept the entire company amused with his interesting stories. I felt really happy and had a great night.

I packed up before I was due to leave because we'd an early start. When I finished, I decided to visit the grotto for the last time. As I walked towards the lift, I fainted in the hallway. I woke up to find one of the hotel porters checking through my suitcase. The hotel staff thought I was a diabetic and were checking my luggage to see if I had any medication that would help me.

'You have to go to the hospital,' one of the staff told me, as soon as they realised I was awake.

'No, it's grand, I really don't want to go,' I told them.

'I'm afraid it's hotel policy,' they replied.

I'd no choice. I was kept on a drip in casualty overnight. I was unsettled being back in hospital and wanted to leave. It reminded me of how unsafe I'd felt in Galway Hospital.

The doctor ensured that I was all right for getting a flight before he discharged me. I was so relieved to be heading home. When I boarded the plane, the air hostess approached me and asked: 'Is there anything I can do for you? I've been told that you're not well. If you feel unwell at all during the flight, call me immediately, won't you?'

I got a bus from Shannon up to the church in Galway where my mother and sisters were waiting for me. My mother greeted some of our neighbours and heard that I'd fainted. I said not to worry but I was glad when we got home.

As I lifted the souvenirs I had bought in Lourdes out of my case, my mother and sisters began to laugh. They especially liked the little donkey who spat fire from his rear end.

'Did you bring back any religious souvenirs?' Suzanne asked me, when I had emptied my case.

'No, actually, I haven't,' I replied.

I felt keyed up after getting back from Lourdes. That night as I lay awake in bed, I heard the sound of a car engine coming up the driveway. I jumped out of bed quickly and looked out the window. The driver was going very slowly, with the car headlights full on. I immediately knew it was my father.

I left the light off in the bedroom and crept out of the room.

'Go back to bed, Barbara, it'll be OK,' Mam shouted upstairs. She was awake as she'd heard the car coming before I had.

I looked out at the car. Strangely, it wasn't the same car that my father owned. It was a Peugeot.

I went back to my bedroom and grabbed the little red pocket knife that I had bought in Lourdes. I was thinking back to the comment my father had made three weeks before, when he tried to choke me to death.

'I have to kill the evidence in case you ever come forward,' he had said.

I sat on top of the stairs in silence, waiting for a knock on the door. I looked through the window at the side of the stairway to see if I could spot him.

He had parked the car beside an old shed and was sitting alone in the dark. From time to time he would start the car and drive around the house to try and scare us.

I stood there and kept staring out at the car. Instinctively, I knew he was sitting there, wondering what to do next.

My mother was looking out from the bedroom

window. She was afraid, wondering what my father was going to do, especially as Paul wasn't home that night. He was staying at Maamcross.

I remained standing there, on top of the stairway looking out the window, until the car pulled off.

I was beginning to wonder if I'd done the right thing.

FOURTEEN

Betrayal

The following morning, my mother and I were discussing my father's strange behaviour the previous night, when Paul arrived home.

We told him what had happened the night before.

'I'm sorry I can't be around as much as I'd like because of work. I won't have any contact with Dad over what's happened. He tried to contact me at work a couple of times but I made myself unavailable when he showed up,' Paul said.

Despite what he said, I was still suspicious that he was in contact with our father. My friends had told me that my father and Patrick would show up in Maamcross and collect Paul. Since I'd come back from hospital I'd noticed Paul's mood changing. Whenever I saw him, he was always in a hurry and seemed hyped up. He didn't seem to want to talk to me.

A day or so after this, my father dropped Patrick off to visit my mother. I was resting in bed and my brothers and sisters had all come in to have a chat. I was trying to get rid of them when Paul started giving out to me. He started ranting and cursing like my father. His face was going red. When he raised his hand to hit me, I was shocked.

He was annoyed because I wasn't responding to his foul language and he slapped me on the nose.

'What was that for?' I yelled at him.

'The story about the abuse shouldn't have gone public. You shouldn't have told anyone at work about it. Now the family will be shamed forever,' he raged. 'You should have kept quiet.'

At the time, I was unable to retaliate. It was only a few weeks since I'd been in hospital and my arms were still bruised after the drip. The Lourdes trip had tired me out a good bit and I was feeling weak. I touched my nose and looked at my fingers; there was blood dripping off them.

I was sure my father had put him up to it. They sounded like my father's words. I was upset when I realised that Paul, like Patrick, was no longer on my side.

'It's true what happened to Barbara,' Suzanne told my brothers.

'Listen, Patrick, the stories our father's telling you about being suicidal, coughing up blood or chest pains are the same stories he used to tell me after raping me,' I said. 'He's trying to manipulate you and turn the whole family against me.'

I noticed that Patrick was looking in the opposite direction as I attempted to explain what my father was doing. He didn't want to listen to my side of the story at all. Instead, my brothers made what they presumed were funny comments about me being raped by my father. They sat on the bed and laughed.

I thought that they were as bad as him and wished I had the strength to throw them out. I was really glad Patrick was no longer living with us. He hadn't proved to me in any way that he was a man. My big brother never stood up to our father and confronted him about what he had done to me.

They both left after that and I wasn't sorry to see them go.

Paul had stood by us for a while but I'd known it was only a matter of time before he fell under my father's spell. My father could be very convincing.

I avoided Paul for the next few days and kept reminding myself that I couldn't rely on him for anything. My mother and I weren't getting on again either and I felt really low.

I was making myself breakfast in the kitchen a few days later when I got into an argument with my mother. Paul walked into the middle of it and that just made it worse. I didn't want to talk about my business while he was around. He'd heard myself and my mother screaming at each other and asked what was wrong.

What did he think was wrong? I couldn't talk to him and just stormed out of the house, crying. His instinct kicked in when he saw me heading back towards the sea and he ran after me.

As well as being physically abused by my father, I had been emotionally traumatised. Physically, my father had violated me but he had also managed to leave me with many mental scars. Arguing with my mother seemed to bring it all to a head and I just couldn't cope. Suicide seemed the only viable solution to my dilemma.

I went down the road to the sea. I ran up to the rock and was approaching the oncoming tide when my brother walked up behind me and grabbed my arm.

He looked really concerned.

'Things aren't as bad as they seem. Your situation will improve,' he reassured me.

He was shocked to see that I was so serious about throwing myself into the sea. I could hardly see him I was crying so much.

'Come on back to the house. Please, come on back. Don't do anything drastic. I promise, while I'm around they won't argue with you. I promise,' he told me.

'Move away,' I screamed. 'There's no need for you to try and save me. You just care about yourself and the family name. You promised you'd be on my side and suddenly when I came out of hospital, all your sympathy is for your father. You've pushed me away and don't care if I recover. All you've told me to do is brush everything under the carpet and move on. You've no consideration for how hard it is to heal from what happened.'

He began to cry and that shocked me so much, I calmed down.

I was stunned when he started crying.

He stuck his arm out and asked me to give him my hand. He noticed I was shaking and so he grabbed my arm and helped me climb back up the rocks.

As we walked back, he said he knew that I was up to my eyes with the family and that I'd lost my self-control because I was so angry. I explained that I wanted to get rid of the scars by drowning myself. I was trying to get him to understand but I didn't feel like I was getting through to him.

As soon as we returned to our house, Paul started to remonstrate with my mother. 'Barbara needs your full support,' he told her.

It felt good to hear him sticking up for me but I was afraid my father would wrap him around his little finger again. I resolved to try to reconcile myself to my brothers' betrayal. It was hard to get over it, but I knew I needed to move on. Otherwise I knew there would be more heartache on the way. Somehow, I managed to resist the constant feeling that my life had no value. I needed to concentrate on getting better. It wasn't easy when neighbours were staring at me and wondering if I was telling the truth. May God forgive those who thought I was lying.

I tried to dress nicely and appear to be happy in front of others. I was living a lie, however. I believe that most people can look well if that's what they wish but it is merely an external image and doesn't portray the inner being. I used to change my image all the time. I suppose that was a way of trying to get comfortable with my inner self. At the time, I had little reason to be happy with my appearance. My father had spent years convincing me that I was an ugly human being, of little value. As my sisters grew older, he'd gotten them to join in on occasion, which hadn't helped. I also heard all sorts of hurtful comments about my situation.

'I heard she's making these allegations against her father because he wouldn't let her go to the local disco with her friends,' one lady from the neighbourhood said.

'It's because her father was having an affair and she's angry with him,' another man said.

'Maybe she dressed to seduce him,' I overheard one of my mother's relatives saying.

'Only stupid people are raped,' Alison told me. I was hurt and disgusted by my sister's comment. I knew that I had saved both her and Suzanne's childhoods.

Every time I went to Galway in the car I was reminded of the locations where I was abused, including the lake in Tully. I hated seeing that place. All the painful memories would flood back into my mind. I knew that I had to stop thinking about all of them and that it was time for me to heal but I couldn't see it happening in Galway.

I didn't know what to do next.

One night a few days later, I awoke to hear loud banging on our front door. My mother got out of bed and put on her dressing gown. I got out of bed and listened at the side of the stairs.

She answered the door and I could see Patrick and my father coming into the house. They were both drunk and began interrogating my mother. I could only hear half the words but they seemed to be telling her that she should tell me to keep my business to myself as everyone in the village was convinced that the abuse had taken place. They said that she should be able to get me to change my story to stop people talking. My father shouted at her to tell people that I had lied.

She was sitting on the couch and I heard her fixing the turf in the fire a few times with the tongs. I hated them for coming into the house. They only stayed for a few minutes so I resisted the temptation to go downstairs.

A few nights after that, my father returned with Patrick. This time I opened the door.

'If you want to visit us, Patrick, don't bring your father with you,' I told him. 'If he enters the premises again, I'll contact the police and press charges.'

Patrick came into the house and spoke to my mother.

'Mam, Dad wants to speak to you, he wants to straighten things out,' he told her.

He persuaded her to speak to my father.

While my mother was outside speaking with my father, Patrick told me about his plan.

'I'm going to get Mam and Dad back together,' he said.

'If that happens, I'll move out. I will never live under the same roof as that man,' I told him.

'Dad said that he'd take care of Mam, Suzanne and Alison,' Patrick explained.

I became very angry.

'Under no circumstances would I allow him to live under the same roof as Suzanne and Alison. They wouldn't be safe,' I told him.

My mother returned to the house while we were still arguing about it.

'I'm going out for dinner this evening in Clifden

with your father,' she said to me. 'He's trying to get things back to normal between us.'

I was furious.

'You're breaking a promise you made to me,' I shouted at her.

I was also very annoyed with Patrick. He wanted our neighbours to see my father accepted back into the family. He still wanted to create the impression that everything was fine and that the allegations of abuse were untrue.

Even though I was angry with Mam, I couldn't relax later that night until I heard her return home safe and sound.

I didn't realise at the time that my father was with her.

I was disgusted when I saw him coming out of my mother's room the following morning. He had obviously slept with my mother the previous night. He made some comment about my bag, trying to make conversation.

I didn't say a word to him.

She was washing clothes in the bathroom and was tearful when I approached her.

'He suggested that I'm having an affair with my own father,' she said.

I was shocked but hoped that maybe now she'd see sense. I'd thought my mother would never sleep with my father again. As far as I was concerned, she was finished with him. I didn't understand how she could want to be with a man like that again.

It was a relief when he left soon afterwards.

Later that day as I lay in bed resting, I heard someone banging on the front door. I thought Mam was in her room sleeping so I looked out the window. I wanted to find out who was there before I opened the door. It was Patrick and I could see my father sitting in the car. He kept on knocking so I dressed, went downstairs and opened the door halfway.

'Is Mam in?' he asked.

'I don't know. I'm only out of bed. I think she's sleeping,' I replied.

'Well, go on and check her bedroom,' he instructed me.

I checked her room but couldn't find her there.

'She's not there,' I told Patrick.

'Not to worry, I have a good idea of where she is,' he replied and turned to walk away.

'Don't ever come back to this house with our father,' I shouted to him as he left.

I watched my father and brother drive off.

I was getting sick of my father's harassment. He just wouldn't leave us alone. I wasn't convinced that my mother had come to her senses either. I couldn't get the vision of my father sitting in the kitchen out of my mind.

That weekend, I dropped into our local hotel. In the bar, I overheard people discussing details of my story. It was now common knowledge in the locality that my father had sexually abused me. Sadly, the story was being embellished all the time.

'I heard you gave birth while you were in hospital and you were beaten black and blue,' one man told me.

'People are adding to the story. I didn't have a child. Some work colleagues came in to see me in hospital, saw bruises on my arm and presumed I'd been beaten up. When really I had bruises on my arms because of the drip,' I told him.

I hoped this would help settle some of the rumours going around about me.

* * * *

I barely noticed that three months had gone by with everything that was going on. I woke up one morning to let my uncle, my mother's brother, into the house. He immediately began shifting all our furniture out of the house.

'What's going on?' I asked Mam.

'We're going to live with my father,' she replied.

I was distraught. I had little trust in men and no trust in elderly men. I begged my mother not to bring us to her father's house.

'This is the first time in years that I have a sense of peace. Please, Mam, don't make us move,' I pleaded.

However, my mother was not to be swayed.

I knew I had to get away from all of them. I'd been too ashamed to return to work but this was the kick I needed. I had to get some money together. I was also determined to find out about the support on offer from social welfare for someone in my circumstances.

By the afternoon, all our furniture and belongings were in my grandfather's house.

I didn't know him very well. He had intermittently shown my mother signs of paternal love but I'd only talked to him on a handful of occasions. I was also worried that there would be trouble because Paul was still staying in the house most weekends and he didn't get on very well with our grandfather.

A week later, I arrived home from Galway City to discover that Paul had moved all his stuff out. He wouldn't be coming back. There had been an argument between himself and my grandfather.

I had a few words with Paul a few days later when he rang looking for Mam:

'Our aunt, Anne Naughton, got an apartment for me. She's financially supporting me until I can support myself,' he told me.

I asked my brother to have as little contact with his father as possible.

He wouldn't promise anything.

We'd only been in his house two weeks when one night I heard a car pulling up outside my grandfather's house. He got out of bed and went down to investigate. Before he opened the front door, the car sped away but a white bag had been left beside it. We later discovered that the white powder it contained was for poisoning animals. It was an obvious warning.

This incident made my mind up for me. I was convinced that my father had left the bag outside my grandfather's door.

I'd had enough of all the harassment. My mother and I sat down one day and finally discussed whether or not I should bring charges. I was still very confused. In many ways I had no desire to prosecute my father, even though he had ruined the best years of my life. I knew what an ordeal it would be and dreaded the court case it would lead to. On the other hand, when I went to hospital I had been determined to prosecute him and had sworn to get justice after he tried to strangle me. It had been easier to agree with Mam and the rest of the family, to just try and leave it all behind me when I left hospital. But my father's harassment was making that impossible. In the end, I didn't think I had a choice. It was time for me to press charges against him.

The next step was contacting the police in Salthill, Co Galway.

I felt strange making that phone call. I knew it was going to change everything.

The police were very helpful and arranged a time for me to make a statement. I was really nervous when the day arrived. When they'd got me settled, they asked a lot of personal questions. I found the experience very embarrassing and told the policewoman that I didn't know where to start. So she decided to make things easier for me and told me to go away and write down all that I could remember about the past. We organised a new time for me to come back with the notes.

I sat in my bedroom on my own for hours, writing the details about how I was sexually abused. I had to list the locations where my father had raped me and to some degree describe the type of abuse that had taken place. It was extremely difficult trying to remember everything as I had blanked out a lot that happened to me.

It was a very painful exercise because I started to get flashbacks. I had to relive many negative experiences that I wanted to forget. I knew it had to happen if I wanted to get justice, so I persevered.

I wrote about 30 pages altogether and handed them back to the police.

Shortly afterwards, I was interviewed by the same policewoman for hours in Salthill police station. Once everything was in order, I signed my signature to all the statements.

My father was brought in for questioning to the local police station a few days later. Initially, he refused to answer any questions that the police asked.

In the end, he began to communicate but only to deny everything and call me a liar.

He tried to confuse the police and mentioned names of people who had long since passed on. The police gradually became exasperated with his behaviour. They released him after several hours of questioning.

A policewoman visited me a week later.

'Your father was very unhelpful. He wasted the time of the police officers who questioned him. Do you still want to pursue the charges against him?' she asked.

'Yes, I do,' I replied.

A file was sent to the Director of Public Prosecutions in relation to my allegations.

My father and Patrick were nowhere to be found and I began to suspect that my father had left the country but I was wrong.

Two weeks later we received a phone call from Patrick one evening. He told my mother that he had fallen down a flight of stairs in Corbett's Court, while working as a security officer. He hadn't gone to England at all.

We were shocked to hear that he was lying in a bed in Merlin Park Hospital.

None of us asked him about our father but Patrick brought up the subject himself.

'I don't have any contact with my father, I've no idea where he is,' he told my mother.

I was not convinced.

My mother said she'd drive over to see him immediately. She gathered my two sisters and drove to Merlin Park Hospital. She told me later that five minutes after they got there, my father arrived in with Paul. Apparently my younger brother was now living with my father somewhere in Galway.

My parents spoke for several minutes and then my mother left with my sisters in tow. He tried to follow her out of the hospital but she was no longer interested in hearing his lies.

When my mother returned home, she rang the police station in Salthill and informed the officer on duty that my father had been in the hospital.

'I'm disgusted with Patrick,' she told me. 'My own son couldn't look me straight in the eye when I arrived.'

'You should never have gone in there,' I said. 'I got cold feet when I heard the tone of his voice on the phone.'

I was surprised at my mother and sisters. I thought they would have realised that it was a set-up.

'I was only a few minutes standing at his bed, looking at his hand up on a sling, with plaster on it, when your father rushed in,' she said.

My sisters joined in and said that it looked like it was planned between Patrick and my father.

'When I heard your father's voice at the door I grabbed your two sisters and rushed to the lift with them to go home,' Mam said.

None of them believed that my father had ill health or that he was coughing up blood as Patrick claimed.

'I knew all along that he didn't have any of these fairy-tale illnesses,' I said.

'He'd run down the stairs with Paul and beaten the lift so he'd be waiting for us.'

Alison said: 'Paul was standing right beside him and Mam shouted that he had taken her two sons away and hypnotised them. Then our father said that he never asked Paul to follow him and that he was free to go back to her. Mam dragged us off to the car before Paul had a chance to do anything.'

I was stunned listening to what my sisters had experienced.

Patrick phoned from the hospital that night and spoke to my mother. I stood beside the phone and listened when I realised it was him.

'I swear to God, I had no idea Dad would be visiting at the same time,' he told her. 'I'll be getting out of hospital in a couple of days.'

Mam didn't reply so my brother asked to speak to me.

'Listen, Barbara, I'm very sorry I haven't been more supportive of you,' he said.

I thought I could hear voices in the background so I

listened harder. I could make out my father's voice
giving my brother orders. He was telling Patrick to
persuade me to visit him in the hospital alone.

When I said I couldn't come to the hospital, I heard
my father telling my brother to ask if I'd look after him
while he was recovering. Patrick said I could get a bus
to the station in Galway and that he'd meet me.

I was really upset and hung up the phone.

Mam rang the police and told them my father was at
the hospital again.

From that day on, I have found it very difficult to
trust anybody.

FIFTEEN

Moving On

My father was brought in for questioning a second time that winter. When he went to Merlin Park Hospital to bring my brother some clothes the police were waiting for him.

Later that evening, Patrick telephoned my mother.

'Why did you inform on Dad?' he asked. 'It's just wrong for the police to bring him in for questioning.'

Patrick was annoyed as he had been waiting for his father to bring his clothes into the hospital for him.

'Because it was the right thing to do,' she replied.

My father again denied everything and was released later that evening. He later made a written complaint about the female police officer investigating the case.

The tension began to mount as we all realised that it could take years for this to end.

As we waited for an answer from the DPP, life had to move on. My sisters went back to school and I knew I had to start working again.

I'd left the job in Spiddal because I found it too embarrassing to remain there.

I was still attending counselling in both Galway Hospital and the Galway Rape Crisis Centre and decided to join a year-long course in office skills in Carraroe. I thought it would add to the skills I'd gained on the course I'd done a few years earlier. I still wanted to start saving so I started working in the evenings. I wanted to get enough money together so I could move out. I got a job with my mother in Spiddal every evening in one of the factories. My mother used to collect me from the course and drive us over.

My aunt, my father's sister, was also working there at the time. Any time I tried to make conversation, she ignored me.

I was feeling much stronger since I'd given my statement to the police and decided to have it out with her.

'It's time to cut the bull. Why won't you speak to me?' I asked her one day.

She mumbled something about my mother.

'Whatever happens between you and my mother is nothing to do with me,' I said. 'I heard that some of my father's relations have said that I'm telling lies and that my father never touched me. Do you know anything about that?'

'Well, I've never called you a liar in public. If Patsie did commit any form of abuse then I hope he will be sent to jail for a very long time,' she said.

We went our separate ways after that but I was glad I'd talked to her.

Unfortunately, I had to leave the job soon afterwards. I was walking home from the course one night when I collapsed on the side of the road. When I awoke I was lying on a couch in the doctor's surgery in Carraroe. After the doctor treated me, he rang for an ambulance and I was transferred to Galway Hospital. They told me that I was exhausted and it was too demanding on my frail health to attend the course and work at the same time. I decided to stick with the course as I thought it would give me a chance to get the skills I needed to ultimately move out of Galway.

The tension continued to mount at home. We weren't on good terms with my father's family members at the time and I wasn't surprised when Alison got into trouble with one of our cousins in school. She had a fight with her cousin over something stupid. Apparently the teacher had given our cousin pages to pass around in class.

'She just threw the pages down on my desk and didn't place them neatly down like she did for all the other students,' Alison explained to me.

Outside the school, after the class, Alison slapped her cousin.

Our local priest spotted her though and gave out to her about her 'unladylike behaviour'.

Alison knew that our aunt would send the police to our house.

'She'll have me charged if she can get away with it,' she said.

Sure enough, a policeman arrived at our house the next morning.

'I'll be questioning Alison Naughton at the school this morning,' he informed my mother.

'There's no need to speak to her at the school. Sure that will only embarrass her. Alison's very sorry for what happened and she's promised that nothing like this will happen again,' I told him.

I had a chat with him about all the issues going on with my father's family and our own family and he finally changed his mind. He agreed not to question her.

Suzanne also had a few problems at school. She returned home one afternoon and went straight to her bedroom. This was very unusual behaviour for my sister. She was a talkative 12-year-old at this stage.

I followed her into her bedroom.

'Are you all right, Suzanne? What's wrong?' I enquired.

It took a lot of prodding but eventually she told me: 'I was bullied at school today.'

I was upset to hear that. It reminded me of when I was her age.

The following day I spotted the girl who had bullied my sister. She was with two of her friends and was walking towards the beach.

I approached her.

'Don't pick on my sister again. School life is hard enough without children bullying each other,' I said.

I'm glad I did this because the girl apologised and said that it wouldn't happen again. After that, the situation in school improved for Suzanne and she eventually became pals with the girl.

The tension was getting to all of us. One positive thing for me was that shortly afterwards, I had my first real boyfriend. He really helped to take my mind off everything. His name was Eamonn and he lived outside Galway City. He used to bring me out in his hometown. His brother-in-law was a Country and Western singer in that area. Eamonn was a lovely person and treated me very well. He used to get me beautiful gifts and bring me out to clubs. My health was still quite bad and I had one embarrassing night with him when I collapsed in my local pub in Carraroe. I was only drinking sparkling water and I'd been talking away when suddenly I couldn't speak. I grabbed my boyfriend by the arm and attempted to ask for help but my voice was gone. I don't recall falling on the floor. I woke up with half the pub around me and thankfully it didn't happen again.

It was good to be out of the house because we all seemed to be getting on each other's nerves.

Sometimes I felt like my family were driving me insane. Living with them was getting more and more difficult for me. It was a relief that I was still able to go for counselling.

Meeting the counsellor was a very positive experience. I felt good after I opened up a bit and we talked about the difficulties I was having with my family. I explained how I felt trapped inside and sometimes I just wanted the ground to open up and swallow me. I knew I needed to take the appropriate steps forward in life but I was torn. The counsellor made me feel that I wasn't alone with all that was going on around me.

I arranged through my doctor to go for further counselling in Woodquay in Galway City, which helped me to get through the difficult time. They were also a help when I ended it with Eamonn after about six months. I couldn't see myself settling down and living in the countryside. I knew I wanted to travel and still dreamt of going to America. He seemed to understand and we parted on good terms.

When the Director of Public Prosecution ordered my father's arrest a few months later, he was nowhere to be found. We thought he'd fled to England with my two brothers. The police said they were powerless and could do nothing until my father returned to Ireland. Extradition proceedings would also take years and they felt it would be better to wait until he came back.

I was afraid he wouldn't come back because he knew about our two statements.

I was beginning to feel like a fool for having bothered with the whole thing. I was wondering if I should just leave it for a few years and see if he came back or would I be better served bringing a solicitor on board at that stage. I thought justice would never be done.

I knew my father was under the impression that he was a free man.

My health deteriorated over the following months and I was in and out of hospital having tests. Eventually my mother brought me to a healer in Ballinasloe, Co Galway. This appeared to improve my health and the fainting episodes ceased. I worked as a waitress during 1999 in the Carna Bay Hotel and tried to move on with my life.

I was still going to counselling but I took a couple of months off as we entered the new millennium. My mother and I were called to a case conference meeting with the police, a psychiatrist and a social worker to discuss what was happening. My father was still missing, presumed to be in England somewhere.

During the conference, the psychiatrist asked me how I was getting along in counselling. I explained that I'd stopped going as I didn't think it was benefiting me. I didn't have a great relationship with my counsellor. The psychiatrist was very good and set me up with a new counsellor shortly afterwards. I found my new counsellor very communicative and we had a positive relationship.

I finally left home towards the end of that year and stayed with a friend. I was working as a part-time machinist. Relations at home had soured and due to the ongoing pressure I felt, I decided that it would be better for all concerned if I moved out. I concentrated on saving money as I was determined to get to America in 2001.

That February, my two younger sisters received a surprise telephone call from Patrick. We hadn't heard from my brothers in years.

'I'm back in Ireland,' he told them. 'I'd like to meet you both somewhere locally.'

Paul wasn't with him and seemed to still be living somewhere in England. The girls agreed to meet Patrick and later that evening, he arrived at the family house. Mam had asked me to call over. Patrick refused to speak to her and quickly got the girls into the car.

Suzanne told me afterwards that almost immediately he asked them: 'Would you speak to Dad if he came home to Ireland?'

'We wouldn't know what to say to him,' Suzanne replied.

'Come on, I'm taking ye for a drive to a friend of mine's house,' he told them.

Before they left, my sisters ran back into the house to tell my mother that they were going out with Patrick.

'No way are ye going off with Patrick by yourselves,' I told them.

They insisted that they were going.

'Fine,' I said. 'But I have to go too then.'

We all got into the car and set off. Patrick dropped up to one of his friend's but then he drove towards my grandparents' house in Kinnvarra.

'Where are you going?' I asked him.

'I'm dropping up to our grandparents,' he replied.

As soon as we arrived, Patrick jumped out of the car and approached the front door.

Suddenly, my father appeared at the wall of the front garden. I was both surprised and frightened to see him.

I looked at my sisters.

'Just stay calm,' I told them.

My father got into the passenger seat of the car. Patrick returned and sat in the driver's seat while my father spoke to my sisters.

I ignored him and gave Patrick a dirty look. He had arranged all this.

My father looked at the house where we had lived until I was 16.

'I'm sad we sold that house. It holds a lot of fond memories,' he said.

'I want to go back to Carraroe,' I said to Patrick.

'Well, keep in touch, girls,' my father said to my sisters and got out of the car.

I remained silent.

Patrick pointed to my father standing at the back of the house where we used to live.

'Dad has a lot of regrets, you know,' he said.

'Well, he didn't think hard enough before he raped me,' I said to him.

'There's no need to bring that up,' Patrick replied and then changed the subject.

As soon as he dropped us off, my sisters ran into the house and told Mam about meeting their father.

'He's come home for his birthday. He's planning to have a meal with his parents to celebrate it,' they told her.

My mother immediately phoned the police and informed the officer on duty that my father was back in Ireland.

'If he realises the police are after him, he'll get the first boat heading to England. The police better send plainclothes officers,' I said.

My mother agreed with me.

'I'll tell them that. I have to go with them to direct them to his parents' house in Kinnvarra,' she told me.

That night, I travelled with her to my father's family home, with the police following behind.

On the main road near the house, we noticed my father's brother passing in the car. We were worried that he had noticed us and would turn back to tell my father. Thankfully he didn't see us.

When we arrived, loads of police officers jumped out

of their cars. They hid in various places surrounding the house. There would be no escape for my father this time.

I went to the front door.

'Patrick,' I shouted. 'Patrick, come out!'

I could hear several voices coming from within the house.

My granny came out first.

She was surprised and seemed a little hesitant about talking to me. We hadn't spent much time together since everything that happened.

'Come on inside, Barbara,' she said to me.

'No thanks, I'm actually in a hurry,' I told her.

Seconds later, my father stepped out and greeted me.

I found out later the police didn't rush in then to arrest him because they didn't recognise him. He had his hair shaved off.

'Patrick, Barbara wants to see you,' my father shouted into the house.

Patrick came to the door.

'Do you want to go for a drink?' I asked him.

I was hoping that he wouldn't see the police or hear my mother because she was talking behind the wall. I was nervous in case she would shout or something.

He looked surprised and replied: 'No, I'm too tired. I'm just going to go lie down for a bit.'

I turned to walk back to the car.

'I'll walk you back,' Patrick offered.

I was nervous that he would see the police hiding. I knew he would get a shock if he saw them.

'There's no need to come all the way to the car,' I told him.

'Ah, it's grand. Who is Mam visiting in the area?' he asked.

I didn't drive so he knew Mam must have driven down.

'Just the lady across the road there,' I told him.

My mother was actually still with the police, hiding behind the wall.

Suddenly Patrick spotted a man with a navy jacket, standing at the back window of Granny's house. Luckily the man had the jacket zipped up so my brother couldn't tell he was police.

'Who's this? Is he your boyfriend?' Patrick asked me.

I remained calm while Patrick stared at him.

'Come here. What are you doing there?' he asked him.

The policeman walked towards him slowly. He pulled the zip down on his jacket.

'I'm a policeman,' he told Patrick.

My brother shouted so loudly in rage that all the neighbours must have heard him.

My father rushed from the house. 'Is something wrong?' he asked Patrick.

Patrick tried to speak but his lips wouldn't move. He was in shock.

My father kept calling his name, as his parents came outside.

'What are you doing on my premises?' my grandfather called out to the man beside me. He wasn't close enough to realise that it was a policeman.

The policeman said nothing and walked closer to my father.

Without warning, he suddenly started reading my father his rights and reached out to put handcuffs on him.

After years of waiting and uncertainty, my father was arrested.

He was speechless. His parents paled as they saw the rest of the police officers streaming over the wall.

Patrick looked distraught. My father was numb and looked like he couldn't move.

Two police officers went on either side of him and started walking him to one of the police cars. They stopped at the top of the gate when they heard a loud voice in the background.

'Where the hell do you think you're going?' Anne Naughton shouted.

The policewoman looked back at me and asked: 'Who on earth is that lady?'

I identified my aunt and could hear her asking them: 'Where's the warrant to arrest my brother?'

The police continued to escort my father up the hill towards the police car and the rest of the officers were right behind them. I followed them and began to look around, wondering where my mother was. Suddenly I spotted her standing at the top of the hill beside her car.

My father was stunned when he came to his senses and saw all the police officers. He gave me a dirty look as he went by.

I sighed with relief as they placed him into the back seat.

Patrick's voice had returned and he reassured him: 'Don't worry. I'll bail you out first thing tomorrow morning.'

He pointed at one of the police officers and told him that if he ill-treated my father while he was in custody that he would suffer the consequences.

The police asked me who he was and I told him that he was my older brother, Patrick.

My father was clearly relieved that Patrick had come to his aid.

We got into Mam's car and I saw my father's eye, looking back at us as he was taken away. I got a bad feeling and wasn't surprised when the wheel went into a drain as my mother tried to turn the car.

My mother was panicking.

We couldn't afford to get stuck beside my father's family home so I rushed out and asked the police for some help. They got us out and we followed the police car out of there. As we passed my grandparents' house they were standing outside their gate. My grandfather put his hand up to wave to his son. They had been celebrating my father's birthday.

Two days later, my father appeared before the Circuit Court in Galway City.

My brother offered to post £10,000 bail, which the judge accepted.

I was disappointed when I was told that my father was to be released on temporary bail.

After my father's arrest my relationship with my mother and two sisters deteriorated. Whenever I saw them, we never seemed to stop talking and arguing about the case and what was going to happen. We were all on edge. The arguments between my sisters and I became more heated. I was glad I wasn't living in the house but in the end I felt that it would be best if I went away for a few months before the trial. I had saved up enough money and I decided that it was time to pack my bags and head off to the United States. I felt drawn to the country. I thought it would be the best place for me to live as it seemed like the land of opportunity.

I left my family under the impression that I would be returning within a few weeks so they wouldn't ask me loads of awkward questions. But as I packed my suitcases, I knew in my heart that it would be a good few months before I saw Galway again. There was no date for my father's trial and I was hoping I'd have a bit of a break before it came to court. I wanted to start, what I hoped at the time, would be my new life.

When I arrived in Boston, it felt like I had entered another world. My cousin (on my mother's side) collected me at the airport. I felt happy to be far away from everything.

Before I knew it, I was working in a model agency during the day and taking care of an elderly lady at night. My life blossomed. She was 102 years old and one of the happiest people I had ever met. Over a period of months, she told me about her life and her husband whom she'd adored.

As I started to earn a living, I began to go to some of the Irish bars in Boston, where most of the Irish-Americans hung out. One evening, I was in one of the Irish pubs when my friend introduced me to an extremely attractive man. He was of Italian extraction and had a gorgeous face. I loved how he dressed because he looked so smart in a stylish black suit. He had spent years in drama school and, like other actors, had dreams of going to Hollywood. When I discovered that he was an animal lover, I was even more attracted to him.

We talked for ages that night and I was delighted when he asked me out on a date. We went to see the musical *Les Miserables* and I was thrilled with the whole night.

I couldn't wait to see him the next day and I had butterflies in my tummy as I arrived at the pub where we were supposed to meet. We had a great time together that night and as the weeks passed, we just got closer.

Three months later, I was watching TV when he suddenly asked: 'Can I move in with you?'

'Yes,' I shouted. 'Of course!'

I was delighted.

I sensed this was the man for me. He had a wonderful extrovert personality and I always had a great time when we went out. He knew that I used to travel regularly to New York City for auditions and work as a model.

One night, at his local pub, we were drinking with a group of his friends. When my boyfriend went to the toilet, one of his friends turned to me.

'Maybe you should go out with a real man,' he suggested and wrote his name and number down on a piece of paper. I was completely surprised as I had believed that this man was one of my boyfriend's best friends.

When we left the pub I told him what had happened. He wouldn't believe me at first but when I then showed him the note, he immediately recognised his friend's handwriting. My boyfriend couldn't believe that his friend had done such a thing.

'I've got no interest in him,' I reassured him, as we walked home.

My boyfriend used to write me wonderful poems. I would come home from work to find notes on the bedroom floor with love hearts and poems. I was also very happy with my job and was now helping to arrange fashion shows. Every morning, I went to the gym and exercised for a couple of hours before work.

My life felt complete. I knew, however, that I couldn't fully relax into my new sense of happiness because the trial was still on the horizon.

One afternoon a few weeks later, in the middle of August, I received a telephone call in work from my mother. 'Your father's trial is coming up,' she told me. 'You'll have to come home for it.'

As I spoke to my mother, part of me wanted to ensure my father was punished for what he had taken from me but another part of me wanted to remain in

America. I wanted to focus on building a life for myself. I was really in two minds about whether to return or not. Everything was going well for me in Boston. I was busy with my job and all aspects of my personal life were rosy. Returning to Ireland would only bring unwanted pain. A big part of me didn't want to go through the ordeal of a trial. The thought of strangers hearing how I had been violated as a child repulsed me.

All these thoughts were mixed up in my head.

Finally, I told my mother that I would think about it and call her back in a few weeks.

I put it out of my mind and time seemed to fly by. It was almost a month later, in September, before I heard from her again

I got home from work and she'd left a message on my answering machine. It was September 13, 2001, two days after the World Trade Center had been destroyed. I rang her back immediately.

'I just wanted to make sure you were OK,' she told me. 'I was worried because I know how you're always visiting New York.'

I reassured her that I was safe and sound in Boston.

'The police have been in touch. They would like to liaise with you before the trial begins,' she explained.

Alison suddenly grabbed the phone.

'Mam's really upset and anxious over the trial coming up,' she told me.

I felt torn in two. I didn't want to go back but I knew I had to.

'Hand the phone back to Mam,' I said.

I knew I had to tell her how I felt.

'I've rebuilt my life here. I just feel that nothing but pain is waiting for me back in Ireland,' I explained.

My mother sympathised with me.

'But if you want justice then you'll have to face your father in court,' she said.

Finally, I agreed to come home. I knew she was right.

'I'll arrange my flights before the end of the week,' I told her.

My boyfriend must have overheard some of my comments to my mother because when I got off the phone he asked: 'Why does your mother want you to go home?'

'I'm needed as a witness for a trial back in Ireland. I've no option but to go back,' I replied.

As I had not confided my family history to him, I found it difficult to know what to say next. At the time, I was extremely embarrassed about my past. I was going to counselling once a week in Boston but I had no intention of discussing this thorny issue with him.

'My mother needs me. As soon as I've finished with matters in Ireland, I'll come back to Boston immediately,' I said. 'I promise.'

He looked at me quizzically.

'Is there anything you want to tell me?' he asked. 'Is everything OK at home?'

'There's something I need to take care of,' I replied.

He looked at me in surprise: 'What is it?'

I prevaricated and replied: 'It's a legal matter.'

I walked into the kitchen to end the conversation.

It pained me that I couldn't confide in him.

Later that evening, I received a phone call from the police in Ireland. It was Noreen Feeney, one of the officers who had taken my original statement.

'I've been speaking to your mother,' she told me. 'I just want to check in with you to see if you have any concerns about the trial.'

'What happens if I don't go back?' I asked.

'The DPP would probably apply to have you subpoenaed,' she replied.

That was the end of my indecision.

I said: 'To be honest I wasn't sure about coming back because I've started a new life in Boston. I was in two minds about it but I spoke to my mother earlier today and she's convinced me it's the only thing to do. I don't need to be subpoenaed.'

She rang off but an hour later, I received a second call from the police in Galway. This time another female officer informed me: 'It's easier to prosecute your father if you return home as soon as possible.'

Slowly, I realised that I had no option but to return home and that I'd need to go quickly. I told my boyfriend that I had to go back to Ireland urgently.

The next day, I booked my flight back to Ireland and rang my job to tell them I'd been urgently called home. I organised for my mother to meet me in Shannon two days later.

The following evening, I dropped down to the local pub to have a final drink with some of the friends I had made in Boston. They all told me that they were sorry to hear that I was returning to Ireland but hoped that I would be back as soon as possible.

I really wished I was staying there. I felt empty inside as two days earlier I'd been more concerned about doing overtime at my job than rushing back to Ireland.

Later that evening, when I got back from the pub, I sat in my bedroom and lit some candles. I prayed that justice would be done.

The following morning, on the day of my departure, my boyfriend asked me: 'Do you intend to come back to Boston?'

'Of course I do, I'll be back as soon as I can,' I reassured him.

Shortly afterwards, my pal Mohammed arrived. He grabbed my bags and drove me to the airport.

Three hours later, I was on a plane heading across the Atlantic Ocean.

I wasn't looking forward to it at all. I was sitting on the plane, looking at a calendar, working out how soon I could book a flight back to Boston.

My mother and sisters didn't recognise me at first because of the colour and length of my hair but I recognised them immediately. My two sisters threw their arms around me and grabbed my suitcases. My mother followed them over and gave me a hug.

Although I was happy to see them again I couldn't stop feeling on edge. I kept telling myself that it would all be over in a few weeks and I could finally put it behind me and move on.

On our way back to Galway, I told my sisters all about my new life in Boston and about my current boyfriend.

The subject of the trial was never raised.

When I arrived back to the house, Carraroe looked a lot smaller to me.

For the next few days, I remained at home in my grandfather's house, feeding the ducks and hens.

Over the next few weeks the police constantly rang my mother checking details of the upcoming trial. It didn't take me long to realise that there was no need for me to be back so early but there was nothing I could do about it. The police also arranged accommodation for us all in Dublin.

On October 21, 2001, the day before the trial was due to begin, my mother, my two sisters and Susanne, a member of the Galway Rape Crisis Centre, and I all headed for Dublin on the train. When we arrived at Heuston Station, we took a taxi to the hotel where we would be staying for the duration of the trial.

That night, I headed to bed early.

I spent the whole night staring at the ceiling. I couldn't stop thinking about the embarrassment of having to reveal the disgusting stuff my father had done to me in court the next day.

I was dreading it.

SIXTEEN

Talking to Strangers

Central Criminal Court, Dublin

The trial started on Monday, October 22, 2001. That morning, I got dressed and prepared myself for the upcoming ordeal. I felt a bit nervous but I wanted to try and eat breakfast so Mam didn't get worried.

At 10.30am, we left our hotel and headed to the Four Courts. As I entered the courtroom, cold shivers ran down my spine. Although I had wanted justice, the reality of what a court case would entail slowly began to dawn on me. I would have to give evidence in front of strangers and describe events in my life that I had done everything I possibly could to forget.

As I sat in my seat, the judge entered the room. Everyone in the courtroom stood up immediately. I felt like I was back in Mass and that the priest had walked in.

I looked around the room and I spotted my father standing in the dock. I noticed that he was still overweight and he was staring into space. A police officer stood right beside him. There was an elderly man with grey hair standing directly beneath my father.

'He's an interpreter. Your father will be responding to all the questions in Irish,' Susanne from the Galway Rape Crisis Centre whispered to me.

When I turned to my mother and told her what was happening, she smiled.

'Don't worry, Barbara, it'll all be fine,' she told me.

I looked around the court and spotted Patrick sitting at the back with Anne Naughton. I hadn't seen him in months, since the night my father was arrested.

Shortly afterwards, the counsel for the State, Patrick Gageby, stood up and began detailing the history of the case, which took us into the afternoon. As he continued to read, I noticed that my father was staring at my mother and my two sisters. I began to get upset and started crying when Mr Gageby went into details of how exactly I was abused. I tried to control myself but I couldn't. I felt angry and sick to my stomach.

When he'd finished, the judge adjourned the court until the following day. As I stood up and looked around the courtroom, Patrick and my aunt were nowhere to be seen. I was glad not to have to talk to them.

We all left the court and spent what was left of the afternoon walking around Dublin.

When I returned to the hotel later that evening, I needed to relax so I took a bath.

As I lay in the bath I started to wonder how the trial would go. I tried to recall some of the instances of abuse and work out how I would relate them to a packed courtroom. It felt like an incredibly daunting task and I knew that I would have some difficulty. My memories of some of the instances were blurred. Over a period of years I had tried to forget these experiences and I'd come to realise that my mind had no wish to relive these matters. However, I no longer had a choice.

Susanne had told me: 'Barbara, you'll have to be very strong during your cross-examination. It's going to be a lot harder than when Mr Gageby was asking you questions.'

I wondered what was going to happen. I decided I needed an early night. I was tired worrying about what he might ask me.

I was just getting out of the bath when I heard someone banging on the door of my hotel room.

'Barbara, Barbara, open up,' I could hear my mother and sisters shouting outside.

'I'm in the bath, I'll be there in a minute,' I called back.

As soon as I opened the door, they rushed in.

'Patrick's down in the hotel bar. He wants to see you alone,' my mother said.

Although in some ways I had every wish to see my brother, I clearly remembered everything that had happened before I went away. I didn't even want to think about what would have happened if my father had got me alone before he was arrested. I knew I couldn't trust Patrick but I still wanted to hear what he had to say.

As I walked down to the bar by myself, I did have a small hope that he'd come to his senses and wasn't going to take my father's side anymore.

Patrick barely said hello to me before commenting: 'Dad's staying in a B&B while he's out on bail for the trial. His health isn't good.'

I realised, once and for all, that my brother's only interest was in my father's welfare and that he had no interest in my life. I felt stupid because I'd really wanted him to be on my side.

'Do you have any concept of what the trial is going to do to him?' he asked me.

He seemed to want to make a last-ditch appeal to me to withdraw the charges. I thought he was mad.

'I don't care,' I replied. 'I'm more interested in building a life for myself. That man raped me. You should be offering your support to me, not our sick father.'

He looked at me as if I was crazy.

I told my brother that I was heading off to bed for the night as I had a heavy day ahead of me.

It took me a while to get to sleep.

* * * *

The following morning, as I lay in bed, I wondered how the day would pan out. I was very nervous about taking the stand. I heard a knock on my hotel room door. It was my mother.

'Come on, hurry up, we're late,' she said, getting me moving.

I got out of bed and dressed quickly.

Twenty minutes later, I walked into the courtroom with my mother and two sisters. It was packed. I was surprised and wondered where everybody had come from. I looked around in shock as I walked over and sat down.

The judge arrived and shortly afterwards, Mr Gageby called me to the witness stand.

I felt shivers as I approached the stand. I wasn't sure what to expect. He realised I was nervous and his initial questions were quite non-intrusive. He was trying to make me feel as comfortable as possible while I sat in the witness box.

'Can you give your name?'

'Barbara Naughton.'

'Where do you live?'

I gave my Galway address.

'Where were you born? What year did you move from there?'

As I looked around the room at the jury, members of my immediate family and my father, I began to realise, although I probably always knew, that there would be no winners in this case.

Mr Gageby moved on to more intrusive questions.

Could I recall the first time that my father sexually abused me?

He told me to explain in detail how it actually happened.

I told him that I was raped at home and that I found going into the graphic nature of the incident embarrassing. Nevertheless, I tried to answer his questions as best I could. I had to pull certain painful instances of abuse out of my memory.

I was very honest and accurate in my statement and I didn't embellish anything.

As I started to relate the more sordid elements, the courtroom fell quiet.

Mr Gageby continued to ask me questions and I continued to provide as much information as I possibly could but I was relieved when the judge interrupted.

'We'll be breaking for an hour for lunch,' he announced.

I'd spent a lot of time in the witness box and I felt dizzy when I stood up to leave.

Helen, a representative from the Victim Support Group, asked me if I would like to have lunch with her. I immediately accepted and my mother and sisters accompanied us. We spent the following hour in the Smithfield area of Dublin where we chatted and took our minds off the trial.

All too soon, it was time to return to the court and continue my story. I walked into the courtroom and spotted Anne Naughton.

I walked up to Mr Gageby and asked: 'Is it possible to have her removed from the courtroom?'

He told me to just continue on with my testimony.

I returned to the witness stand and continued detailing the instances of abuse. As I carried on with my testimony, details of locations where my father had raped me streamed into my consciousness. I began to clearly remember the exact locations where I had been raped.

It was like reliving the abuse all over again.

'I'm not sitting in this witness box to seek revenge on my father, I'm here to show him that what he did was wrong,' I told the court.

I looked across at my father who was sitting a few yards away from me. I saw tears coming from his eyes.

'My father is a cruel person. He's not aware of how cruel he is and that's the other reason I'm sitting here. I want to tell him how difficult it was to survive around him as an infant and a teenager. He set one person off against the other in our home. He easily managed to manipulate my brothers. My sisters weren't as gullible. He never wanted to see any man approaching our house in order to see my sisters or me. He was so possessive when boys from the locality were chatting to me. He would tell me that he knew what they were thinking about. He thought just because he had a sick mind that everybody else would think the same. He cut conversations short with a boy from the neighbourhood who was a couple of years older than me. My father said that the boy spent too much time staring at me whilst chatting to my father. I felt trapped. I couldn't go for a walk with my sisters without our father following us. It became more embarrassing as I got older. One of my neighbours mentioned that she was no longer interested in coming in to visit us because she was fed up with my father grabbing my knee and making crude comments about me to her.'

I looked at my father as I recounted this and I saw his legs shaking with embarrassment.

The silence in the courtroom was comforting.

I was tearful most of the time as I was getting flashbacks of what had happened to me over the years. As I went through the horrendous part of the story about the night my father tried to strangle me, I noticed a lot of people in the court were crying.

My mother had told me not to tell the court that a man came to the car and saved my life in case the jurors thought I was unbalanced. But as I sat in the witness box, I felt that it was important for me to say it.

I didn't want to leave anything out.

'The man who saved my life in the early hours of the morning had walked up from the mountain. I don't know whether he was a real person or not,' I told the court.

'My father threatened to kill me if he is convicted and sent to jail,' I concluded.

When I finished giving my testimony, the barrister turned to the court.

'Everything Ms Naughton has told the courtroom matches the statement that she previously made to the police. She was accurate on all details,' he announced.

I noticed that my father had his head down and was studying his nails. I looked around me and spotted Patrick crying. I realised that this was the first time my whole family had heard the full story. I had asked a member of my legal team if it would be possible to have my family members removed from the courtroom as I felt details of my abuse might be too painful for them to hear. They had told me to leave my family in there, that they should hear the whole story.

My father's barrister then stood up and began to cross-examine me. I don't remember everything he asked me but some of his questions have stuck with me. At first, he showed me a drawing of my original home in Kinnvarra and asked me several questions about the house.

'Are the walls made out of concrete?'

'Yes, I believe they are.'

He wanted me to describe the layout, where all the rooms were located and where my bedroom was located in relation to my parents' room. He seemed to think I wouldn't remember.

After I explained the set-up, he said: 'This map is at variance to what you've just described.'

'The map you have is probably quite dated. My father built a wall in the sitting room and made several structural changes to the house over the years.'

'How can you be so accurate about dates and locations of the alleged incidents when some of these incidents happened very late at night?'

Before I could respond, he handed me a photograph with a picture of an old gate on it.

'Do you recognise this gate? Can you tell me its location?'

'It's at Furbo. He raped me there one night.'

'How can you be so certain of the location when it happened late at night?'

'There were lights on in my father's car.'

People started laughing and the judge ordered everyone to be silent.

'It's as if I had an accident at that location. That place is printed indelibly on my mind.'

'Did you have a boyfriend when you were 18?'

'No, I had friends but no boyfriend. I found it practically impossible to have a boyfriend at the time as my father was constantly controlling my life.'

The cross-examination finished shortly afterwards. I left the witness box and sunk into my seat. It had been quite a test and I was exhausted.

Mr Gageby next called my sister, Alison.

My father was visibly stunned as he watched Alison approaching the witness box. As he cleared the sweat from his forehead, he looked at me with hatred in his eyes.

Alison told the courtroom about the things my

father used to tell her about me: 'He told me never to believe a word that came out of Barbara's mouth as she was a confounded liar. I thought it was strange that he never stopped telling us how bad a person Barbara was.'

She then recalled an incident where she had heard our father threatening me when I was younger.

'I was in my bedroom when I heard shouting coming from the downstairs kitchen. I recognised the two voices as being my father's and Barbara's. I heard him threatening her but I had no idea why.'

As she concluded her testimony, Mr Gageby thanked her. Her cross-examination didn't last long and Suzanne was called next. As she was only 16 years old at the time, she was given the option to give evidence in camera or directly to the courtroom. I was proud that she had decided to take the stand to talk about how my father had treated me. As she sat in the witness box, my father started to go red and again gave me an angry look.

Suzanne told the courtroom that my father constantly told her never to believe a word I said. 'He also told our neighbours never to believe a word out of Barbara's mouth as she was worse than his sisters for telling stories. I remember once how he called me aside and asked me what sort of conversations I had with Barbara when we went for long walks. I told him that we spent most of the time talking about school and music. I felt very uncomfortable when he asked me those sorts of questions.'

She spoke about how she had overheard my father threatening me in the kitchen on the morning of the day I collapsed at work. Suzanne had listened as my father promised he'd never touch me again and warned me to look bright and cheerful at work.

Shortly after that, my sister finished her testimony and my father's barrister began to cross-examine her. He kept asking her about that morning and how she could be so sure about what she'd heard. I felt he was quite tough on her but it ended eventually and Suzanne sat down.

As she finished, I looked down at my finger. It was swollen and quite painful. I didn't know why it had swollen up out of the blue.

The judge then asked about Paul Naughton. Paul's statement had been submitted as part of my case but he hadn't come back to Ireland with my father and Patrick. I wasn't sure if he was even still living with them in February when my father was arrested. I was annoyed that he hadn't come back from England for the trial. I presumed he still sided with my father and that was why he didn't want to read out his statement in court. My defence team thought it would be helpful to my case to get him to come back. I wasn't so sure.

The judge ordered that my younger brother be in court to give evidence and then adjourned the case for the day.

Helen, from the Victim Support Group, leaned towards me. She'd noticed my swollen finger.

'Do you want to go to hospital to have your finger examined?' she asked.

I nodded and as I stood up, I spotted Patrick sitting at the back of the courtroom.

He looked at me and smiled.

I didn't smile back.

As soon as we left the Four Courts, I explained to my mother that Helen was driving me to the Mater Hospital. When we arrived, we had to wait for two hours before I was treated. They said it was an infection, possibly related to stress.

I left the hospital that night with a bandage on my finger and returned to the hotel.

As Helen dropped me off I wondered what was going to happen the next day.

The following morning we arrived at the Four Courts early and took our seats.

Shortly afterwards, the judge arrived and started proceedings.

'Have the police managed to contact Mr Paul Naughton?' he enquired.

A policewoman approached the judge's stand.

'No, we are still trying to contact him,' she told him.

The judge then adjourned the case for the remainder of the day.

I returned to the hotel and a police officer arrived to talk to me.

'Although we've managed to contact your younger brother, we are having difficulties persuading him to return to Ireland to give testimony,' she explained.

I hadn't realised they'd actually managed to get in touch with him. I was disgusted that my brother was still refusing to give evidence. I had travelled back from America for the trial, even though I didn't want to because I knew how upsetting it would be.

'Can you give me his phone number? I'll ring him myself to try and get him to come back,' I told her.

As soon as I returned to my room, I rang Paul. At first he refused to speak to me and hung up. I rang again and he stayed on the line.

He complained about how the Irish police were treating him.

'They threatened me with jail if I refused to go back,' he told me. 'I've no interest in going back to Ireland.

The case will have to go on without me.'

'The case will be struck out if you don't return to give evidence,' I insisted. 'If you don't come willingly, then the police could apply to have you extradited, like they do in the United States. It would be much better if you came of your own accord.'

As I continued to try to persuade him, my mother and two sisters entered my room and joined in.

Slowly, his mood began to change.

'If you don't come back to give evidence, I'll never speak to you as long as I live,' I warned him, not knowing if it would do any good.

He finally agreed to come back and we talked about other things for a while. Everything was quite friendly by the time I hung up. My mother and sisters had rushed downstairs to tell the police that I had managed to persuade Paul to come over.

The police sergeant arrived in my room and thanked me.

'Do you know what flight he's arranged?' he asked.

'He said he'd ring back as soon as he's booked a flight,' I replied.

The phone rang just after that and Paul said: 'I'm having trouble arranging a flight.'

The police officer told me to tell Paul that the police would arrange his flights and that I could ring him later on and give him the details.

I was delighted he was coming and told him I'd see him the next day.

Later that evening, Patrick arrived at the hotel. He was very surprised to hear that Paul was travelling over from England to give evidence.

I told him: 'You'd better not try and contact him and tell him not to come. The police are arranging his flight for him.'

He got annoyed and left soon afterwards. I knew he was only coming to see us to try to get information that he could give back to our father.

The next morning, I stood in the main hallway of the Four Courts with my mother and Susanne, the counsellor, waiting for Paul to arrive.

My two sisters remained outside watching for his taxi. As soon as they saw it, they ran back in.

'He's arrived; he's here,' they shouted. They were excited as none of us had seen him in years. We were wondering what he'd look like as he was now 22 years old.

I spotted Patrick chatting to Paul as they entered the Four Courts. He didn't look too different. They then came over to us and Paul gave us all a hug. He began speaking to Mam and my sisters.

I overheard enough to know that although he sympathised with me, he still felt bad about my father. Paul still wished that I had never pressed charges against him.

I began to worry about what my brother was going to say on the stand. He was being a bit stand-offish around me and that made me more anxious. I watched him talking to Patrick and I wondered what they were discussing.

I didn't say anything and we all walked into the courtroom and sat down. Paul sat beside my counsellor.

As my father came in, he immediately saw Paul and gave him a look.

The judge arrived and began to address the court. He confirmed that Paul was in the courtroom. I found it difficult to concentrate. I was beginning to worry that the worst thing that could have been done was putting Paul and Patrick on the witness stand.

My mother was then called to give evidence and she started by describing my father's personality: 'He's a manipulative individual who has managed to get his own way on a constant basis. He also constantly lies,' she told the court.

She also said that she now realised that he was manipulating her so that he would have time on his own to abuse me.

The barrister asked my mother many questions and she managed to answer the majority of them. She didn't talk about everything, however. I was hoping that she would mention the night when she caught him in my bedroom. I was also waiting for her to say that he had the habit of going back to my bed and sleeping there during the day on Sunday when he would have drink on him. Or that he used to wreck everything in my bedroom but I think she was still afraid of him.

When Mam stepped down from the witness box, my father laughed at her and leaned down to say something to the interpreter. I'm sure whatever he said wasn't nice.

Then there was an unexpected turn of events. As Mr Gageby was addressing the courtroom, he inadvertently informed the court that a barring order had been placed against my father from approaching my mother's dwelling place.

My father's barrister jumped to his feet immediately.

'What relevance does this comment have on the ongoing case? This is a slur on my client's name. This remark could unjustly influence the jury's decision,' he told the judge.

The judge adjourned the case for the day.

'There's going to be a legal argument regarding my remark. This issue has to be resolved before the case can continue,' Mr Gageby explained to me.

There was nothing else to do so we went back to the hotel.

Later that evening, my mother, two sisters and I had dinner with my two brothers. The police had gotten Paul a room in our hotel. I wasn't going to join them but I went along at the last minute to try to find out what my brothers were planning to say the next day.

Paul and Patrick told me that they were very worried about taking the stand and that they were afraid of what the barristers might ask them.

I told them that barristers aren't strict and that it wouldn't be hard.

We spent the rest of the evening catching up and trying to avoid awkward subjects. I no longer felt I could trust my brothers but I still cared about them. When dinner ended, they walked us up to our rooms.

When we got to my room, Patrick wanted to double-check what floor I was on.

I was surprised that he wanted to know this.

'Is it the first or second floor?' he enquired, walking towards my bedroom window.

'We're on the first floor,' I told him, as he looked out.

My two sisters came in as well and heard what Patrick had said.

Suzanne went and stood beside him at the window.

'That's a nice stairway, leading right up to your window,' she commented.

Shortly afterwards, my mother told them that it was time to leave: 'Come on, you'd better go,' she said. 'We all need a good night's sleep.'

They all left but then Susanne, my counsellor, knocked on my door. I was very happy to see her.

'So how are you feeling?' she asked.

'I'm nervous about what my brothers might say tomorrow,' I told her.

We talked for a while and I went straight to bed as soon as she left.

At 3am, a loud knocking sound woke me up. First I thought somebody was knocking on the door and I wondered who was there at such an hour. Slowly, I realised that the noise was coming from the window, at the other end of the room.

It was dark so I couldn't see clearly as I tip-toed over. The curtains were partially pulled. Suddenly I saw the outline of a person standing in front of the window. I thought I was imagining things.

As I pulled back the curtains, I realised that my father was standing outside. I was so shocked. At first, I thought I was going a bit mad because of all that was happening with the case and that I was seeing things.

As soon as he saw me, he began to knock louder.

I turned and rushed out of the room as quickly as I could. I ran down the hall and knocked relentlessly on my mother's bedroom door.

Eventually she opened it.

'What room is Paul in?' I asked her. 'Where's Paul?'

He was the only one I could think of who might be able to help.

She realised that I was in a state of panic and tried to calm me down.

'What happened? Are you OK? Calm down, take a few deep breaths,' she tried to reassure me. 'Paul's in room 12...' As soon as my mother told me his room number I ran as fast as I could and started banging on his door, shouting at him to open it.

I was trembling with shock.

When Paul opened the door, I told him what had happened. He dressed quickly and dialled the reception number from his bedroom. He then tried to phone the police on the mobile numbers they'd given us but couldn't get through.

'Go back to Mam's room. I'll go down to reception and get the police from there,' he told me.

When I returned to my mother's room, I told her what had happened.

'Don't worry, he's obviously desperate and will try anything,' she replied.

After a few moments, Paul returned.

'They've looked outside and there's no sign of him. If he was outside your window, he's gone now,' he told us.

'Are you OK to be in your room on your own?' my mother asked me.

'I'll be fine,' I replied and went back to my room.

I wasn't surprised when I had a very restless night after that.

The following morning, I was practically asleep walking into the courtroom. As I sat down, I prayed to my great-grandmother to be with me.

A police officer approached me and apologised: 'We're very sorry you had difficulty contacting us last night.'

Shortly afterwards, the judge arrived and Patrick was the first witness called.

During my brother's testimony, he confirmed some of the statements that I had made but was on occasion unable to confirm others.

'Do you recall an occasion when you were jogging with Barbara and your father arrived and drove off with her in the car?'

Patrick confirmed this incident.

Although Patrick was hesitant in responding to many of the questions the counsel for the State asked him, I felt that overall he was honest while he was on the stand. He then answered my father's barrister's questions to the best of his ability and seemed relieved when he was told to leave the witness box.

As soon as Patrick was finished, Paul was called. My younger brother's testimony in general was not supportive of my case. When he finished giving his testimony, I noticed that my mother was upset with the comments he had made in the witness box. I couldn't even look at him.

Paul's cross-examination ended soon afterwards and the judge adjourned the case for the weekend and told us to return the following Tuesday morning.

Before we left, I asked Mr Gageby how it had gone and he said it was hard to say what the jury would decide at that stage.

As we walked out of the courtroom, Patrick was beside our father and Anne Naughton.

My mother was still fuming with both her sons.

'Thank you very much. You weren't a bit supportive of Barbara. It looks like you enjoyed what happened to her. I will never see you again as my son over what you've done. You failed to answer some of the questions you were asked on purpose,' she shouted at Patrick.

My father's legal team were stunned as they walked directly into a slanging match between my mother and Patrick. My father and his sister simply walked past my mother and didn't engage in the row.

'You're a disgrace for siding with your father,' she continued shouting.

Patrick looked at her and said that he didn't side with his father and that she wasn't perfect either as a mother.

I grabbed my mother's arm.

'Patrick actually told the truth, to the best of his ability,' I told her.

My mother looked at me.

'It was Paul's testimony that was hostile. If you want to accuse anyone of letting me down, then you should direct your anger at him,' I said.

As Paul had left earlier, my mother gradually calmed down.

Patrick came over to me and told me: 'I didn't protect my father.'

'I have no problem with your testimony, you were honest in the witness box,' I replied.

We returned to the hotel to gather our belongings and get the train back to Galway for the weekend.

We'd a bit of time so we decided to have a drink before we left. We were sitting in the lounge of the hotel when I saw Patrick and Paul approaching. I stood up to go.

'I'll meet you at the train station, Mam,' I said.

Before I could leave, my brothers arrived at the table.

'Would any of ye like a drink?' they asked.

I turned to Paul and said: 'I've no intention of remaining in your company.'

I couldn't believe this was the same person who had helped me the night before. Looking at him now, it was so hard to remember all the good times we'd had together as children and all the pain we'd shared.

'Dad's going to kill you for making the allegations that you made in court. Even if he is found guilty, Dad's lawyer told him that he believes his sentence would be lenient.'

As my brother continued making these hurtful remarks, I wondered if he'd have been saying the same thing if he'd seen my testimony. I turned to my mother, Alison and Suzanne.

'How can you listen to this, when he's so obviously taken his father's side?'

Nobody said anything.

'You're very lucky the case wasn't thrown out of court after Mam accosted me outside the courts,' Patrick then said.

I couldn't listen to any more of this. I got my bags together but before I left I had one last question to ask: 'Paul, tell me this, why haven't you the guts to stand up to your father? At least I have the guts to stand up against my father for what he has done to me,' I said.

Paul stood there speechless, as I walked away.

As soon as I left the hotel, I burst out crying.

Later, on the train, my mother and two sisters began chastising me for the comments I had made to Paul. They wanted me to sit there like a dummy and allow myself to be insulted by my spineless brother. They told me that I should have kept my voice down in the lounge in front of other people.

My mother kept giving out to me. I finally told them that I looked forward to the day I could get away from them all and moved to another seat.

I felt very alone.

Thankfully, Susanne was there and I told her what had happened.

She reassured me that she'd have a word with Mam. Next thing, my sisters arrived back to me in a fury.

'That counsellor's after giving out to Mam. She told her she was jeopardising the case. That's disgraceful. You shouldn't have gotten her involved,' they said.

I was glad I had. I felt that my counsellor was someone who saw through them and she was doing her best to help me win the case.

SEVENTEEN

The Verdict

When we arrived in Galway, my mother collected the family car, which was safely at her uncle's house. As we drove through Connemara I began to relax a bit. I was glad to get away from Dublin and the trial.

The following morning, I rang a travel agent and booked a flight back to the United States for a few weeks later. I was confident the case would be finished by then and I wanted to get back to my life.

Later that afternoon, I received a call from my boyfriend in Boston.

'What's going on? When are you coming back?' he asked.

'I just have some family business to finalise. Don't worry, I've already booked my flight back to Boston for three weeks' time.'

He tried to get me to say more but I changed the subject and gladly talked about life in America for a while. I was looking forward to getting back to it.

That evening, one of my old classmates dropped around to the house. We discussed old times and we got around to talking about my new life in Boston.

'Well, I love my job and I have a fantastic man. I've a great life over there. I think I have an excellent future,' I told her.

I didn't tell her that being in America enabled me to leave my shameful past behind.

I found a photo of my boyfriend to show her.

She looked at the picture of the man I intended to

marry one day and said: 'He's ugly.' She then ripped up the photo in front of me.

'Why did you rip it up?' I demanded to know.

She just looked at me.

'You could do much better for yourself,' was her reply.

I said nothing and thankfully she left shortly afterwards.

When I awoke the following morning, I heard several voices in the kitchen. I could make out the voices of my mother and several neighbours. They were discussing the case. The neighbours sympathised with my mother and called my father every name under the sun.

'If he's convicted she should "name and shame" him. He deserves it,' I heard one of them say.

I stayed in bed until I was sure the last of them had left. When I reached the kitchen, my mother and grandfather were still discussing the case. As soon as I walked in they both rounded on me.

'You better "name and shame" after the case if he's convicted. You'll have to, Barbara,' I was told.

I was in two minds. I had no desire for any publicity and was hoping to quietly leave the country as soon as it was over.

I sat down at the table and told them: 'I don't know. I don't want the attention that would bring. I just want to head back to Boston in peace. I've no desire for revenge. I just want closure.'

My grandfather stood up, looking furious.

'You would not be welcome back in this house if you don't do what your mother asked,' he bellowed, standing over me.

I felt both intimidated by my grandfather and overwhelmed. When I looked across the room at my mother, she repeated what her father had said.

I started to feel trapped. I was dying for the trial to end so I could fly back to the US.

The next day, I returned to Dublin with my mother and two sisters on the train. Mam was still talking about 'naming and shaming'. I really had no desire to name my father publicly, as I felt it would merely attract further negative attention. But the trial had been quite exhausting and had left me drained. I didn't have the strength to argue with her.

When the train arrived at Heuston Station, we all jumped into a taxi and went back to the same hotel.

The next morning as we entered the courtroom, I overheard my father's barrister speaking to my father and his sister, Anne.

'It would be better if you took the stand,' the barrister was telling my father.

'Would it benefit his case if they're able to produce a psychologist's report indicating his ill health?' Anne Naughton asked the barrister.

'It would have little or no bearing on the case at this stage,' he replied.

My father was called to give evidence shortly afterwards.

My mother looked surprised as the interpreter stood beside my father.

'Where are you from originally?' my father's barrister asked him.

'I was born in England,' he replied.

His voice was quite loud and he had no need of the microphone that was positioned on the witness stand. As the barrister continued, my father began answering all the questions in Irish.

'Was Irish your first language?' my father's barrister asked.

'Yes,' my father replied. He looked over at his interpreter to translate.

My father's barrister asked him a few more general questions and then sat down.

Mr Gageby, barrister for the DPP, then stood up and began his cross-examination.

Initially, he asked him several introductory questions.

This continued for a while. Then he asked my father to describe the relationship he had with his children.

My father nearly choked and angrily asked what he meant.

'I'm just asking about the general relationship you had as a parent with your children.'

My father calmed down and said that the relationship was 'like all normal families have with their children'. He mentioned sitting around and watching television and said he'd bought the TV for us. My father claimed he'd only ever watch TnaG, the Irish language station.

The State's barrister went on to ask him about his other interests. This was all leading up to the more serious questions. He then asked my father if he had any idea why his daughter would be making such allegations against him.

He asked: 'When did all the trouble start?'

My father responded that the trouble began in 1978.

'Would you explain that, please?'

'That's the year she was born. That was the year all my troubles began.'

My father began telling his life story and explained how a member of my mother's family had stabbed him. He unrolled his sleeve, to show everyone his scar, but mixed up the arm it was on.

The whole courtroom erupted in laughter.

My mother's face went red like a tomato and she was filled with shame.

When Mr Gageby tried to resume, my father ignored his questions and continued retelling the more sorrowful episodes of his life. As Mr Gageby was not a fluent Irish speaker, he had no idea my father was ignoring his questions until the interpreter translated my father's remarks from Irish to English.

As my father continued telling his story, he began to act it out with his hands. I thought his testimony was becoming farcical. He recounted a story about when his brother-in-law forced him to buy several bottles of *poitín*.

As the interpreter translated, cries of laughter could be heard around the courtroom.

Eventually, Mr Gageby asked my father if he could possibly answer the questions he was asked and not spend the day regaling the courtroom with stories.

When my father finally finished, the barrister asked him again why his daughter had made such allegations.

'Her mother put her up to it.'

'Why do you think your wife would want to do that?'

Without hesitation, my father replied in English: 'She would do it out of spite.'

The barrister then lifted up my 30-page statement.

'What do you think about the statement your daughter made to the police?'

'*Malaí Breaga* [a bag of lies],' my father replied aggressively.

At this stage, he began responding to Mr Gageby's questions in English. My father looked directly at him and repeated in English this time: 'A bag of lies.'

My sister Suzanne, who was sitting beside me, began to laugh from nerves. My father heard her laughing and started to lose control. He lost track of what he was saying as he kept his evil eye on her.

'Were you able to speak English as you were growing up?'

'No, my English was poor and they generally only spoke Irish in the area.'

'What standard of English do you think you have now?'

'I have very little use for English.'

Mr Gageby then produced a letter.

'Would you please read this out to the courtroom?' he asked my father.

He handed the letter to my father.

'Do you recognise the signature at the bottom?'

My father faltered for a moment.

'It's my signature,' he quietly replied.

'Sorry, could you repeat that, Mr Naughton, so the whole court can hear?'

My father repeated it, louder this time, and started to read out the letter as Mr Gageby instructed. It had been written in English. He was mumbling so it was hard to hear, but I think he was complaining about the policewoman that arrested him. When my father finished, Mr Gageby said: 'No further questions.'

We returned to court after lunch and the two barristers made their final presentations. The judge then asked the jury to retire and consider a verdict.

We returned to the courtroom at 7pm that evening.

'Have you reached a verdict?' the judge asked the foreman of the jury.

'No, we haven't. We need more time,' the foreman replied.

They were sent to a hotel for the night but had to reconvene the next day and try to reach a verdict.

I was concerned that the jury wouldn't convict him as my brothers siding with my father had complicated everything. It all seemed to be up in the air.

I don't know how we got through that night.

The following morning, we entered the courtroom and were told that the jury still hadn't made a decision.

The day dragged and we were all waiting around outside. Finally that afternoon, we were all called back to the courtroom. There was an atmosphere of tense anticipation as we filed back in.

'Have you reached a verdict?' the judge asked.

'Yes, we have.'

When I heard those words, I felt a tremor of fear and adrenaline shoot through me.

There was not a sound in the courtroom. It seemed like everyone was holding their breath.

I looked over at my father who was slumped in his chair. He looked like he was crying.

The foreman of the jury announced that the verdict was guilty.

I felt a huge sense of relief.

Patrick Naughton, my father, had been found guilty. He was going to be punished for abusing me.

My father nearly collapsed as the verdict was announced.

My brothers and sisters were silent after the verdict and quietly exited the courtroom.

Several people surrounded me and I was congratulated on all sides. I watched as my father was taken into custody to await sentencing.

A big part of me couldn't believe it had happened.

The rest of the day was a blur.

* * * *

I found it hard to know what to do after the guilty verdict. I'd booked my flight back to Boston but I didn't seem to want to go anymore. I didn't feel that the case would really be over until the sentence hearing, which I'd been told wouldn't be until after the New Year.

I went back to Galway at first for a few weeks but it was the wrong place for me to be. I lost contact with my boyfriend and relations at home were strained. I finally moved to Dublin where I got an apartment.

After two more months passed, I decided to return to New York for a few months. I worked in a talent agency there but couldn't stop thinking about my unfinished business in Ireland. I was compiling a Victim Impact Statement to read out at the hearing. I had to track down medical records, including reports from hospitals and counsellors I'd attended in America, as they were all part of the statement. I wanted to include everything.

Once the sentencing date was announced for early April, 2002, I immediately made arrangements to return to Dublin.

When my father appeared in the Central Criminal Court, Dublin, for sentencing, I was called to the witness stand by the judge, Mr Justice Philip O'Sullivan.

I had to read out my Victim Impact Statement to the courtroom. It contained statements made by a psychiatrist and a counsellor I had attended, as well as my personal statement.

I felt very strongly about one section of it and read: 'I am aware of cases of this nature where people convicted receive very lenient custodial sentences. I feel that such sentences are unfair on the victims. If my father is found guilty, he should be sentenced to 18 years, the amount of time I lost due to his despicable behaviour. I'm glad I survived to tell my story as my father tried to murder me. I hope this judgement will help other victims of such crimes throughout rural Ireland come forward and confront their abusers.'

I finished reading the Victim Impact Statement and sat down.

The judge, Mr Justice Philip O'Sullivan, announced that he was sentencing my father to 11 years' imprisonment. Patrick Naughton's name would be placed on the register of sex offenders and he would have to remain under supervision for 12 years after his release.

My father looked stunned.

Anne Naughton started crying.

I felt a massive sense of release. When my father had told the court that all my allegations were 'a pack of lies' I was afraid they'd believe him. Not only did 11 years vindicate my actions in bringing my father to court, it also meant that I was safe from him for many years to come. I was still terrified that he would follow through on his threats and try to kill me but at least now he'd be out of my life for years.

Two police officers moved towards my father and started to lead him from the courtroom. As he passed my mother and me, he began cursing her in Irish and vowed to have his revenge.

I was horrified. My father obviously took no responsibility for what he had done to me. He had no remorse. He was more interested in threatening my mother than in apologising to us.

My mother looked forlorn and embarrassed. She reacted immediately and urged me to name my father to the awaiting press.

This incident convinced me that it was the right thing to do.

I saw my father staring at a man who worked for the Irish language station, Raidio na Gaeltachta. I think that brought it home to him that everybody in our local area would soon know what he'd done.

Epilogue

My nightmare did not end the day the abuse stopped, or the day my father was jailed. The case against my father had split my family. My brothers sided with him and Anne Naughton, my aunt, went to extraordinary lengths to try and influence the outcome of the trial. It was hard for me to get over all that.

Subsequent to my father's sentencing, relations with the rest of my family soured. Whenever I tried to contact them, I felt they treated me as if I was a stranger, and we rarely talk now. Physically, I still suffer from a serious stomach disorder, have teeth problems from grinding them in my sleep, am afflicted with bulimia, panic attacks and I have attempted suicide.

I am trying to move on with my life, however. I visited a spiritual healer in the United States in an effort to retrieve some of my lost childhood. It made me so much stronger in myself. I have also attended past life regression and hypnotism sessions in Ireland. In many ways I feel that I have now retrieved my soul and am in a position to move forward. I've managed to surmount my illnesses and very understandable anxiety in order to come forward and speak the truth.

I am now pleased to be living back in Ireland – in Dublin – where I have made some wonderful friends. As a child, I always loved singing but due to my painful childhood experiences, this talent was suppressed. Thankfully, I have now renewed my love affair with music and I am writing my own songs.

My father was released in January 2010. I intend to

have no contact with him and try to take comfort in the fact that, at least, justice was served. There is hope. The future now is up to me.

Barbara Naughton
May 2010

Acknowledgements

I would like to express my heartfelt thanks to: Kevin Kilraine for his constant support; the Galway Rape Crisis Centre for their support during my father's trial. My counsellor Susanne for helping me during the trial and showing me a light at the end of the tunnel; Jim Mitchell (RIP) for his assistance during the trial and Alan Carroll for his assistance and advice after the trial; Chris Giblin who was very supportive and helpful after the trial; Peter McGarry, solicitor, for his legal advice and friendship; Kate Mulkerins for her constant support; Caoimhin O'Caolain, TD, for his efforts on my behalf; Katherine Dewar, a beautiful human being (shamanic healer and soul retriever) from Boston, for her inspiration, guidance and healing.

Finally, I would like to thank my editor, Aoife Barrett, for asking all those insightful questions and guiding me through this process, and to all at Merlin Publishing for making the publication of my book a rewarding experience.